W9-BTC-682

EAST CENTRAL
32050008067297
973.929 K
Kyle, Dolly.
Hillary : the other woman : a
 political memoir

WITHDRAWN

NOV 2016

HILLARY
THE OTHER WOMAN

HILLARY

THE OTHER WOMAN

A POLITICAL MEMOIR BY

DOLLY KYLE

 WND Books

HILLARY THE OTHER WOMAN

Copyright © 2016 by Dolly Kyle

All rights reserved. No part of this book may be reproduced in any form or by any means—whether electronic, digital, mechanical, or otherwise—without permission in writing from the publisher, except by a reviewer, who may quote brief passages in a review.

Published by WND Books, Washington, D.C. WND Books is a registered trademark of WorldNetDaily.com, Inc. ("WND")

Book designed by Mark Karis

WND Books are available at special discounts for bulk purchases. WND Books also publishes books in electronic formats. For more information call (541) 474-1776, email orders@wndbooks.com or visit www.wndbooks.com.

Hardcover ISBN: 978-1-944229-45-0
eBook ISBN: 978-1-944229-46-7

Library of Congress Cataloging-in-Publication Data available upon request

Printed in the United States of America
16 17 18 19 20 21 LBM 9 8 7 6 5 4 3

I dedicate this book to survivors of sexual abuse and rape.

CONTENTS

FOREWORD

This book *Hillary the Other Woman* is as timely as tomorrow's news-paper, and its author Dolly Kyle is as fascinating as any person I have met. Moreover, the events, characters, and encounters described in these pages reveal Ms. Kyle's firsthand knowledge obtained over many years.

My conclusion that Ms. Kyle is narrating the truth was first based upon lengthy and specific investigations conducted by the staff of the House of Representatives Judicial Committee in the course of the impeachment of William Jefferson Clinton. As a consequence of our find-ings, we intended to put forward Dolly Kyle as our chief witness at the anticipated Senate trial. Unfortunately that trial never took place thanks, in the main part, to the craven cowardice of the Republican leadership.

Based upon my knowledge of her character and integrity, I can say without qualification that Dolly Kyle's word is as solid as gold.

Most people knew little or nothing about the Clintons until they appeared in the 1992 presidential campaign. Dolly Kyle, on the other hand, has known "Billy," as she calls him, since they met when she was an eleven-year-old girl and he was a thirteen-year-old boy. Their friendship, always close and often intimate, lasted until "Billy" was campaigning for the presidency of the United States.

Because their relationship extended over many years, Dolly Kyle was able to learn the most interior thoughts of her friend Billy Clinton. She observed the radical changes over the decades in his character, attitude, and loyalty to his friends, associates, and benefactors. The morals and motives of William Clinton will become clear in this book.

By the same token, Ms. Kyle met and became acquainted with Hillary Rodham before she became Mrs. Clinton. From observing Hillary's actions, personality, and temperament over several decades, the author is able to disclose the true character of the woman who wants to lead the free world.

At this time in our history, our nation is confronted with perhaps the most vital presidential election ever to take place. Currently, it appears that the Democratic Party will again turn to the Clintons to carry the party standard. In 1992, the candidate Bill Clinton stated that by electing him you would get two for the price of one (Bill and Hillary); so too, it is essential that the electorate realize that again it will elect two for one—this time, Hillary as President and Bill as First Spouse.

The two-for-one election potential is what makes this book essential reading for any citizen who intends to vote in November, and cares about the outcome.

Neither the Clintons nor their vast array of supporters will like what they read here; they will, no doubt, mount their usual campaign of lies, half-truths, and attacks against the author Dolly Kyle. So be it. There is no doubt in my mind that every statement in this book is absolutely true and correct.

It is, therefore, a singular honor that Dolly chose me to write this foreword.

—DAVID P. SCHIPPERS, ATTORNEY AND CHIEF INVESTIGATIVE COUNSEL FOR THE U.S. HOUSE JUDICIAL COMMITTEE FOR THE CLINTON IMPEACHMENT

AUTHOR'S NOTE

I am telling this story the way I saw it, in roughly chronological order with flashbacks, but I will occasionally cover a bit of the same ground more than once in this book. I'm doing this intentionally because I want each chapter to stand alone, for several reasons.

I know from experience that radio, television, and print journalists typically do not take the time to read an entire book before interviewing the author. Therefore, with my format that deliberately includes some overlapping of explanations, I will be able to refer an interviewer in advance to the appropriate chapter or chapters for a particular audience.

Readers with questions should feel free to contact me through my website: www.DollyKyle.com.

Joseph Farah of WND Books enthusiastically embraced this project and rallied his team to produce a timely, quality publication. THANK YOU, Joseph, Geoffrey Stone, and Mark Karis for your vision, professionalism, and flexibility.

I'm grateful for the steadfast support of a small cadre of previewers who faithfully read my "dailies" and sent constructive feedback. This wonderful group includes people of differing political ideologies who live in different locations on different continents; they share a commitment to truth, integrity, and the importance of an informed electorate. THANK YOU to my daughters Paula and Leesa; to my long-distance friend Charles Morgan who should be writing; to my artist friend Heideli Loubser in South Africa; to Renaissance Man George Russell, who will argue cogently with anyone anytime on any topic; and to those friends who have chosen to remain anonymous . . . just in case.

1
WHY WOULD I WRITE THIS BOOK?

As I was debating with myself about whether or not to write this book about Hillary "the Other Woman," I suddenly recalled with discomforting clarity the two events of my teenage years that formed an ideological foundation for my later decision-making.

When I was a sixteen-year-old freshman in college, I took a part-time job at the locally based People's Indemnity Life Insurance Company in Hot Springs, Arkansas. The founder and president of the company was related to family friends, so I felt comfortable there. I started as a receptionist, answering the phones a couple of days a week. Soon, I was assisting the president and other executives with their correspondence. Later, I was asked to help in the accounting department.

While making routine written entries in the books, I saw that the commissions being paid to the salesmen, as well as the overrides being paid to the president of the company, had no logical relationship to the premiums being collected. I quickly realized that the company was a sham, a fraud, a house of cards doomed to collapse.

The company was running on and depending upon a continuing influx of "investor funds" from family and friends in Hot Springs. There was no underwriting, no financial security, no chance that the company could pay life insurance proceeds to beneficiaries when and if a significant number of policyholders would die in the near future.

What were the chances that policyholders would die in the near future? Pretty good odds. The company's salesmen were hocking those life insurance policies on military installations around the country to young soldiers who were being shipped overseas to serve our country in Vietnam. The death toll from Vietnam was already frightening.

Initially, I had trouble believing what I was seeing on the books at the insurance company. How could anyone be so blatantly dishonest? How could anyone be telling lies this big? How could anyone deliberately prey on those young men who would die for our country?

Regrettably, my daddy was dead, so I couldn't discuss the situation with him. Fortunately, he had been in the insurance business and he had taught me something about the way it was supposed to work. Even without that background, however, I would have realized that a company should not be paying commissions and overrides that were ten times higher than the monthly premiums paid by the policyholders. In my mind, that "commission" money could only be coming from the trusting investors who were funding the business.

I talked to my mother about it. She couldn't believe that these nice people, who were friends of our family and families of our friends, could do such awful things. I couldn't find anyone who wanted to hear what I was seeing, thinking, fearing, so I said nothing further about it. After a while, I quit that job, and I tried to forget about People's Indemnity Life Insurance Company.

I don't remember the exact time frame, but it wasn't too long until the insurance company's house of cards did collapse, as I had anticipated. Friends of family and families of friends lost untold amounts of money that they had unwittingly invested in the scam. I had not, however, anticipated how wide and deep the ripples would spread in Hot Springs; I was sickened when I heard about the resulting bankruptcies, foreclosures, divorces, and families ripped apart.

Elsewhere, there was no telling how much damage had been visited upon the young widows and orphans of the gullible teenaged and twenty-something soldiers who had tried to provide for their survivors with a life insurance policy. The company president went to prison for his crimes, but there was no justice for the victims of that huge, deliberate fraud.

I was devastated that I had not done anything to prevent the inevitable tsunami that resulted from that company's scam. The entire matter, however, seemed to be an isolated incident and not a life-influencing event for me at that moment.

When I married and moved to Little Rock at the age of eighteen, I enjoyed life there in a beautiful, quiet neighborhood where the street formed a large circle. People walked their dogs in the mornings and evenings, and everyone knew everyone on a first-name basis.

There was a monthly garden club for the ladies. At my first meeting, I discovered that my next-door neighbor Mrs. Powell would not be attending any of the club events because she was dying of cancer. Back then (1966), people whispered the word *cancer* as if mere articulation of the word would cause it to spread and infect everyone in the room.

After my daughter was born, I would put her in a big, old-fashioned, leather baby buggy every day, and walk a couple of times around the three-quarter-mile circle for air and exercise. I'd slow down as I passed in front of the Powell's house, hoping I would see some sign of life, or some excuse to drop by to meet my next-door neighbor, but I never did.

The idea that I should be visiting with Mrs. Powell began to prey upon my conscience, daily, but I told myself that I shouldn't intrude. I was thinking, fearing that I might not be welcome. I did not want to face the unknown consequences of knocking uninvited on her door.

Finally, of course, Mrs. Powell died. I baked a couple of chickens and carried them next door for Mr. Powell and the mourners who would come to pay their respects. The maid Ruby greeted me at the carport door, and I started to introduce myself.

"Oh, I know who you are!" Ruby exclaimed. "You're that cute Miz Dolly who lives next door. Miz Powell used to watch you out the window every single day, and she always said, 'I wish that pretty young lady would come visit me and let me see her baby.'"

Once again, I was devastated that I had failed to act—to do something, anything, about the situation in front of me.

I sobbed myself to sleep that night.

The next day, I vowed that I would never again fail to step forward. I would never again fail to act—to do something—regardless of the consequences. I vowed to step forward whenever it was the right thing to do. This is such a time. Publishing this book is the right thing to do.

Hillary Rodham Clinton is running for president. She is morally and ethically bankrupt.

I am in a unique (though highly uncomfortable) position to disclose what I know about this blatant coconspirator and enabler of former President Bill Clinton, a sex-addicted serial abuser and attacker of women. Hillary's supporters surely must suspect at some level that she is a liar and a frantically ambitious person who will do anything (including attacking women while purporting to support them) to assuage her unfillable, addictive, emotional need for power.

Somehow, so far, these facts about Hillary do not seem to matter to her female supporters, but I think that they must be in some sort of denial about who she really is. I intend to show quite clearly that Hillary's past (as well as present) behavior disqualifies her to be president.

In a country of over 300 million people, there must be a woman who is ideally suited to be the first female president of the United States of America. Hillary is *not* that woman. This country does not need to stoop to elect a woman who got where she is by clutching the coattails of a rapist/serial sex abuser. This country can do better than supporting the Clintons in the vicious, unrelenting attacks upon any woman (or man) who would dare to expose the truth about them.

There are over 80 million millennials in the United States who do not know anything about the Clintons except the pleasantries that the mainstream media have chosen to share with them. If they have heard anything about the long ago and far, far away impeachment of President Bill Clinton, they think it was a partisan effort to punish him for having oral sex in the Oval Office with an intern young enough to be his daughter.

The millennials (and many others) do not know that the Clinton impeachment charges were based on perjury, witness tampering, and obstruction of justice in a federal lawsuit. What people have learned by implication from the Clintons is that it's okay to lie under oath. It is *not* okay to lie under oath, and the entire judicial branch depends upon the upholding of *truth* in sworn testimony.

As a lawyer and an officer of the court, I had a sworn duty to uphold the judicial system of the United States. It was also the sworn duty of President Bill Clinton to uphold the Constitution of the United States. Instead, he, as the head of the Executive Branch of government, assaulted the Judicial Branch, as he assaulted women (and men) who confronted him about his antisocial, sociopathic, and criminal behavior.

Many people remember (and many don't remember) that Bill *and* Hillary Clinton ran for the presidency in 1992 on a slogan of "two for the price of one." Hillary claimed to be a co-president along with Billy in their White House years.

Hillary's copresidency is the main "accomplishment" on her resume and travelogue. Later, as secretary of state under Barack Obama for four years, Hillary flew nearly a million miles around the world, and gained nothing for the United States of America. We are still learning about what she gained for herself and gave away to the detriment of our country.

It's time to take a serious look at what these co-president/co-conspirators did "together" for the past forty-plus years. They are still clawing and trampling people in their quest for power, just as they did in the beginning. In fact, many of their same supporting characters are still on the scene . . . or, more correctly, still slinking behind the scenes to suppress the *truth* in whatever way they are compelled to do it. This is not a pretty picture, and I'm not thrilled to be in the position of painting it for those who need to see.

Exposing the power-mad Clinton couple is not a pleasant thing to do. As Dave Schippers warned in his foreword to this book, the Clintons will, "no doubt, mount their usual campaign of lies, half-truths, and attacks" against me as a consequence of my daring to tell the truth about them.

The Clintons have been allowed to rewrite history, thanks to the cowardly complicity of Congress and the media. Billy and Hillary Clinton have convinced a slumbering electorate that the impeachment was only about sex in the Oval Office, and that the charges against the president were fabricated by Hillary's imagined "vast right-wing conspiracy."

Nothing could be further from the truth. The impeachment of the "co-president" was for crimes against the people and the Constitution. Hillary and Billy were complicit in those crimes as well as countless others. The biggest problem is that the problem is so big. Most people find it intellectually difficult to believe that all this happened and no one reported it at the time.

I lived it, I watched it, and even I didn't comprehend the full extent of the Clinton travesty as it unfolded before me. Now I am in a unique position to reveal the truth about Billy and Hillary that no one else can tell. I'm exposing decades of their abuse and corruption as clearly and concisely as I can in this book. I have written it raw and unedited so that the reader can "hear" my voice through these pages.

What the reader does with this information is not in my control. I hope that, at the very least, everyone who reads this book will start to ask questions and will persist with the important follow-up questions too.

Standing up and speaking for the truth and for what is right may be a difficult choice, but it is a choice that each of us must face many times in our lives. I am the first-born daughter of a long-ago-buried United States Marine, and I cannot turn away in cowardice.

2

ON MEETING BILLY CLINTON

"Admit it, Dolly!" Geraldo Rivera said forcefully from his television studio in New York. "Admit that you were attracted to President Clinton when he was the governor of Arkansas because of the power of his office!"

I laughed at the popular television interviewer and shook my head. Geraldo was comfortably seated fourteen hundred miles away from my little stool in the remote television studio in Dallas. I looked directly toward the tiny red light that indicated where the camera was in the very dark room.

"No, Geraldo, that's not even close."

"Then what was it?"

"I met Billy Clinton on the golf course at the Belvedere Country Club in Hot Springs in the summer of 1959. I was eleven years old and Billy was twelve, going on thirteen. He was taller than *I* was!"

What I said to Geraldo about meeting Billy Clinton was true, although it wasn't the whole truth. There is never time for the whole truth in a medium dominated by sound bites.

The larger truth of my meeting Billy Clinton on the golf course in the summer of 1959 involved the psychological and emotional dynamics of intertwined family histories and shared experiences in a small, though somewhat cosmopolitan, Southern town.

Mostly, and most importantly however, even though we were so very young, our first encounter was all about what my mother and her Italian family called "*colpo di fulmine*"—the thunderbolt.

Some readers may recall that there was a case of the thunderbolt described in *The Godfather*. Dare I mention *Romeo and Juliet*? Or, more recently, *Titanic*?

J. M. Darhower, in *Sempre*, paints a vivid picture:

> *Colpo di fulmine.* The thunderbolt, as Italians call it. When love strikes someone like lightning, it is so powerful and intense it can't be denied. It's beautiful and messy, cracking a chest open and spilling their soul out for the world to see. It turns a person inside out, and there's no going back from it. Once the thunderbolt hits, your life is irrevocably changed.

I imagine that a description of the thunderbolt may sound overly dramatic to anyone (especially a non-Italian!) who has not experienced it. I also know that people have debated for years about the romantic notion of love at first sight.

It is not my intention to present a philosophical argument for the existence of the thunderbolt or love at first sight. I'm simply stating what happened to Billy Clinton and me.

Our thunderbolt, obviously, did not lead to our living happily ever after. It did, however, bond us together in a liaison that evolved from puppy love to dating to friendship to a passionate love affair. We talked, flirted, laughed, cried, prayed, sang, walked, danced, wrote letters, made love, broke up, reconnected, and did it all again and again and again. Whatever that thing was between Billy Clinton and me, it lasted for decades—transcending state lines, oceans, marriages, societal prohibitions, and political considerations.

* * *

In order for a reader to understand my relationship with Hillary Rodham Clinton and the source of my observations of her behavior over time, it's necessary to know a bit more about my relationship with Billy Clinton.

I was a songwriter even before I started writing novels; a childish ditty that I composed about Billy decades ago provides a quick overview of the way it was back then:

> The day that I first met you, I was just a little child,
> But I still recall the feeling that you gave me when you smiled;
> Now the years have gone by, and I can still truly say,
> That the feeling you gave to me has lasted to this day.
>
> And I knew, I always knew,
> What that feeling was, but didn't know what to do,
> And so I'd write down your initials,
> And then six more letters I—L—O—V—E—U.
>
> The times we shared in high school were spent playing cat and mouse,
> When I finally got a car, I'd drive each day right by your house;
> When I dated your friends, I always acted so cool,
> But when I was with you, I'm sure I acted like a fool.
>
> In my book, you wrote in blue,
> "It's been fun to know you!... Good luck!... and God bless you!"
> But what I wanted by your initials,
> Was just six more letters I—L—O—V—E—U. . . .

The first two verses and the choruses of that little song establish the early scenario between Billy and me. I'll hold the third verse for later, when it figures prominently in the story at a much more grown-up level.

In actuality, it was Billy Clinton who drove by my house daily when we were in high school. On a rare truthful day, he will admit to that. Having skipped two grades, I was a fifteen-year-old senior and too young to get a driver's license, so I didn't ever drive very far alone.

Billy did not live in our old neighborhood in the older part of town, but in a small new subdivision several miles away. Gas was cheap and Billy didn't have an after-school job as many other kids did in high school, so it was easy for him to drive by my house "on his way home."

For parts of our young lives, Billy's mother, Virginia, was married to Roger Clinton, Sr., whose brother Raymond owned the Buick dealership in Hot Springs. Thus, Virginia and Billy always had nice big Buicks to drive, even in the "divorce" interim between Virginia's two marriages to the alcoholic Roger. By coincidence, the third Clinton brother, Roy, worked for my daddy for a while.

People in Arkansas (and other small places) inherently understand the nature of relationships that develop in these tight environs. If you meet someone from Arkansas while you're traveling through Europe, you can play the "do-you-know" game. Your fellow traveler will probably know and/or be distantly related to the person you ask about in Arkansas. At least, he will know someone who knows that someone. Really, it's that tight . . . and that was even truer back in the 1950s when Billy and I were growing up in Hot Springs.

I'll interject here an explanation for those who think Billy grew up in Hope, Arkansas. Billy was born in Hope (his mother's hometown) and he used the clever line "The Man from Hope" for his presidential campaign in 1992, but his childhood years after age seven were spent in Hot Springs where Virginia moved after marrying Roger Clinton.

Billy first attended St. John's Catholic Elementary School, but Virginia put him in a different school when I entered St. John's in 1954. Otherwise, we would have met much sooner.

At any rate, Billy and I graduated from Hot Springs High School in 1964. HSHS, by the way, was still a racially segregated school when Billy and I graduated . . . and that was seven years after the infamous

1957 "integration" of Little Rock's Central High School.

That integration story merits a whole other book that has not been written yet about the behind-the-scenes political reasons for the actions of the Democratic Governor Orval Faubus in calling out the National Guard to block the entry of nine "Negro" students—"The Little Rock Nine"—from attending Central High. The quick-and-easy bottom line is that Faubus wanted to run for an unprecedented third term as governor and he needed an "issue" to rally support around him.

Republican President Dwight Eisenhower sent federal troops to Little Rock in support of integration, which had been mandated three years earlier in the landmark Supreme Court case of *Brown v. Board of Education*. My Aunt Mary called from Philadelphia and invited us to stay with her during what she called "the insurrection" in Arkansas. It became quite a mess in Little Rock, but I'm thankful that we stayed in Hot Springs and did not move to Philadelphia.

Central High School in Little Rock was closed for the year, and "white flight" to old and brand-new private schools began. Phil Stratton, the Faubus aide/confidante/lawyer (and a close friend of our family) who should have written a book about what was happening behind the public scenes of the 1957 integration crisis, died November 9, 2014, taking most of the story to his grave.

If anyone wonders why Billy Clinton could use the phrase "G**damn nigger" (which I heard him say frequently) while he was the governor of Arkansas, that person needs to understand the environment in which we were raised. I'm not condoning it, but that is the way it was. Granted, Billy should have outgrown that habit before he became governor, but he still has trouble controlling himself when he's angry.

It seemed to me that I might be rambling here, but, upon reflection, I realize that all these paths are critical to understanding the children we were and the adults we became. To say that Hillary Rodham didn't "belong" in Arkansas is a gross understatement. Billy may have been more comfortable with the epithet "G**damn nigger," but ask the Chicago native if she ever used the terms "stupid kike" and "f***ing Jew bastard" before condemning all Southerners for racism.

Billy and Hillary have a history of racial discrimination. Even today, anyone who sees Hillary's interactions with young black women who ask questions can observe the disdain and arrogance with which Hillary puts down the questions and the questioners. In addition to the one-on-one situations, there was the systemic racial discrimination that resulted in lawsuits filed during the Clinton governing years in Arkansas; Clinton lost. I will write more about that in a later chapter.

History is not always pretty, especially when told truthfully and not rewritten by people with a political agenda. I watched Billy Clinton grow up, and I watched Hillary Rodham bring her carpetbag to Arkansas. I know what really happened.

The Clintons and their misled supporters have rewritten history to suit their political agenda, which is to get votes to get power to get money to get more power to get more money. The Clintons' vicious cycle of intertwining greed and power addictions will have no limit, unless someone stands up and announces, "The emperor has no clothes!" Here am I.

3

I DID NOT HAVE SEXUAL RELATIONS . . .

Billy (yes, that's the name still used by many of his childhood friends) Clinton and I had an unusual relationship during my two years of high school. This is significant for understanding many of the events that came later, including our triangle with Hillary. This triangle should *not* be confused with a ménage à trois!

Triangulation is a complex psychological phenomenon, but the basic version can easily be understood by kids in junior high school: Amy likes Bobby and Bobby like Carla, but Bobby also likes Amy. When I was in junior high school, information like this was passed around on scraps of paper in the classroom, at the risk of having it intercepted and read aloud by the teacher. Today, messages are sent via text and Twitter and who-knows-what-else; the risks are much greater.

At Hot Springs High School, Billy and I dated in the traditional (back then) sense of a boy calling a girl to invite her to a particular event, such as a party, a dance, a movie, etc. Both of us dated other people as well, and we never "went steady."

In addition to our traditional dates, Billy and I frequently would run into each other when we were "out" with different people, whether at Cook's Ice Cream after a football game or at a weekly dance at the YMCA or whatever. Rather than acting awkwardly in these situations, Billy would walk by and whisper in my ear, "Can you ditch So-and-So? I'll take my date home and pick you up in a half hour."

Most of the time, I agreed. Most of the time, Billy was late. Usually, on these "after-date" dates, we would have serious, in-depth conversations. Yes, we also "parked" in our favorite spot on West Mountain, but we drove around town first, singing together with the songs on the radio, and talking, talking, talking.

In case anyone is wondering, Billy Clinton and I did *not* have sexual relations in high school. Let's not get started on the definition of sexual relations here; there was enough of that in later depositions. I was a virgin throughout high school and I do *not* know what Billy was doing sexually elsewhere. There were always rumors from other cities, and he did travel around the state frequently (band contests, DeMolay events, etc.), but I do *not* know anything about that for a fact.

One night, on one of our after-date dates, Billy told me that he wanted to be president.

"You mean, of the United States?" I asked.

He nodded.

Although Billy confessed his desire to be president to me when we were in high school, he must have also told other "kids" in our Class of 1964. Or, they simply perceived it some other way.

Billy's photo with President John F. Kennedy in the Rose Garden of the White House (in the summer of 1963, when Billy was an Arkansas delegate to Boys Nation) was prominently pictured in our HSHS annual, the 1964 *Old Gold Book*. There was a general sense that the political baton had been passed to Billy Clinton from President Kennedy, who was assassinated a few short months after that photo was taken.

After high school, Billy and I were heading in different directions to college. He was going east to Georgetown University in Washington,

DC, and I was traveling west to Dallas to attend Southern Methodist University. Each of us faced the future with the mixed feelings that are typical of teenagers who are leaving family, friends, and hometown for an unknown future elsewhere. Overall, though, I'd have to say that we were excited and hopeful.

August 1, 1964:

I was a 16-year-old virgin when I was drugged and raped by one of Billy Clinton's friends.

August 2, 1964:

I lay still on my four-poster bed, staring at the ceiling. I felt groggy between my ears and sore between my legs. I tried to collect my thoughts. I was raped. Nice girls don't get raped. Why did this happen to me? What did I do wrong? I'm ruined. I'm trash. My life is over. I could die right now. I wish I could die right now. There are guns in the house. I could kill myself. If I kill myself, my mother will be upset. I could tell my mother what happened to me. My mother will be upset. My mother will be upset with me. My mother will think it was my fault. Everyone will think it was my fault. Maybe it was my fault. But, what did I do wrong? Why did this happen to me? Nice girls don't get raped. I was raped. I must not be a nice girl. I must be trash. My life is over. I should kill myself. My life is already over. I am trash and my life is over.

August 16, 1977:

Thirteen years later, I finally told someone that I had been raped. I told Billy Clinton, having no idea that he would rape Juanita Broaddrick the following year. Billy said:

"I'm sorry that happened to you."

August 1, 1987:

Twenty-three years after my rape by Billy Clinton's friend, I told one of my longtime girlfriends what had happened to me back in 1964. She asked me the guy's name. I told her. She knew about two other women he had raped. I should have told someone about the rape when it happened. I should have filed criminal charges against the rapist. I could have prevented other girls from being raped. Nice girls don't let other girls be raped because they are afraid to say anything.

December 30, 2015:

I watched on television as the nationally beloved comedian Bill Cosby was arrested on sexual assault charges. They say he drugged and raped women and young girls. Billy Clinton raped and sexually assaulted women too. To protect him (actually, to protect her own political career), Billy's co-conspirator wife Hillary then attacked his victims . . . and attacked me. Now Hillary is running for president and she pretends to support women; it's time to talk honestly about that great big lie.

January 6, 2016:

Juanita Broaddrick was raped by Arkansas Attorney General Bill Clinton in 1978. She recently sent a message via Twitter about her horrible experience with that long-ago rape:

"It never goes away."

4

LIFE AFTER DEATH

I believe that there are three kinds of people in this world:

1. people (of any sexual orientation) who have never been raped or sexually assaulted;

2. people who have been raped or sexually assaulted, but are in denial about the fact that it happened and/or in denial about how it has affected their lives and relationships; and

3. people who have been raped or sexually assaulted, and have worked hard to overcome it, but still carry traces of something that will never go away.

There are infinite variations on the theme of what people do psychologically in response to being raped and sexually assaulted. Some of the common categories are:

a. many become confused about their sexual orientation;

b. many become frigid, refusing to have sex with anyone or refusing to enjoy sex; and

c. others become promiscuous.

I'm in the 3-c group. I worked hard in individual and group therapy, in twelve-step programs, in prayer and meditation, in reading about dysfunctions and treatment; I even earned a bachelor's degree in psychology. Still, like Juanita Broaddrick, I carry traces of being raped, and that will never go away.

Although I don't know anything about the "confused" response, I firmly believe that both Billy Clinton and Hillary Rodham are in the no. 2 group—sexually abused but in denial. There is no outward sign that either one of them has dealt with that inner demon, even though Billy admitted to me that he was a sex addict, but that's getting ahead of the story.

Billy has been an abuser of women over the course of many decades, and Hillary is his enabler and co-conspirator in those abuses. Without treatment, the abused become abusers.

These "decisions" to become frigid or promiscuous were usually not conscious decisions that we victims made as children or teenagers or young adults. Here's the thought process I subconsciously followed (and consciously figured out later) to deal with being raped:

i. I hated being raped and being unable to stop it; I needed to be in control;

ii. I will never let something like that happen to me again; I need to be in control;

iii. I will always be in control of what I do sexually; I need to be in control;

iv. I will never let a man force himself on me sexually; I need to be in control;

v. I will become the sexual instigator because I need to be in control;

vi. I will have sex when I want and with whom I want, so I can be in control; and

vii. I am in control of my sexual behavior.

I was deluding myself because I was not in control at all. This is analogous to the child who does the opposite of what his parents demand and thinks that it is being in control.

Although the result of being raped was promiscuity in my case, it's easy to see how the opposite could happen.

I say all that to explain, but not in any way to excuse, my sexual behavior after I was raped. One of the unintended consequences of my behavior was that I became pregnant at the age of seventeen. I married the child's father (fortunately, not my rapist) and had a beautiful baby, whom I loved more than life itself.

In fact, it was this new little life that helped me to overcome the kinds of death I had experienced in being raped: the death of my childhood, the death of my sexual innocence, the death of my dreams for happily-ever-after, and more.

While married and having children, I continued to take college classes locally at Little Rock University (now UALR). I also continued to see Billy Clinton when he was in Little Rock or Hot Springs, or when I was in Washington, DC, where he was at Georgetown University.

After graduating from Georgetown, Billy went to Oxford University in England via a Rhodes scholarship that was strongly supported by his mentor Sen. Bill Fulbright.

It's important to this story (and to my relationship with Billy and Hillary) to know that Fulbright had given Billy a job during his student years at Georgetown, had introduced him to everyone who was anyone in Washington, and had provided the kind of invaluable support that only a man of Fulbright's stature and integrity could offer. It is impossible to overemphasize Bill Fulbright's role in Billy Clinton's life and political career.

I did not know until a couple of decades later that Billy Clinton had raped at least one woman while he was at Oxford, which explains why he left after two years and did not finish the three-year program there. I understand why his victim did not press the issue. Billy was not arrested, not tried, and not convicted of that rape in England, so he had no trouble getting into law school at Yale.

Yes, it made me nauseous—physically sick to my stomach—to learn about Billy's rapes, especially after what had happened to me. Imagine how you might feel if someone you loved turned out to be a sick, sociopathic criminal.

Currently, in the United States, more women are coming forward to testify about the sexual assaults by comedian Bill Cosby. At the same time, many more women are becoming emboldened by the example of others and are beginning to test the waters about revealing Billy Clinton's sexual assaults on them. This includes other women in England.

If the guy who raped me (and God knows how many other women he eventually raped) ever had the nerve to run for public office, you can bet that I would do everything I could do to let people know who he really is. I have learned that lesson. Billy Clinton is no different; Hillary is his accessory after the fact.

It's amazing to me that Hillary Rodham Clinton recently had the unmitigated gall to produce a television ad saying that women who claim rape and sexual assault should be believed! She should have added a disclaimer: "*unless* they were raped or sexually assaulted by my husband and coattail provider. In that case, they should be publicly ridiculed and humiliated."

Eventually, and not surprisingly, I was divorced. It was late January 1974. I was twenty-five years old and the mother of three daughters, who were three, five, and seven years old. Decisions loomed.

The previous spring, Billy Clinton had earned his law degree at Yale, where he had lived with fellow law student Hillary Rodham. Their "romantic" story has been printed in other places, but I've never seen any reference to the fact that Billy moved in with Hillary to sponge off her allowance.

Billy told me at the time that he thought his sex life was over, but at least he had a roof over his head. He felt powerless then, and his seething, untreated need for power was percolating beneath the surface. Of course, necessarily without treatment, it would emerge soon enough in more sexual assaults.

It was Hillary's early and continuing role in the Clinton "marriage" to provide finances for the political couple. This fact is critically important in understanding the long-term dynamic of their arrangement. Hillary's role of providing financial security for Billy was part of her motivation for the series of financial crimes (yes, crimes) that she committed over the decades. Hillary was upholding her part of the deal to get Billy elected president, after which it would be her turn to be the first woman in the Oval Office. (She wouldn't want to count the other women Billy had in there before her!)

Ideology, integrity, and love of country were never involved in the "Billary" quest for the White House. It was always a codependent, coconspiratorial grab for money and power and more money and more power. Unfortunately for them, and for the United States of America, there is never enough to satisfy addicts.

5

HOLD THAT PLANE!

As I stated previously, my divorce was final at the end of January 1974. I was twenty-five years old and the mother of three daughters, ages three, five and seven. I needed to make some wise decisions for our short-and-long-term future, whether in Little Rock or elsewhere. Billy Clinton's phone call didn't help me a bit.

Billy called me from Fayetteville where he was teaching at the University of Arkansas School of Law, after graduating from Yale Law School the previous spring. (I did *not* have any idea at that time, or until years later, that Billy was "coming on to" and even assaulting some of the female law students who were in his classes.) Billy was planning to be in Little Rock for a breakfast meeting with some heavy hitters (that's big money, not thugs), and he wanted me to go to that casual little event with him.

As readers of my novels know, one of the most enjoyable aspects of my early childhood was going to breakfast with my daddy and his friends in Hot Springs. They were all involved in politics in some way. Typically, attendees would be the mayor, the tax collector, the chief of police, various aldermen, and state representatives and senators, all of whom I knew from childhood on a first-name basis. They ate breakfast, insulted each other, laughed a lot, and discussed the inner workings of the city and the state. They groused about national politics from time to time, but I think they preferred to talk about the people they knew personally. Only United States Senator Bill Fulbright knew all the national figures, and he really did know everyone.

The breakfast meeting with the heavy hitters was on February 16, 1974, at Little Rock's Holiday Inn Downtown, a pleasant but unspectacular venue. We had a lovely time and lively conversation. At the appropriate moment, I excused myself to go powder my nose, and when I returned the men were waiting to say their good-byes.

I thought everything had gone quite well with these men who had been handpicked by Senator Fulbright; he was not at the meeting, but had rented a room upstairs for Billy.

This was one of Billy's first meetings with potential financial backers in his first campaign. Billy was going after a giant in his first political race; he was running against John Paul Hammerschmidt, the entrenched Republican in the conservative Third Congressional District. Actually, it wasn't his very first political race. Before that, Billy was elected senator at Boys State, launching him into that famous Kennedy photo, and he lost our senior class secretary election to Carolyn Yeldell Staley, his next-door neighbor and lifelong friend.

After that breakfast meeting, Billy could hardly wait to get me upstairs. He was so excited.

"You were spectacular!" he said as we retreated to the privacy of Fulbright's hotel room.

"I had a great time!" I responded truthfully. "Nice guys. Big checkbooks?"

"Oh, yeah," Billy said. "I can see this campaign going very very well."

We talked politics and people for a while, but Billy didn't mention

Hillary, the other woman with whom he had lived at Yale. Despite the adult nature of our relationship at that time, I had no concern about any other woman in his life. I was newly divorced and needed some breathing room. We talked about my plans for the immediate future, which included law school somewhere. Here asked me to go to UA, where he was teaching. I was uncertain about that.

Suddenly, as if he had completely forgotten about it, Billy said that he was going to be late to catch his plane back to Fayetteville. I drove him to the airport as fast as I could, using the back route across Ninth Street that I knew so well because my ex-husband's family had warehouses in the area.

Billy wanted me to run to the departure gate with him, so I left my car parked at the curb. (You could do that back then.) We were about halfway to the gate when Billy asked me if I had a dime because he had to make a phone call.

"Get them to hold the plane!" Billy said, as he picked up the phone receiver and deposited a dime. This is a classic example of his self-importance and my willingness to help.

I ran to the gate (no security in those days), formulating a plan on the way. I asked the ticket agent if she knew the name of the plane's captain. As luck would have it, she did. I went to the gate agent who had just closed the door.

"Sorry," she said. "You've missed the flight."

"I'm not trying to get on the flight, but I must talk to Captain Whoever-He-Was. Urgent!"

In answer to her questions, I told her that I had met him in Dallas at a party near Love Field, and I had to discuss something important with him. I convinced her to open the door and go down to give him the message that Dolly, the blond he had met in Dallas, needed to see him and it was urgent. Back in the 1960s and 1970s, the area around Love Field was a major playground for airline personnel and wealthy businessmen, so I thought my ploy might work. Sure enough, a minute later, the captain appeared. He was frowning.

"Thank you so much for coming to talk to me!"

I put my hand on his arm and we walked about ten feet away from the gate attendant.

"I'm really sorry and embarrassed to do this, but my boyfriend is running for Congress and he seems to think that he's the president already. He asked me to have you hold the plane for him."

The captain laughed, and he may have breathed a sigh of relief as well. We stood there and talked until Billy finally sauntered to the gate area. Yes, sauntered. Either he figured he had already missed the plane or he figured I'd be doing what I was doing. In either case, he did not bother to hurry. I introduced Billy to the captain, who gave me a smile and a salute before he put his arm around Billy's shoulders and headed to the plane.

Billy's antisocial, narcissistic disregard for the comfort, needs, schedules, and convenience of other people is in evidence here, along with his now-famous tendency to be late for everything. Being habitually late is a known passive-aggressive trait, and certainly a form of control. These traits would only get worse as Billy acquired power.

Hillary, on the other hand, is not known for being late. She is known for her antisocial, narcissistic disregard for the comfort, needs, schedules, and convenience of other people. You may have heard some of the stories told about Hillary's arrogance by state troopers in Arkansas and by the staff serving in the White House. Believe them.

Watch the imperious way Hillary treats anyone "beneath" her, especially young black women. Review her last political debate; she didn't even look her opponent Bernie Sanders in the eye when she deigned to give him a perfunctory handshake.

6

MEETING HILLARY— THE BACKGROUND

Many people (but not Arkansans!) have been surprised to discover that I knew Hillary Rodham Clinton personally. Hillary and I were never friends, of course, but it shouldn't be surprising that we knew each other. After all, I had known her husband since childhood, and our families were connected.

Billy Clinton and I both graduated from Hot Springs High School in 1964. Our friendship and dating relationship throughout high school developed into a deep adult friendship and, eventually, into a long-term affair.

I'm not proud (and have repented) of having that decades-long affair with Billy Clinton, but it is a fact. It was our relationship that formed the basis of my connection with Hillary.

In Arkansas, everyone (of the same race and socioeconomic status) knows everyone else or knows someone who knows everyone else. This was especially true in the 1950s and 1960s, when the total population of the small state was under 2 million people.

Members of the Kyle and the Clinton families had been friends for many years in Hot Springs. As a fun piece of trivia, it was "Uncle Raymond" Clinton who taught me to play poker when I was in the first grade.

Uncle Raymond Clinton's brother Uncle Roy Clinton worked for my dad in his insurance business. Billy's stepfather Roger Clinton, Sr., was the brother of Uncle Raymond and Uncle Roy. By the way, Roger, Sr., was the only one of the three Clinton brothers whom I did *not* call "uncle." We were never close and I never had any need to call him anything.

Roger Clinton bought (leased? borrowed?) his cars from his brother Raymond, who owned the Buick dealership; Roger Clinton bought his insurance from his brother Roy, through my dad's agency.

It happened to be Uncle Raymond's son "Corky" Clinton who introduced me to his "cousin" Billy Clinton on the Belvedere Country Club golf course in the summer of 1959. I feel like apologizing for all the quotation marks, but that's the way it is here in Arkansas.

Anyway, Billy and Corky were cousins by marriage, and not related at all by blood. Billy's mother, Virginia, had married Roger Clinton, Sr., in 1950 and moved with him to Hot Springs where she worked as a nurse anesthetist. In 1956, Virginia and Roger had a son named Roger, Jr., who was almost exactly ten years younger than Billy.

Given the small size of the community and the long-term relationships among and between the Kyle and Clinton families (there are many more connections, but they are not necessary to this story), it would have been odd if I had not eventually met Hillary. I adopted another Southern custom and gave her an appropriate nickname: "Chilly."

In the fall or winter of 1972, Billy and I were having a long-distance telephone conversation (which was a bigger deal back then) before cell phones. He mentioned that he had moved in with a fellow law student named Hillary. I don't recall if he said her last name at the time or not. He spoke in an offhanded manner and I took it to be nothing serious.

A few months before that, Billy had been in Arkansas, working on the presidential campaign of Democratic nominee George McGovern. It was during the summer of 1972 when the budding politician Billy Clinton unburdened himself by confiding to me a serious secret that could have killed his political career. I was very upset to have him "dump" that burden on me, but I did keep the secret—all these years.

After a while, I realized that keeping Billy's potentially political-career-killing secret would act as a kind of insurance policy for me. The long-term lesson, of course, is that Billy has no qualms about unloading his problems on someone else. Is it coincidental that it's usually a woman?

With the history that we had before 1972, I certainly knew how to tell the difference between Billy's deeper true feelings and his more typical surface-level "political" persona that he showed (and still shows) to the rest of the world.

In our phone call that included talk about Hillary in 1972, Billy made it sound like the Hillary person had a decent place to live and he had simply moved in with her. Knowing how cheap Billy was and how often he used other people for whatever he needed at the time, I didn't find his away-from-home living arrangement to be unbelievable, nor even out of the ordinary, for him.

Billy said that he had told Hillary all about me. On the other hand, however, he didn't say very much to me about her. He spoke as if she were not, and never would be, an issue between us.

In a strange way, even though Billy and Chilly eventually married, she never was an issue between us, other than an annoyance that had to be considered in scheduling our time together. Hillary was always "the other woman" as far as Billy's attention went.

As adults, Billy Clinton and I were both dysfunctionally comfortable in rationalizing that *our* relationship predated the "Billy and Chilly Show." After all, I was only eleven years old when we met on the golf course in Hot Springs, and he was only twelve, going on thirteen.

It had started innocently enough, and grew into a deep friendship before becoming an affair. Thus our affair was, and always would be to us, somehow okay. Yes, that is classic rationalization.

One can never know exactly what Billy may have told Hillary about me, and when he told her, but I'm certain that she was aware of me in 1972. Most people do give some background information about important old boyfriends or girlfriends when they start dating someone new. Even the compulsive liar Billy Clinton did that. Probably.

Unfortunately, the articulate young politician Clinton did not prepare Hillary or me for our first face-to-face meeting.

Fast-forward a little over a year to February 1974. Billy and I were openly dating, although it was necessarily something of a long-distance arrangement. Arkansans of a certain age will remember that, before the interstate highway was constructed, there was quite a tortuous drive between Little Rock and Fayetteville.

Part of the trek from the state's political capital in Little Rock to the state's sports capital in Fayetteville was called the Pig Trail. It was a play on words regarding the convoluted turns in the highway from the center of the state to the "Woooo Pig Sooie—Razorbacks!" destination in the northwest quadrant.

Young love is persistent, however, and Billy never did require much sleep. He drove to Little Rock frequently and I never had to meet him in Fayetteville, which was nice since I had three young children in my care. In retrospect, I realize that Billy probably didn't want me to be in Fayetteville because of his other extracurricular activities there.

The astute politician did not mention Hillary the other woman to me during the winter and spring months of 1974. He also did not mention how many other women he might have been "seeing" at the time. Stories about his inappropriate advances toward female law students did not surface until decades later.

Nevertheless, knowing that I had taken the LSAT (Law School Admissions Test) and had applied to several law schools, Billy repeatedly asked me to choose to attend law school at UA, the University of Arkansas. He wanted us to be able to spend more time together, and it would certainly be easier if I were living in Fayetteville rather than in Little Rock.

UA was not my first choice of law schools, although I was somewhat tempted by Billy's enthusiasm for the idea. Frankly, I never did like cold, rainy weather, and Fayetteville has plenty of that. Additionally, I wanted my children to be able to visit their father in Little Rock and have him visit them frequently. Fayetteville was not an easy commute by car, and the foggy winter weather could be treacherous for an approaching private plane.

On the other hand, Billy made the idea of going to law school in Fayetteville sound like a fun sort of adventure and a kind of "do-over" for our whole relationship. After graduating from high school together, we had gone to different colleges, and maybe we could recapture that missed era ten years later.

Another plus in the Fayetteville equation was that one of my brothers had recently decided to go to law school there, and he suggested that we (my brother, not Billy!) could purchase a duplex together.

At that point, I was undecided and it was too early to have received any acceptance letters from law schools. Just for the record, I was accepted everywhere I applied.

When Billy decided to run for Congress, early on he had asked me to accompany him to a private meeting with potential financial backers for the race. Other than Uncle Raymond's initial $10,000 contribution, I think that most of the money connections were made for Billy Clinton by Bill Fulbright.

Sen. William J. Fulbright of Arkansas had become a strong supporter of Billy Clinton during Billy's years at Georgetown University while Fulbright was chairing the powerful Senate Foreign Relations Committee. It was Fulbright who supported Billy's bid for a Rhodes scholarship. Bill Fulbright was always there for Billy Clinton when he needed something political.

I enjoyed going to that first "fund-raising" meeting with Billy; it reminded me of having breakfast with my daddy and his political cronies while I was growing up in Hot Springs. Billy was thrilled with the financial backing that he received that day, which typically had been pledged at the end of a meal when I went to "powder my nose," as was expected in Arkansas politics.

Not surprisingly, Billy asked me to be with him when he introduced himself to the Arkansas people at his first televised press conference. I stood beside Billy; my mother stood beside me. George Douthit, a long-time photojournalist, was among the press corps there in Little Rock for the momentous occasion of Billy's first televised foray into politics.

George Douthit's photographic works are now housed in a Special Collection in the University of Arkansas Library. I'm pleased to have my own special mementos from George. On the day of that press conference, George took what I consider to be the best-ever picture of Billy, the young politician. George mailed it to me along with a very sweet note and photos of our group.

I'm glad to have that photo because over the years, too many other photographs and documents have disappeared from various archives as the Clintons and their minions rewrite the history about Billy and me (and everything else) to line up with their lies.

With his permission and his assurance that the photo was mine for all purposes, I used George's excellent picture of Billy in an article that I wrote for the UALR (University of Arkansas at Little Rock) student newspaper, announcing Billy's candidacy for Congress. I was taking a journalism course that semester (in preparation for going to law school) and was pleased that the photo taken by George and the article written by me made the front page of the school paper.

No, I did not call him "Billy" in the article because he was using the name Bill Clinton professionally; I am not, however, the only person from Hot Springs who still calls him by his childhood nickname.

Naturally, I gave a copy of the UALR newspaper to Billy. He was pleased to see the front-page article, but very surprised to see that I had named a third, unannounced person who was planning to run against him in the Democratic primary.

I was tickled to have "scooped" all the major news outlets in Arkansas with that information. No, I never did reveal my source who proved to be 100 percent reliable.

There was no sign of Hillary at Billy's first press conference in Little Rock early in 1974. Although Hillary had flunked the Washington, DC bar exam, she had landed a job working for the Watergate Commission that was investigating the actions of President Richard Nixon.

Ironically, Nixon would resign for crimes that were petty compared to those of the Klinton Krime Kartel in the following years. Hillary stayed in Washington into the summer of 1974, trying desperately to establish herself as a potential political power near the seat of power in the nation's capital city. That is something she was never able to do on her own.

Billy did not mention Hillary to me at all in the spring of 1974. He intensified his uphill battle against the entrenched Republican congressman John Paul Hammerschmidt in northwest Arkansas, but he still found time to visit with me in Little Rock . . . and other women around the state.

Although Hillary was not present at Billy's historic first televised press conference in Little Rock, she had begun to assert her presence elsewhere in a strange way. In the spring of 1974, Hillary sent her father and one of her brothers to Arkansas to "help" in Billy's congressional campaign. It was common knowledge, however, that she had sent them there to spy on the wandering candidate, who was already quite well known for his roving eye.

How did everyone know the Rodham men were there as spies? Easy. It would be comical to think that a couple of Yankees invading the state of Arkansas could add anything substantive to Billy's political campaign. I suppose they could stuff envelopes and put on stamps.

Back then, by the way, it was important to put on stamps slightly crooked in the corner of the envelope so that they did not appear to be affixed there by machines. This was in the "olden days" before everything was digitized, mass-produced, and mail-merged.

I don't know what the men of the Rodham Spy Team were able

to report to Hillary about what Billy was doing with other women in Arkansas. They were very obviously Yankees in a very Southern state, and it was not likely that they could have garnered any insider information.

Hillary herself wasn't able to garner insider information when she moved to the state. She snooped through Billy's papers, but she had to hire private investigators to get the latest news about Billy and his current other woman . . . or women, as the case may be. I'm getting ahead of my story.

In early 1974, Billy was in Fayetteville teaching and traveling for his campaign. I was in Little Rock taking postgraduate classes to get in the groove to go to law school. Hillary the other woman was in Washington doing research about Nixon for the Watergate investigation.

Billy lost that congressional race and continued teaching for a while, biding his time for another campaign. Hillary made such a bad impression on her Watergate boss that he wouldn't give her a letter of recommendation for another job. She would ultimately move to Arkansas, where she would pass the bar exam, after flunking the bar exam in Washington. Billy would help her get a job teaching at the law school with him.

I had no trouble deciding what to do next in my life after seeing what Billy did on the night of the 1974 Democratic primary election as you will read about in the next chapter.

It would later become obvious that spying was not the only technique that Hillary Rodham had picked up in Washington while studying the backroom machinations of President Richard Nixon. She would upgrade her spy team from being only her father and a brother to hiring professional investigators who had no qualms about sending thugs to silence any of Hillary's perceived enemies.

Sending others to do her dirty work of breaking and entering and destroying property and threatening people and doing whatever it took to cover those tracks became Hillary's *modus operandi* in Arkansas . . . and beyond.

I can't fault anyone for having trouble believing that such outrageous behavior went on unchecked and unreported year after year after year. As I will relate in later chapters, this was not terribly off the norm for those of us who grew up in Hot Springs, the playground of Al Capone and other gangsters, but it's not within the realm of experience of Middle America.

The Clinton saga supports the cliché that truth is often stranger than fiction.

7

MEETING HILLARY RODHAM

The night of May 28, 1974, was a significant one. It was vote-counting time for the Democratic primary in Arkansas. It was an especially heady time for the young congressional candidate William Jefferson Clinton and for all of us who knew him as Billy.

Billy would be flying to Little Rock that night from Fayetteville, where he was teaching law while running for Congress. He had asked me to pick him up at the airport to take him to the television station downtown for a live interview. After that, we would go to Sen. Bill Fulbright's campaign headquarters for pictures and a brief show-of-support visit with his mentor. Then I would take Billy back to the airport.

Billy and I were involved in a sexual relationship at the time, and both of us were single, but I had no illusions about spending the entire night with him. He would go back to Fayetteville to watch the returns with his campaign workers, as he should. Billy was making the quick round-trip to Little Rock because it was the only city that had statewide television capability in 1974, and he wanted to take advantage of a free appearance there.

Billy was already thinking about the next political office, as he always was; it would be a statewide race. With a borrowed airplane full of gas and a volunteer pilot (plus my free taxi service), Billy was getting invaluable television publicity that night without any out-of-pocket expense.

On that primary election day, I treated myself to some serious pampering, knowing that Billy always wanted his "Pretty Girl" to look her best. No, I didn't take offense at the pet name he had called me since I was a kid.

I considered what Billy might like me to wear and decided on the new aqua and white knit dress with a jacket that I had worn only once. I had bought it to do a regional television commercial, which hadn't aired yet, so it would be new to Billy. He appreciated seeing his Pretty Girl dressed well.

By the time I left the house about 7:30 that evening, I was refreshed and relaxed for the short drive to Adams Field in Little Rock. The gate attendant, who had known me for years, waved me in with a friendly greeting. I sat in the car with the air-conditioner on as I watched Billy's borrowed plane taxiing toward the general aviation area.

Thanking God that Billy had landed safely, I waited eagerly for the props to stop and the cabin door to open. Billy was the first person off the plane, followed by a dowdy-looking woman who appeared to be middle-aged and three innocuous young men in gray suits. I opened my car door and resisted the urge to run to Billy's arms. In public, I always took a cue from his body language. To my amazement, he extended his right hand in the gentleman's traditional gesture of greeting.

"How good of you to come," Billy enunciated formally.

I stifled a laugh, wondering what he was thinking, but took his offered hand and shook it. Looking into his eyes, I saw confusion, weakness and fear. My heart went out to him, and I wished he had spent at least part of the afternoon with me; he obviously needed some pampering.

The dowdy-looking woman stepped up beside him. I could see

then that she was of our generation, not middle-aged as I first thought.

I couldn't imagine why Billy would haul such a person in the plane with him in public. She was wearing a misshapen, brown, dress-like thing that must have been intended to hide her lumpy body. The garment was long, but stopped too soon to hide her fat ankles and her thick calves, which, to my astonishment, were covered with black hair.

Thick brown sandals did nothing to conceal her wide feet and the hair on her toes. I looked up quickly, embarrassed for the woman and afraid that I had already been rude for staring, as a kid might stare at a deformed or crippled person.

The early training from my daddy took over and I looked straight into the woman's eyes, searching for the good and for our common ground. Her eyes, however, bulged out of focus and seemed to glare at me behind coke-bottle-thick lenses. The dark, heavy frames that competed with thick eyebrows that seemed to stretch from one side of her forehead to the other.

Sensing real hostility behind the glasses, I glanced quickly at Billy for some direction. He hesitated.

In that moment, I noticed that the woman emitted an overpowering odor of perspiration and greasy hair. I hoped that I wouldn't gag when she got in my car.

Finally, Billy spoke.

"Dolly, this is Hillary. Hillary, Dolly."

I was stunned.

I had no idea where Billy could have found someone so bizarre to play this little joke on me. I decided to adopt the poker face I had learned from our Uncle Raymond, and I pretended that I didn't even notice this Hillary-impersonation trick. I wasn't going to let this theater-major, or whatever she was, see how appalled I was at her hideous disguise.

"Pleased to meet you," I said to the hostile woman.

I smiled and extended my right hand in friendship unconvinced that this was the woman Billy said he was living with.

The woman responded only with a glare at me. Finally, seeing my hand still extended, she managed a grudging nod. She did not condescend to shake my hand. I had to admire her for staying in character. After taking acting classes and doing television work, I knew how difficult that could be. She was carrying it off well.

The three young men with Billy seemed pleasant enough, but certainly no threat to Billy's domination in a crowd. He always enjoyed, actually thrived upon—no, really lived for—being the center of attention. A few minutes later, at the television station, it seemed to annoy him that a lot of people were making a fuss over me. That sort of sharing of attention for me had sometimes annoyed him in high school as well.

The sandal-shod woman with lank, smelly hair stood off to the side and glared at everyone. I thought that Billy should have told her to lay off this little joke at the television station because, whoever she was, she would be a terrible reflection on him. He, however, never even seemed to notice she was there.

I vowed to myself not to drive off without the other woman, no matter how bad she smelled.

The interview at the station went well and I was genuinely happy for Billy. Immediately after his camera appearance, the strange woman scowled and gestured at him.

She was trying to direct Billy's attention to the latest election results on the studio monitors. I didn't realize at the time that her big concern was Fulbright's *losing* vote tally.

I needn't have worried about leaving the bedraggled woman behind. When Billy was ready to go, she wordlessly followed him to my car. Billy slid to the middle of the front seat, rubbing against me. The three gray suits sat silently in the back. The other woman plopped into the front passenger seat, as she had done earlier, and slammed her own door.

Driving from the television station lot, I turned to the right.

Billy asked, "Where are we going?"

I silently considered a plethora of cute philosophical replies, but instead answered directly.

"We're going to Fulbright's headquarters, of course. That's what you had planned for this part of the evening."

Senator Fulbright had his campaign headquarters in downtown Little Rock, which was typical for a statewide race. The building was less than a dozen blocks from the television station we had just visited, so it was no big deal to go there.

"It was the plan to go to Fulbright headquarters," Billy said, "but I need to go to the airport. The plan has been changed."

I noted his use of the passive voice: "the plan has changed." He had a habit of switching to the passive voice when he didn't want to take responsibility for something.

A classic example is, "Mistakes were made." I don't think I ever heard him say, "I made a mistake."

"Why has the plan changed?" I asked. Thinking about my sister who was also at Fulbright's campaign headquarters, I added, "Little Sister said the Senator is expecting you."

"He'll understand," Billy said. "You can just tell him that I had a plane to catch."

I couldn't deal with his convoluted logic. Having flown in private planes for years, I knew who should be in charge of the take-off time. I didn't turn the car around, but continued toward Fulbright's headquarters.

"Yes, you do have a plane," I answered, "but you certainly don't have to catch one. It's a private plane, and it's yours for the evening. It's important that you stop by to show your support for the Senator. After all, you wouldn't be this far along in your career, especially at your age, without everything he has done for you."

"Didn't you see the returns coming in on the monitors at the television station?" Billy asked impatiently.

"Of course, I saw them," I replied with some irritation. I hated it when Billy asked me stupid questions. "And, of course, I'm sure that you're going to win the Democratic nomination for Congress."

I did not inject my opinion that the incumbent John Paul Hammerschmidt would whip the bejeebers out of him in the general election the following November.

"Yes, I'll win," Billy replied, "but, Fulbright is *losing*!"

There was no tone of affection, sadness, empathy, or graciousness in his voice when Billy said the name Fulbright. He emphasized the word *losing* as if this *losing* should be an explanation for not going to see his mentor on the most critical night of the elder statesman's thirty-year career.

"Yes, he's losing," I agreed, "and that's very sad, but what does it have to do with you?"

"Well," Billy explained with strained patience, "I don't want to be seen with a loser."

He spat out the epithet *loser* so venomously that I can still hear the reverberation in my mind all these decades later.

I felt a kick in my stomach from my friend and lover.

How could Billy let himself be seen in public with this awful unknown woman in the brown sack? How could he turn his back on his beloved mentor after all these years? How could he call Senator Fulbright a loser?

I truly loved the Senator for the way he had sponsored and mentored Billy, and Billy had always talked to me as if he loved the Senator too.

Bill Fulbright had provided a Senate job for Billy while he was in college at Georgetown University; he had introduced him to powerful people in Washington; he had given him support for the Rhodes Scholarship that Billy received to study abroad; he had provided an impeccable reference for Billy to get a teaching position at the University of Arkansas Law School; and, most recently, the Senator had given his endorsement and had made the introductions to the financial backers for Billy's congressional campaign. The "heavy hitters" whom I had met a few months earlier were all writing checks based on the Senator's endorsement of Billy Clinton.

My own little sister shared my feelings for the Senator, and she was at his campaign headquarters with the elder gentleman and his wife. Although she was a month shy of her sixteenth birthday, she had been flying all over the state with Senator and Mrs. Fulbright, to political rallies, shopping malls, picnics, etc.

The Senator had taken my sister under his wing, as he had done for many other promising young people in Arkansas. Senator Fulbright (who had been a friend of my daddy) also was instrumental in helping one of my brothers to receive a Presidential Appointment to the Air Force Academy, but there was no doubt that Billy Clinton was his bright and shining star.

(By the way, there was not a clear-cut election "win" for Billy that night in May 1974; he did, however, win the Democratic nomination run-off in the following month.)

In my mind, at that moment in the car with Billy, with the strange stinky woman, and with the three hushed gray suits in the back seat, I could easily imagine Senator Fulbright at his headquarters. The Senator surely would have watched Billy Clinton on the Little Rock television broadcast, knowing that he was only a dozen blocks away.

Fulbright certainly would understand Billy's absence from his crowd of supporters that night. The Senator had seen his share of backstabbers in Washington. He was politically astute enough to realize that his young protégé had abandoned him at the mere count of a vote.

I felt hot tears forming in my eyes as I made a left turn away from the route to Fulbright's headquarters and headed back toward the airport.

"Senator Fulbright may not win this election," I whispered. When I realized that my voice was quivering, I took a deep breath and swallowed hard to regain my composure. Then I continued with a firm, drawn-out emphasis on every word, "but, he will *never* be a *loser*."

I made no pretense of further conversation with any of the foreign people in my car. I drove them to the airport in stony silence, dropped them off without a word, and drove immediately to Fulbright's headquarters. There, I found my younger sister in tears, watching the Senator's disastrous election returns on the television set. I hugged her gently.

My sister returned the hug, then looked around and asked me, "Where's Billy?"

"I took him back to the airport."

"I don't blame you. I can't believe what he did to you."

"To me?" I frowned, not knowing what she meant. "What did he do to me?" I asked.

"I heard that he had Hillary with him when you picked him up at the airport and took him to the television station. That's low. That's really low. That's even low for him."

"No! Don't be silly! It wasn't Hillary."

I laughed out loud, but my sister was shaking her head.

"Really, it wasn't Hillary," I explained. "It was one of the most pitiful-looking women I've ever seen. He couldn't have ever lived with someone like that. Are you kidding me? Not Billy. I don't know what was going on with him tonight. I guess he meant that to be some kind of a joke on me, but the joke's on him, having to put up with her all night. You should have seen her. Whew! You should have smelled her! I chose to ignore his big joke, but I have no idea what he was thinking, or where he dug her up."

My sister shook her head again.

"He dug her up at Yale," she announced in her typically blunt manner.

"That can't be right," I argued. "That could not possibly have been the real Hillary. It had to be some other woman."

"That was definitely Hillary," my sister continued. "I just talked to a friend of mine at the television station who had seen and smelled her somewhere before. I was calling over there to find out why y'all weren't here yet, and my friend told me that Billy had Hillary with him. He said that she was really pissed, but you were cool about it."

For the second time in the hour, I felt a kick in my gut.

"I can't believe he would do this to you," she repeated sympathetically, "but, since you weren't mad at him for that, why didn't you bring him with you? The Senator was looking forward to congratulating him for his primary victory. He wanted to have some pictures taken together tonight. He said that tonight is the beginning of his dream for Billy."

"Billy made me take him back to the airport without coming by here first when he saw the returns in Fulbright's race. He said he didn't want to be seen with a *loser.*"

I spat out the horrid word *loser* as Billy had done, and I looked over my sister's shoulder at the tall, slim, dignified Senator Fulbright. His elegant wife stood loyally by his side, a hint of tears brimming in her eyes as she envisioned the end of their thirty years of distinguished service in Washington.

The lights glared harshly on the Senator as reporters fired questions at him.

"Senator, are you ready to concede?"

Fulbright nodded. He smiled graciously in defeat. His eyes searched the faces in the crowd, and he thanked his friends for their support.

To this day, I still believe that Senator Fulbright was looking for Billy Clinton in his crowd of supporters that night. I believe that the pain of losing the senate race was less than the pain of being abandoned by his brightest hope.

Of course, the Senator never mentioned anything like that to any of us. He was not the sort of man who would. Senator Fulbright was a gracious giver. He was an honorable man.

As the Senator gave his concession speech in the harsh glare of television cameras, my sister and I joined the other supporters in enthusiastic applause for the retiring gentleman.

Noticing the tears in my eyes, my little sister said again, "I can't believe Billy would do this to you."

I said, "I can't believe he would do it to the Senator."

8

"LET'S YOU AND HER FIGHT"

I've been asked by many people what in the world Billy Clinton was thinking when he introduced Hillary and me on the evening of May 28, 1974, at the airport in Little Rock. It's not always possible to interpret the meaning of someone else's actions or to know all the purposes of the heart. There are many factors interacting on all of us at any given moment. To say that it is only one thing would underestimate the complexity of the human psyche. What follows in this chapter is a thumbnail summary of my ruminations about the event of meeting Hillary. To say that this is all I have concluded about it would underestimate me as well.

When I picked up Billy at the airport on that election night of May 28, 1974, I was so completely stunned by his traveling companion's odious appearance, smell, and demeanor that I still didn't believe this could be the woman he had lived with at Yale. Even with free rent, she was not his type.

I truly thought that the "introduction" of Hillary was some kind of a sick joke being played on me by Billy. Hillary, on the other hand, did not have the advantage of being deluded about who I was. I'm sure that she was both shocked and upset (and rightfully so!) to see *me* at the airport that night.

I've had plenty of time to consider what was going on, or not going on, in Billy's mind to introduce Hillary and me the way he did so many years ago. I never asked Billy about it. He wouldn't have told me the truth if he knew what it was.

I made it clear to Billy that night that I was beyond disappointed. I was downright disgusted with the way he treated Senator Fulbright. I was always more upset about his abandonment of his mentor than about the way he treated me—*and* Hillary—with that callous maneuver.

In retrospect, I wondered if part of Billy's hesitation before introducing Hillary and me had to do with the question of etiquette and social protocol. Although he had arranged the unfortunate first encounter between two of his "girlfriends," it was obvious that he had not considered his manners in advance.

It was not at all a gentlemanly act to introduce Hillary and me the way he did. He probably had not thought about whose name he should mention first.

Ultimately, at least as far as the protocol of introduction order is concerned, Billy did the right thing. He used my name first: "Dolly, this is Hillary. Hillary, Dolly."

Social protocol requires the older or closer family member or friend to be named first in an introduction. He followed that convention. That's the best I can say for his performance at the airport that night.

Knowing what I know now about Hillary, I'm sure that she later threw a screaming, cursing fit about my appearing at the airport that night. Maybe she was even more furious because Billy introduced us in the order that honored me over her. It would have been clear to any Southerner with manners that Hillary was "the other woman" in that encounter. I don't know if "the other woman" noticed that or not.

Unfortunately for Hillary, she would have had to wait through the long night of election returns before getting Billy alone for her tirade against him. I'm not saying that he didn't deserve it, but it was only the beginning of decades of such tirades.

At some point, even without therapy for her enabling, codependent, coconspiratorial behavior, Hillary finally must have realized that nothing she said or did would ever make any difference in Billy's behavior. Still, she probably felt better after venting since she had, and apparently still has, an incredible amount of pent-up anger.

Hillary's anger frequently erupts at the most inopportune moments, as when testifying before Congress, for example. Hillary, like Billy, believes her own lies, and she can fly off the handle any time she is challenged in the least.

Hillary is fortunate to have most of the mainstream media running interference for her, but her anger is now so close to the surface that even the media won't be able to save her from herself in every instance.

There is no reason to think that Billy Clinton would have told me the truth about the why and how of his introducing Hillary to me. He wouldn't have told me the truth even if I had asked him point blank, and even if he had paused long enough to analyze it.

Like so many compulsive liars and otherwise dysfunctional people, Billy adjusts the truth in his own mind to be something that makes him comfortable. Hillary does the same thing. After making that adjustment to his personal history, he comes to believe his own lies. Believing his own lies helps to make him quite convincing to people who don't know him well.

Although I didn't get the truth about the infamous airport meeting from Billy himself, I did consider two important pieces of family history.

First, Billy was raised by his maternal grandparents until he was nearly five years old. At that point, Billy's mother, Virginia, having finished her nursing training, went back to Hope to claim her emotionally abandoned son.

I am *not* saying that Virginia deliberately abandoned Billy emotionally, but the fact that she left him would have made an indelible impression. When Virginia married Roger Clinton, Sr., and decided to move to Hot Springs, the fight over Billy nearly resulted in a court action for grandparent custody, which was practically unheard of at that time in Arkansas.

Second, I heard something relevant from Billy's half-brother Roger Clinton, Jr., several years later. Roger's situation harkened back to the mother-grandmother fight over the child Billy.

Billy's brother, Roger, was discussing with me the fact that two women were interested in him. Naturally, I asked him which of them he preferred.

The strange answer he gave me was, "They can fight it out. I'll take the winner."

At first I thought he was kidding about that. Then I was shocked to realize that he was serious.

Did Billy have that same attitude? Did he think that it was up to the women to "fight it out" over him? Was this Billy's psychological baggage from the fight between his mother and his grandmother over custody of him? Did Billy expect Hillary and me to "fight it out," and he would take the putative winner?

I had always thought it was the man's place to "fight" for a woman. A real man would court a woman honestly and persistently. He would strive to vanquish any other suitors until the woman he wanted was his.

I had no idea what it would mean for two women to "fight it out" over a man, but I started to believe that Billy might have the same attitude and belief system as Roger did.

Perhaps I was too ingrained in the "old school" to grasp the concept of a woman fighting for a man. I thought that a coy drop of a handkerchief should do it, and the guy would take it from there. I never initiated a phone call to a boy that I liked, and I would have died before asking a guy for a date.

Considering the obvious role reversal that was part and parcel of the dysfunctional Clinton family, maybe I should have noticed that sooner. Billy, however, had always called me; I didn't call him.

Billy had always asked me to go out with him; I didn't ask him to go out with me. He seemed normal enough to me in high school. I didn't dream back then that he had a deep-seated, emotional need to have a woman aggressively pursue him.

Isn't it interesting that Billy later insisted that Monica Lewinsky was stalking him? In fact, he claimed that all those other women with whom he had sexual liaisons were pursuing him. He even complained to his friends and aides that women were everywhere and they all wanted him.

Billy even lied under oath about me, after decades together, saying that I had chased him for years wanting to have sex with him.

Once again, with Monica, Gennifer, Paula, and the others, Billy conveniently shifted the facts to a more comfortable personal scenario. He told himself the lies so many times that he believed them.

As a result of convincing himself that his lying stories were true, Billy's lies became quite convincing to people who didn't know him well. The people who didn't know him well included most of the people on the planet, but especially those who believed that character was not important in a politician.

It would never have mattered to me that Billy needed to feel pursued. I would not have chased after him. I would have (as I did in high school) only let him know with a smile or a look that I was interested.

As politically incorrect or old-fashioned as it might sound in the twenty-first century, I still believe that the major moves are up to the man in a relationship.

I heard the story (as did everyone else) about the way Hillary spoke to Billy first at Yale. She made it clear that she was interested in him. Ultimately, she invited him to move in with her at Yale, rather than vice versa.

Hillary took the role of financial provider from the beginning, or so Billy told me. Hillary's financial support enabled Billy to indulge in his addictions to politics, power, and sex. In the same way, in Billy's childhood home, his mother had assumed the role of supporting the family financially while his stepfather, Roger Clinton, indulged in his addiction to alcohol.

It seems reasonable that Billy had the same attitude that his little brother, Roger, expressed about women fighting over him. "Let's you and her fight."

In that scenario, Hillary would have had the upper hand in a fight with any of the women I ever knew. Neither I nor any Southern woman with options would have considered a guy like Billy Clinton to be a prize anyway.

It's one thing to have an affair with a charming rogue who was sexually addicted and never made a decent income. It would be far less charming to be married to such an out-of-control addict.

9

REUNIONS WITHOUT HILLARY

Even before the disastrous primary election night of 1974 I had decided not to go to law school at the University of Arkansas where Billy was teaching. Instead, I was going to Dallas to attend SMU School of Law, which enjoyed a much better academic reputation than UA. There was no doubt that the weather was better, and I would never have to run into Billy Clinton on campus.

After my divorce was final in January 1974, I had purchased a home right down the street from my mother's house in Little Rock. In June, I ran an ad in the newspaper:

LEASE: Lovely updated three-bedroom, two-bath colonial brick home with double garage and large fenced yard. Exclusive neighborhood near shopping and schools. Three-year lease ideal for medical school resident.

The first person to answer the ad said she was the wife of a medical school resident. The very pregnant young woman arrived promptly as scheduled at one o'clock on Sunday afternoon, with two small children in tow. She loved the house and asked me if I would allow dogs; they had two Irish Setters.

I cringed, thinking of the white carpet in the living and dining rooms, but I had a good feeling about the woman and was impressed with her punctuality. We immediately signed the lease agreement; I called the newspaper to cancel the ad.

"I can't believe you're actually going through with this," my mother said when she heard that I had leased my house. "At least, don't go all the way to Dallas. Why don't you go to Fayetteville with your brother? You'd be a big help to each other and I could visit you both in the same town."

It was somewhat tempting to go to Fayetteville, especially considering the cheap in-state tuition there. It would take every nickel I had to pay the private school tuition at SMU, but I thought it would be worth the investment. SMU School of Law had an excellent reputation for real estate and tax law, the two topics that interested me the most. I have never regretted the decision to go there.

My brother, on the other hand, found Fayetteville to be perfect for his requirements, so he went to UA School of Law where he renewed his childhood acquaintance with Billy. My brother was a brilliant guy, with undergraduate degrees from the University of Miami in both electrical and mechanical engineering; he had also completed some graduate work at Georgia Tech in engineering before deciding to go to law school. Additionally, he was a pilot, which was about to factor into his new life in Fayetteville.

At that time, Hillary was still working in Washington, DC, and she was still trying to become a political force under her own steam. It was a futile attempt.

Eventually, Hillary's job with the Watergate investigation ended. Although I don't believe she was fired from that position, I do believe that Hillary was devious and underhanded. I do believe that Hillary showed the same lack of integrity there that would later get her into more serious trouble. I also believe that Hillary's boss on the Watergate job had very little respect for her as a young lawyer, and he doubted that she had any potential to bring honor to the profession.

Hillary was still in Washington as I was moving to Dallas in that summer. Billy was teaching part time when he was in Fayetteville; he was campaigning hard in the Third Congressional District.

Moving to Dallas and attending law school was an exciting new chapter for me as a single mom with three children under the age of eight. I was highly organized, to say the least, and I did develop a lot of great ideas for surviving and thriving in such a situation. People used to laugh when I told them (tongue-in-cheek, with some typically Southern hyperbole) that I moved into an apartment in Dallas that had less square footage than our yacht on the Arkansas River, and I lived on a budget that was less than I had formerly paid my full-time maid.

Determined people adjust. I adjusted.

I felt a dramatic sense of relief when the last piece of my massive furniture was carefully placed in my charming apartment. I had discovered that "charming" was a real estate euphemism for a really tiny place.

Still, everything was going smoothly, and I felt good about my decisions, even though everyone in Arkansas had repeatedly suggested that I was crazy. I plugged my phone into the wall jack, sat on the sofa, and, before I had a chance to dial my mother's number, the phone rang.

It was Billy.

"I heard a rumor that you were moving to Dallas. I guess it's true," he joked lamely.

"Where'd you hear it?"

"Jim McDougal. He's working on my campaign now. So is Senator Fulbright."

"How nice for you," I replied. "Political friendship is a strange and wonderful thing."

"Come on, Dolly," Billy whined. "I don't want you to be mad at me."

"*Disgusted* would be a more accurate word."

"Well, then, don't be disgusted. Don't you know what day this is?" he asked petulantly.

"Yes. It is the day I start my life over in Dallas and make some choices that are good for me."

"My Pretty Girl, surely you know what day this is."

"I told you. It's the day I start my life over."

"Okay, then, what happened fifteen years ago today?"

"I went to the country club to play golf. If I had had any sense at all, I would have stayed home and cleaned my room."

Billy laughed.

"You can't mean that. We wouldn't have met."

"We would have met anyway, in high school, but I would have been older and had better sense. A person shouldn't make subconscious, life-long decisions at the age of eleven."

"Or, thirteen."

"You were twelve."

"Going on thirteen."

"Fine. So we made some bad decisions."

"I don't think they were bad decisions. I don't want to leave it like this, Pretty Girl. Talk to me."

I didn't say anything.

"Are you coming to the reunion?" he asked.

"What reunion?"

"The Class of '64. Next weekend."

"With moving and all, I forgot about it. I don't think so."

"Please, come. They'll have a great party. Afterward, you and I can get together to talk. We need to talk. I really don't want to leave it like this after all these years."

I considered what Billy was saying for a moment.

It had seemed awkward to end something as intense and important as our relationship with silence rather than a real word of good-bye. The primary-election-night-drop-off-at-the-airport had been a very summary dismissal, though not inappropriate in my mind.

I thought it might be reasonable to see Billy alone and listen to what he had to say. I hated to seem unreasonable.

"Please," he said softly into the silence. "I really want to talk to you. Alone. Surely I deserve that much."

"Fine," I agreed.

"Great! Meet me at the Velda Rose, in the ballroom, at seven next Saturday. We'll hang around for a while to see everybody and then we'll go somewhere private to talk. Just us. It's important to me. Thanks."

I hung up the phone and sighed, no longer in the mood to call my mother to give her the latest news. I looked for the large oil painting that had always hung over my sofa. Finding it but not the hooks or tools to hang it, I placed it on the back of the sofa and sat in the large wing chair to enjoy the tranquility of the painting and to think about Billy.

Suddenly, on the first day of my new life, it was important for me to understand more about my old life with Billy. I sifted through the pieces one by one, beginning with our meeting on the country club golf course.

Eventually, I focused on the night near the end of high school, when Billy and I almost had sex. He had said that he wanted to be president of the United States, and he insisted that I should marry for security.

I turned that over and over in my mind. I had only been interested in marrying for love, not for security. Security was Billy's big concern for me.

For the first time, I saw clearly what I should have noticed when I took Psychology 101. Billy's insistence on security was pure and simple projection.

Security was *his* big concern, and no wonder!

I recalled the gossip and stories about Billy's early childhood. His father had supposedly been killed before Billy was born; it was later revealed that his putative father was overseas in the military when Billy would have been conceived.

When Billy was an infant, his mother left him with her parents for years so she could finish nursing school. She wanted to finish school so she could have security. She must have carried a lot of fear about security and projected that fear onto Billy. He must have felt emotionally and psychologically abandoned by his mother, even though that certainly could not have been her intent at the time when she left him to further her education.

Having established that security was at the root of Billy's motives, I reviewed what I knew about Hillary. She was extremely unattractive, but with contact lenses, electrolysis, and a major change of eating habits, she could be made presentable.

She would also need to attend some sort of Southern charm school to get rid of her hostile Yankee attitude. All things considered, at this point, she would not cause Billy any concern that other men would be after her, and this would provide a kind of relational security.

Then I considered what Hillary's socioeconomic status might be. She did not have the air of aristocracy, which I had observed in my own mother and her friends who were raised in extreme wealth on the Philadelphia Main Line.

Nor did Hillary have the mark of poverty, so prevalent all across the South. I had noticed that really poor people who managed to get a decent education and to start moving up in society were always very careful to be clean, well-groomed, and as well-dressed as they could afford.

I concluded that Hillary was neither rich nor poor. She simply showed all the signs of a middle-class kid who was in some kind of rebellion against her family's values.

Finally, Hillary was a lawyer, a graduate of Yale, and reputedly smart and highly ambitious. She wanted a career in Washington. How perfect. With her personality, she needed someone charismatic like Billy, and he needed someone willing to work, as his mother had, to provide his security.

Billy had also complained that I was a distraction to him. Clearly, Hillary was not.

Then I remembered his comment two years earlier, in a friend's backyard under the trees in the moonlight that he had thought his enjoyment of sex was over. He thought he had outgrown it.

I had not understood what he meant at the time, but it was obvious now that Billy must have already been physically involved with the smelly, unattractive Hillary. No wonder he thought his sex life was over!

My major professor had warned his classes repeatedly not to perform amateur psychoanalysis on family members and friends. Even after thirty-nine hours of psychology classes leading to a bachelor's degree, spanning my seven years of college (interrupted by the births of three children), I had never indulged in amateur analysis.

I had taken my professor's warning about amateur analysis seriously, but I decided that my analysis of Billy and Hillary fit very nicely. Until I discovered otherwise, I would proceed as if it were true.

This analysis gave me the options to continue seeing Billy as before, fully understanding who he was and that we would never marry, or to end the relationship forever and forget about him.

Apparently Billy didn't want to end it forever or he wouldn't have called me. The choice was now mine. Coming to this point gave me some comfort, although I was still deeply troubled by his betrayal of his mentor Senator Fulbright. It seemed as if the Senator had already gotten over it. Politics.

I spent the rest of the week concentrating on putting my new home in order for the start of school and retrieving my children who had been in Little Rock with their father and their grandparents. I went to Hot Springs to attend my tenth high school reunion and then I would pick up the girls to start our new life in Dallas.

Within thirty minutes of arriving at the Velda Rose in Hot Springs on that Saturday night, I was sorry that I had made the effort to go. The few people whom I wanted to see were not there. With the general election looming in November, Billy was being the consummate politician, as he always was, but I failed to be charmed by it.

Billy gave me a hug and a kiss on the cheek, and then he turned to give an identical greeting to one of the popular girls in high school who now weighed two hundred fifty pounds.

Sensing my displeasure, Billy pulled me to him and whispered,

"Don't forget I want to see you. I want to talk about us. We'll leave early, okay?"

I nodded and sensed a *déjà vu*. Billy used to do this to me at parties and dances all through junior high and high school. Why did he want to see me later, but not with his friends? I could have understood it if I looked and smelled like Hillary.

A girl whom I had barely known in high school came up to me and said, "I always wondered why you and Billy didn't get married."

I just stared at her and frowned.

"So," the interloper went on, "I figured that since you're divorced, maybe there's something going on with you and Billy again. Want to tell?"

"You'll have to wait for the book."

I smiled and excused myself.

At that point, I had not ever consciously thought that there might be a book some day. It is ironic the way true words are often spoken in jest.

After a couple of hours, I was ready to leave. Billy was in the throes of hand shaking and hugging. I decided to take a walk down to the fountain at the junction of Central, Park, and Whittington Avenues, one long block away.

I walked toward the doors of the huge banquet room. Before I could get there, Billy had disengaged himself from a group and was at my side.

"You're not leaving?" he whined. "You promised we'd have a chance to talk."

"I'm just going to get some fresh air. When will you be ready to go?"

"Give me ten minutes."

I nodded and left for twenty minutes.

When I returned, Billy was still engrossed in conversation, though the crowd had already begun to disperse. Small cliques, leftover from ten years ago, were arranging to meet at various homes and clubs to extend the evening.

There was a slight buzz of excitement as a couple of reporters entered with cameras and started taking pictures of the young congressional candidate. An attractive woman, who identified herself as a stringer for *People* magazine, asked Billy several questions about his campaign strategies. Finally, she included some personal questions about his current love life.

With Hillary on the hook in Washington and with me standing ten feet away knowing that he wanted to resume our relationship where I had dropped it, Billy looked at the reporter as if he would consider bedding her.

"There is no one special in my life right now," he said, "but I am always hopeful."

My inclination was to leave immediately, but I was so fascinated with Billy's glib ability to lie that I found myself watching and listening to his every word.

When the woman writer was leaving with her assigned photographer, she scribbled something on her business card and gave it to Billy, along with a meaningful look. The rest of the reunion crowd dissipated quickly after that.

There were only twenty-five or thirty die-hards still milling around. I walked over to Billy to let him know I was ready to go.

"Just ten more minutes," Billy requested, as if he had not said that an hour earlier. "There are some people I want to talk to."

"There are always some people you want to talk to, Billy. I'm tired of being at the bottom of that list!"

"You're not leaving, are you?" Billy asked, as I turned away from him.

Over my shoulder, I said, "I'm already gone."

Billy took a couple of steps toward me and grabbed me gently by the elbow.

"Dolly," he whispered. "My Pretty Girl, how can you leave? I want to see you alone. What about our last wonderful weekend together?"

I turned back to face him squarely and spewed, "Consider it a campaign contribution!"

Billy didn't follow me as I stormed out through the double glass doors without looking back. I'm sure he stayed there politicking and shaking hands until the last dog died.

* * *

For whatever it may be worth historically, Billy went without Hillary to our tenth Hot Springs High School reunion. He also went without Hillary to the fifteenth reunion, and to the twentieth, and to the twenty-fifth, and to the thirtieth. The thirtieth included the infamous scene between the two of us that was immortalized under oath in the impeachment investigation. Hillary also did not attend the forty-fifth of the fiftieth reunions.

Anything I might have to say about that would be tacky.

In case you noticed that the thirty-fifth was missing from that list, I'll explain. Billy cancelled his reservation for the thirty-fifth reunion when he found out I was planning to be there. By that time, I had testified against him in the *Jones v. Clinton* case. I had also filed my own federal R.I.C.O. (Racketeer Influenced and Corrupt Organizations) lawsuit against Billy (President Clinton) and a half-dozen others in the Klinton Krime Kartel for trashing me to prevent the publication of my first novel.

Oh, yes, I had also filed a criminal contempt action in federal court charging Billy with perjury, witness tampering, and obstruction of justice.

For once, Billy Clinton was in no mood to see me.

10

BRICOLAGE OR POTPOURRI OR MIXED BAG

Although there are many articles online that say Hillary Rodham was fired from her job as a legal clerk for the Watergate Commission, I don't believe that to be true. I do believe that Hillary's behavior was unethical and that her superiors were not pleased with her lack of integrity, which is crucial to an honorable career in the legal profession.

I also believe the report that Hillary's boss there refused to give her a letter of recommendation for another job. In any case, after Hillary flunked the Washington, DC, bar exam, she moved to Fayetteville, Arkansas, to live with Billy, who had lived with her at Yale.

Billy had started teaching law at the University of Arkansas the previous year, and he paved the way for Hillary to teach there too.

Hillary's move to Arkansas in 1974 was many months after she had sent her father and one of her brothers to spy on Billy while he was running for Congress. Clearly, she would not have sent the spies if she didn't have plenty of reason for suspecting that Billy was running around on her.

The Rodham moles were most likely not able to catch Billy in anything since they were "furriners" from Chicago and no one in Arkansas would trust them or confide in them.

After the tenth high school reunion fiasco in Hot Springs in the summer of 1974, I went back to Dallas and started my three years at SMU School of Law while Hillary started teaching at UA with Billy.

I was so disgusted with Billy Clinton after the way he turned his back on Sen. Bill Fulbright that I destroyed our old photos, letters, and other memorabilia. I knew that I knew that I knew that he would become president and that those items would have historical value someday, but I didn't care. I didn't dream at the time that there would be more letters and more photos later, as our relationship resumed. Again.

While at SMU School of Law, I met and dated a fellow law student. We got engaged to be married in the summer of 1975. Billy called my sister to ask if the rumor of my impending marriage was true. He couldn't ask me because I had quit returning his phone calls.

My sister confirmed the wedding date. The day *after* our marriage, Billy called my sister again, to ask her if I had actually gotten married. She confirmed that as well.

Billy and Hillary married less than two months later at their house in Fayetteville, with a justice of the peace presiding. Hillary wore a dress that she purchased in a department store the night before the ceremony. Of course, I wasn't privy to the vows that they took, but that might make an interesting study.

Not long after Billy and Hillary were married (October 1975), Billy sent a "personalized" form letter saying that he was going to run for Attorney General of Arkansas. It's interesting that he addressed the letter to my husband and not to me.

Billy crossed out the form letter salutation and handwrote my husband's name. Believe it or not, at the end of the letter, Billy scribbled, "Give Dolly my love . . . tell her to call me the next time she's in Little Rock . . .

hugs and kisses to the children . . . Bill."

Stupidly, and not knowing anything about Billy's rape of Juanita Broaddrick, I did go to see him on one of my frequent visits back to Little Rock. Billy was serving as Arkansas Attorney General by then, and he invited me to visit his office and meet his staff, including his personal secretary who would be with him for years.

The date of my first visit to Billy's A.G. office is easy to remember because it was the day that Elvis died (August 16, 1977)—the same day that I told Billy about being drugged and raped by one of his friends right after we graduated from high school.

"I'm sorry that happened to you," was all he said.

I wonder if Billy was really sorry about my being drugged and raped by his friend. I wonder if he has any idea how devastating a rape or sexual assault can be to a young girl—or to anyone for that matter. I wonder if he ever had any remorse, guilt, or repentance for raping Juanita Broaddrick. I wonder if he ever had any remorse, guilt, or repentance for all the other women he attacked sexually—whether or not Hillary found out about them and added her own attacks.

At any rate, my visit to Billy's bland, paneled, government-issued attorney general's office on August 16, 1977, could have put me back on Hillary's radar screen. I'm not sure, though, because I don't know who would have told her that I was there. Billy's secretary and staff were always on his side and protective.

In defense of Billy's staff, I don't think that a single one of them had any idea of the brutality that Billy was capable of inflicting on women. He really could pull off the Dr. Jekyll and Mr. Hyde routine. Hillary had seen it by then, but I had not.

Hillary's inability to get the scoop on Billy's behavior has been an ongoing issue for her, and it continues to this day.

It is common knowledge that Billy's Secret Service agents and Hillary's Secret Service agents coordinate. They are careful to make sure even today that there will be no other woman with Billy at their "residence" in Chappaqua, New York, on those occasions when Hillary visits.

While she is running for president in 2016, Hillary flies with her entourage to make campaign appearances in small towns in Iowa, New Hampshire, and other key states. Don't be misled by seeing her emerge from a bus.

Hillary prefers to fly to a neighboring town where a bus is waiting for her and then take a short ride to her campaign sites. Once there, she has "meaningful talks" with a few chosen residents and some local media people in a little mom-and-pop restaurant.

When someone asks her a hard question, as young black women have been doing lately, Hillary has them escorted from the room, often with a haughty, disparaging laugh behind their backs as they are removed from her presence. Then she says, "Let's get back to the issues."

Hillary refuses to answer any hard questions and then she flies "home" to Chappaqua to rest for a few days. I'm quite sure that the stress of fearing a pointed question about the Klinton Krime Kartel's past transgressions truly is exhausting. Hillary needs the rest. Campaigning and traveling is strenuous for someone carrying that much baggage.

Hillary can't catch a break from her Secret Service support either. Ever since Billy and Hillary had state police protection while he was the governor of Arkansas, Hillary has shown her complete and utter disdain for law enforcement officials and military personnel. Apparently and understandably, the feeling is mutual.

The professionals who are sworn to guard and protect Hillary don't like her. The state police in Arkansas didn't like her. In fact, most of the people in Arkansas didn't like her. Hillary was a big factor in Billy's losing the governorship in 1980. She made a major accommodation in 1982 by taking the name "Clinton" rather than insisting on using her maiden name. It was all show and no substance, but it served her purpose. Again, I'm getting ahead of my story.

When the professionals who post the guard have a choice between protecting Billy's secret life (enabling him) and ratting on him to Hillary, there's no contest. Billy has gotten where he is by being charming and charismatic.

Hillary is not charming, nor is she charismatic, although she can fake it for very short periods of time. Usually, however, she doesn't even try.

Billy needs people; Hillary needs the power that they represent. Billy can also be manipulative and ruthless; Hillary may have the edge on him in the ruthless contest. It's hard to say which one is worse.

Because Hillary did not have people who liked her, she did not have friends who would tell her the truth about her wandering husband. Therefore, she had to hire private investigators to track Billy and to target the women he was dating—or attacking.

She had to keep his nose clean in the public mind because she was intentionally riding his coattails to political power. If she had been able to succeed in public life on her own, she would have stayed on the East Coast where the power was. Maybe she was afraid to flunk the Washington, DC, bar exam a second time. She told a "romantic" story to cover that trail.

Hillary certainly began hiring private investigators in Arkansas in the late 1970s when Billy was governor. It's possible she even hired investigators previously because she knew about Billy's rape of Juanita Broaddrick that occurred while he was campaigning for governor.

If you have any trouble believing Juanita Broaddrick's allegations that she was raped by the aspiring politician Clinton, consider Lisa Myers's powerful interview conducted with Juanita. A transcript of the interview can be found online. The prerecorded interview with Juanita Broaddrick was supposed to be aired on *Dateline NBC* on January 29, 1999. The Clintons pressured NBC to sit on that explosive piece. (Parts of that Myers-Broaddrick interview are on YouTube.)

A flood of inquiries, requests, and complaints from Internet news junkies finally forced NBC to air the show nearly a month later.

After the show was aired, Clinton sycophant supporters pushed the story that Juanita Broaddrick's account was not believable because she couldn't remember the exact date of the rape. Saying that Juanita's story is not believable is the same as calling her a liar. As far as I know, there were no apologies for that inexcusable affront to the woman who had already suffered enough.

Juanita was later able to establish the date of being raped by Billy Clinton when she checked her old schedule for a convention that she had been attending in Little Rock. Billy Clinton's public records confirmed that he was in Little Rock at the same time.

The Clinton White House declined to comment on Juanita's interview. Billy sent his attorney David Kendall to make a perfunctory denial of the old rape charge; that kind of dishonest behavior gives lawyers a bad name.

No one with eyes, ears, and a functioning brain could doubt Juanita Broaddrick's allegations of rape after seeing her interview.

11

KEEP IT SIMPLE, SAY IT OFTEN

Whether you are pro-Clinton or anti-Clinton, your eyes probably glaze over when you see something written about all the Clinton scandals. I get it. I understand why most people don't have a clue, and why they don't want a clue, about the breadth and depth of the Clinton crimes and immorality.

It's all too complicated. It's too broad. It's too deep. It's too convoluted. It is also outside the realm of experience of most people. The average person cannot comprehend that two politicians could have managed to get where they are with so many crimes in their wake, and so little reporting about it.

That is exactly what Billy and Hillary Clinton did, however, and I'm going to put it all in little nutshells to make it understandable—one scandal at a time.

To paraphrase a quote that has been attributed to novelist, poet, and philosopher George Santayana: "Those who do not learn from history are doomed to repeat it."

As it applies here, the history lesson is that Billy and Hillary Clinton continue to be lying, cheating, manipulative, scratching, clawing, ruthlessly aggressive, insatiably ambitious politicians who are giving public service a bad name—and nothing about them has changed in the past forty-plus years, except that they have deluded more and more people.

Some people are still blind. Some people are in denial. And, bless their hearts (a Southern euphemism for "how dumb can they be?"), some of them simply refuse to believe any of it.

As Hitler reportedly said, "Make the lie big, make it simple, keep saying it, and eventually they will believe it." So, the bigger the lie, the more people believe it. And this from the man whose eloquence and deception resulted in his takeover of Germany, and the systematic extermination of approximately 6 million Jews in the 1930s and 1940s. One wonders how this could have happened in an apparently free country until one observes the Clintons close up over a number of decades.

I was in the unfortunate position of being one of the targets of the Clintons, so I saw firsthand how most "journalists" in the mainstream media were complicit in spreading, or at least allowing, the Clintons' lies. Many journalists failed to research and report the truth. One very well known American journalist originally confronted me in a telephone call with the question: "Aren't you lying about your past sexual relationship with President Clinton?"

"Why do you think I'm lying?" I asked him in return.

"If you were telling the truth, there would be some reports in the media confirming your story."

I had to laugh. If no one knows my story, then it doesn't exist? Is that the way it works now?

Cogito, ergo sum. "I think, therefore, I am." If the media don't know who I am, then I am not?

I'm not going to divulge here the name of that journalist because he soon thereafter read my novel and called me back to say, "That's a true story, isn't it?"

I can't recall that there was a single journalist of any ilk who didn't believe me after having a conversation with me, either privately and off the record or on television or radio. That doesn't mean that the journalist ultimately had the *cojones* to write a true story, but at least she *knew* the truth.

The bigger the lie, the more people believe it.

Hitler's henchman Joseph Goebbels repeated that paraphrase in a later article in "*Die Zeit ohne Beispiel*": " . . . when one lies, one should lie big, and stick to it. They keep up their lies, even at the risk of looking ridiculous."

"I did not have sexual relations with that woman, Miss Lewinsky."

"What difference, at this point, does it make?"

"It depends on what the meaning of the word *is* is."

Bless their hearts, some people still believe that the earth is flat, and some people still believe the lies of the Clintons.

12

SICK AND TIRED OF ALL THE GATES?

Am I the only person who is sick and tired of seeing the word *gate* appended to the Clinton scandals?

Did the mainstream media start using the moniker from pure D laziness, as we would say in the South? Or, was there a concerted effort to think of a way to denigrate the seriousness of the various Clinton scandals?

What better way to make something sound trivial and old-newsy than to stick a "gate" at the end of it?

Chinagate.

Travelgate.

Filegate.

Monicagate.

Lootergate.

Enough.

Says who?

Says I.

Of course, this scandal-naming trend was a takeoff on the name "Watergate."

Watergate is a complex of condos, apartments, a hotel, and offices in Washington, DC, where burglars were arrested inside the offices of the Democratic National Headquarters early on the morning of June 17, 1972. An alert security guard called the police, and the intruders were caught attempting to wiretap phones and steal documents.

It is still unclear whether or not President Richard Nixon knew in advance about the misguided attempt to help his presidential campaign by spying on the enemy. The real problem for Nixon was that he apparently participated in or orchestrated a cover-up of the affair with:

hush money for the burglars;

interference with the FBI's investigation;

destruction of evidence; and

getting rid of (firing, not the Al Capone solution for getting rid of) staff members who wouldn't cooperate with the cover-up.

You can see where I'm going with this one, right? It will ring a bell in your head if you are already familiar with the Klinton Krime Kartel's *modus operandi*:

hush money;

interference with FBI investigations;

destruction of evidence; and

getting rid of staff members who wouldn't cooperate.

The Klinton Krime Kartel, orchestrated primarily by Hillary Clinton, also added the following and more to the cover-up arsenal:

threats;

intimidation;

physical assaults;

physical batteries;

home burglaries;

business burglaries;

spying on the enemy;

manufacturing of false evidence; and

publishing of false articles in the mainstream media to discredit any woman (or man) who dared to raise the TRUTH about what the Clintons were doing in Washington and beyond.

Now, back to the original Watergate.

There was a congressional investigation of Nixon's actions in regard to the burglary and cover-up. The players were known as the Watergate Committee, and the recent law-school graduate Hillary Rodham was a junior staffer there, although she had not passed the bar exam and was not a practicing attorney.

By August 1974, it was obvious that President Nixon had been involved in some sort of conspiracy. This led to his being the only president in American history to resign. Nixon's resignation happened concurrently with my entry into law school, and it was a hot topic in our classes at SMU School of Law.

Although I do not condone Nixon's actions in the cover-up, I do have to commend his doing the honorable thing by resigning. Vice President Ford assumed the presidency; Gerald Ford immediately pardoned Nixon for all the crimes he "committed or may have committed" while in office.

Billy Clinton, on the other hand, when investigated for his various crimes and cover-ups (which were far more extensive and serious than those of President Richard Nixon), lied and lied and then he lied some more, rather than doing the honorable thing of resigning:

he lied under oath in the *Jones v. Clinton* federal lawsuit;

he lied to the American people when he looked right into a television camera and stated, "I did not have sexual relations with that woman, Miss Lewinsky"; and

he lied under oath in his Grand Jury testimony, wherein he also spouted one of the most oft-quoted and ridiculous sentences in American political history: "It depends on what the meaning of the word *is* is."

All this time, Hillary the co-president knew exactly what her uncontrollable husband was doing in the Oval Office—and elsewhere. If she did not know, then what in the world was wrong with her? Arguably, no one liked her, so no one ratted on Billy, the same as it was back in Arkansas.

Still, is this the kind of perceptive abilities that would help qualify Hillary for the leadership of the United States of America? Don't we want a leader who can figure out what's happening right under her nose?

Can you imagine having a leader with a finger on the nuclear trigger without any psychological insight into the big picture? That is scary. Very, very scary.

Hillary can't have it both ways. Either she knew what was happening with her co-president, or she didn't know. If she didn't know, why didn't she know? Denial? Repression? Fear of the truth? Fear of rejection?

We had this self-proclaimed "two-for-the-price-of-one" co-presidency. Hillary was the first First Lady to have a presence in the West Wing of the White House. What was she doing there?

If there is any doubt that Hillary viewed herself as the co-president, consider what she said when White House files were subpoenaed: "I'm not going to have some reporters pawing through our papers. *We are* the president."

This type of arrogance fueled Hillary's belief that she is above the law. Her mental disconnect from reality explains an awful lot about what crimes Hillary had the audacity to commit during the decades of her coattail-riding quest for the White House.

I say, let her have her fantasy about being the co-president back then. Two terms of being co-president is more than enough of her. Hillary is a female affront to honorable women, and the evidence of that will continue to mount.

13

JUANITA BROADDRICK

As of the writing of this chapter, I have not met my fellow Arkansan Juanita Broaddrick, whom I have mentioned in earlier chapters. I first heard about Juanita Broaddrick by name when I was subpoenaed to testify in the case of *Jones v. Clinton*, wherein the young state employee Paula Jones accused the president of sexually assaulting her when he was the governor of Arkansas.

Some of the disgusting details in the Jones allegations involved Billy's dropping his pants, exposing his penis, and asking Paula Jones to kiss it.

In support of the plaintiff Paula Jones, Juanita Broaddrick was asked to testify about her own allegations that she had been raped by Attorney General Bill Clinton in 1978.

My testimony was to focus on Billy's admission to me that he was a sex addict. Naturally, the lawyers for Paula Jones wanted that information to show that his egregious "kiss it" behavior was part of a pattern and practice of sexual misconduct. Otherwise, such absolutely brutish and outlandish behavior would sound crazy to a jury of persons unfamiliar with an untreated sex addict.

Billy Clinton's admission of his sex addiction took place after midnight on the night of May 17–18, 1987, at the Airport Marina Hotel East in Dallas. What Billy told me was that his plane from Washington, DC, to Little Rock had been diverted from Atlanta to Dallas. Who knows why he was there? At any rate, we were in the hotel together.

Juanita Broaddrick and most of the other women who had been found and asked to testify in the *Jones v. Clinton* case were threatened by the Clinton's minions to discourage their testimony. I don't know for a fact all the particulars about each of the other women's experiences, but I do believe Juanita's public statements about the rape *and* about her subsequent intimidation by Hillary Clinton.

Reluctantly, Juanita gave an interview to Lisa Myers of NBC. It was a powerful piece of journalism—that was FINALLY aired on *Dateline NBC*, on February 24, 1999.

There are several things I'm going to emphasize here to put all this in perspective. Juanita Broaddrick was raped in 1978 by Arkansas Attorney General Bill Clinton. Juanita Broaddrick suffered intimidation afterward by both Billy and Hillary.

Know this:

1. In 1978 women (and girls, and boys) did *not* report rapes; it's scary enough to do that in 2016;

2. Juanita Broaddrick owned and operated a nursing home;

3. Nursing homes in Arkansas at that time were regulated by the attorney general's office;

4. As the attorney general, Billy Clinton could have wreaked havoc on Juanita Broaddrick's nursing home and her source of income by the simple use of nit-picking regulations, onerous requirements, uncalled-for investigations, etc.;

5. The mainstream media called Juanita Broaddrick a liar who was only interested in a book deal and making money off her accusation of the poor innocent president;

6. The mainstream media generally agreed that if Juanita went back to Arkansas, did not seek a book deal, and did not try to make money off her accusations against the poor innocent president, then they would believe her; and

7. Juanita Broaddrick did go back to Arkansas, did not seek a book deal, and did not try to make money off her accusation of the poor innocent president. Isn't it time to believe her?

Another important fact is this: If Juanita Broaddrick had filed criminal charges against attorney general Bill Clinton for raping her in 1978, she could also have filed criminal charges against Hillary Clinton as an accessory after the fact.

I was raped in 1964 by one of Billy Clinton's friends. I did not file charges. Juanita was raped by Billy Clinton *and* intimidated afterward by Billy *and* Hillary. I understand why Juanita did not file charges.

What I don't understand is the very poor memory of the mainstream media sycophants who have forgotten what they said about Juanita. She is to be believed!

Billy Clinton's decades-long evasion of justice, plus Hillary Clinton's campaign ad saying that rape victims should be believed, must have piled on the last couple of straws to break Juanita's long silence. These recent events certainly induced me to break my long silence and start writing this book.

I hope that other Clinton victims will feel validated now and will be encouraged to step forward. The accessory-after-the-fact crimes of threats and intimidation are still in play for anyone who is afraid to talk.

If you were a victim of the Clintons and you are afraid to say anything, then the intimidation is still working. How long can people with information maintain a fearful silence?

A scene from *Cat on a Hot Tin Roof* by Tennessee Williams comes to mind. This is Big Daddy talking here:

> When something is festering in your memory or your imagination, laws of silence don't work. It's just like shutting a door and locking it on a house on fire in hopes of forgetting that the house is still burning. But not facing a fire doesn't put it out. Silence about a thing just magnifies it. It grows and festers in silence, becomes malignant.

I do hope that more and more of the untold numbers of Clinton sex and intimidation victims will come forward now and break their long silences. There is no need to let the secret wounds fester to the point of malignancy. The Clintons are the festering sores on the face of America, and it's time for a cleansing.

14

BEHIND THE GATES

The Arkansas governor's mansion faces north near the front of an 8.5-acre parcel of land in the historic Quapaw District of Little Rock. The large "block" that the mansion occupies is surrounded mostly by equally large and lovely homes, but there are smaller ones on the south and east sides. Towering deciduous trees shade the neighborhood's sidewalks that have those typical bulges caused by invading tree roots.

Billy and Hillary lived in the Governor's Mansion before it was extensively renovated in 2000. There was a huge addition on the south side in 2002. It's a lovely, historic, honorable name in Little Rock.

On the west side of the governor's mansion is a hard-to-notice driveway that is heavily shaded. A wrought-iron gate swings in to allow the entry of expected and approved visitors.

There is a small guardhouse on the left of the driveway, before the parking places. I parked there and used the kitchen entry when visiting Billy privately. For parties, receptions, formal dinners, and such, I used the front gates.

Billy loved the "perks" of being governor. He especially liked to have a team of Arkansas state policemen who variously served as his drivers, bodyguards, and running buddies. Hillary, on the other hand, didn't enjoy the perks, and she appeared to hate much of the political life that she was determined to live. She usually dressed inappropriately, and she treated the state troopers with disrespect on a good day, and with utter disdain the rest of the time.

Perhaps Hillary suspected that the men on the security detail were covering Billy's tracks when he was with me (and too many other women). She would have been correct in that suspicion. Billy called her "the Warden," but inside the gates at his prison compound/mansion, all the guards were definitely on his side.

Much has been written about Hillary's foul language and anger directed toward the security detail in the White House. Such odd, unacceptable behavior was her pattern in the governor's mansion as well. I often had gossipy talks on the phone with troopers when Hillary was taking longer than usual to leave for an engagement. We had some tasty chats. Anyway, Hillary was gone a lot, both before and after Chelsea was born.

Hillary resented having to dress according to the accepted norms for Southern women, not to mention the expectations for the wife of a governor. Hillary frequently visited a couple of the best women's shops in Little Rock wearing baggy sweat pants and an ill-fitting top. She would look at the nice clothes, but generally not buy anything.

Hillary and Billy hosted a garden party one afternoon at the mansion. Hillary wore a gauzy white skirt, which might have looked dreamy on the right woman with the right accessories. Unfortunately, Hillary was wearing a pair of brightly printed full brief panties (aka granny panties) that were clearly visible through the fabric.

Some of the best-dressed women in Little Rock attended that party, but as far as I know, none of them ever copied her new trend. No one liked her enough to suggest that she go inside to change rather than to make a fool of herself. That's sad and pitiful, but true.

* * *

"I want to have a baby," Billy announced to me one evening. We were in the Arkansas governor's mansion together while the Warden was out of town, or who knows where.

"Do you really think that's a good idea?" I asked.

Billy frowned. Then he laughed.

"Oh, I didn't mean with *you*!"

This strange conversation took place at the end of March 1979. Billy had been governor for only a few months, but he was always in the process of making political plans, and this smacked of another campaign maneuver to me. I admit I was a little miffed, first at my own naiveté, and then at Billy for thinking that I would want to have this conversation with him.

"Then why are you telling me? It's not my business."

"I'm having a problem."

"What? You have to have sex with the Warden first?"

Billy laughed again, and then he got very serious.

"I have a low sperm count."

"So what? It only takes one of those little swimmers to do the job for you."

"We've tried and tried."

"Maybe you need to put your heart into it," I suggested, as generations of Italian superstitions came to my mind.

"No, it's a problem. A fertility expert says it's my fault."

"Why are you so dead set on having a baby anyway? It doesn't appear that you have the time to take care of one."

"Politically, it doesn't look good. We need to have a baby so we can appear to be a normal couple. We need to do something serious to take attention off the Warden's lifestyle."

Billy did *not* use the word *lesbian*.

"I guess you're telling me this for a reason. What do you want me to do about it?"

"You didn't have any trouble getting pregnant," Billy said.

"There's an understatement for the world, but you said you didn't want to have a baby with me, so what do you want?"

"I want you to pray about it."

As unbelievable as it seems, that is absolutely what he said. Draw your own conclusions about my immediate, intense, jumbled, and convoluted feelings about Billy's request.

"I want you to pray about it," he said.

I nodded and said that I would.

"But, you have to do your part," I reminded him.

"I know," Billy said with a sigh. "I will."

I did pray about it, and the baby, who would be named Chelsea Victoria Clinton, was born less than a year later. Chelsea would be the only child of Billy and the Warden.

A strange and completely unexpected thing happened when Chelsea was born. Billy fell absolutely head-over-heels in love with his little daughter. Hillary? Not so much.

In an early scene in *Gone With the Wind*, the heroine Scarlett O'Hara had become a widow after the husband she cared nothing about died almost comically. There was a dance to raise funds for the Confederate war effort, and Scarlett was stuck behind a table in her widow's rags. She tapped her little shoe in time to the music, obviously wanting to dance. This was Hillary after Chelsea was born. She could not wait to get out of the house and back to work where she could feel important.

My older friend Louise stopped by the governor's mansion to deliver a gift. (Louise and her son had known Billy for years.) Hillary confided to Louise that she had no idea she would feel so trapped by being at home with a baby.

"How long do I have to stay at home with this kid?" Hillary asked Louise. "What would look right to the people around here?"

Hillary was the widow wanting to dance. Louise told her that she should not go back to work for at least three months. Hillary was not pleased with that suggestion, but started counting the days.

* * *

It seemed that Hillary liked her work at the (now named) Rose Law Firm, but I don't think she ever realized, or cared to face the facts about, why she had been hired as the first female *associate* of the Rose Law Firm. Billy had been the attorney general of Arkansas, with a promising political future ahead of him. I'm sure that no one in the Rose Law Firm had heard any rumor about Billy's rape of Juanita Broaddrick at the time, or everything would have been different. The Rose Law Firm has always been a paragon of legal practice in Arkansas. The original firm (with a longer name) was founded in 1820, and was the first law firm west of the Mississippi.

Fast-forward a couple of years. Billy was governor and Hillary was named the first female *partner* of the Rose Law Firm. Any lawyer will tell you that no one is named a partner in a prestigious firm without many years of outstanding legal practice or some portable business that she can carry in the door. Obviously, as the wife of the governor, Hillary had plenty of potential for obtaining business. The business that Hillary handled, however, and the way that she handled it, would not turn out so well as the senior partners had hoped, but I'm getting ahead of my story.

Hillary spent her time practicing law, traveling around the state, and generally inserting herself into Billy's political affairs to his detriment. She had insisted on keeping her maiden name, which did not sit well with the traditional Southerners in Arkansas. Perhaps if she had treated Billy and his friends, associates, security guards, and constituents with some respect, she might have gotten away with her maiden-name act of independence.

That may not be a correct assessment, either. People in the South have little patience for hypocrisy, and Hillary showed herself to be at least two-faced from the beginning. I believe that Diane Blair, whom she met in Fayetteville, was the only real friend that Hillary ever had in Arkansas. Hillary did confide in Louise from time to time because Louise knew everyone and could answer any "society" questions. Of course,

Louise never said anything about me to Hillary in those conversations.

Hillary looked down her Yankee nose at Arkansans, and it was obvious to everyone that she couldn't wait to leave the state. What Hillary had in mind, of course, was moving on up to the White House, but for a while that dream appeared to be in shambles.

As I've said in several ways, people all over Arkansas talk to each other. A lot. Call it gossip, if you wish. Word about Hillary's far-left political views and her unhinged anger tirades spread like wildfire.

Everyone knew that Hillary would throw dishes at Billy in the kitchen and that she even broke a door off a kitchen cabinet during one of her hissy fits. This did not sit well with anyone in Arkansas, and no one seemed to understand why Billy would put up with it. People would have had to understand his chaotic, abusive childhood to understand that.

When public sentiment wafted its way into the governor's office, which it frequently did because no one minded complaining to Billy about his Yankee wife, Hillary would then grab her political-pawn baby Chelsea for a few good photo-ops to show that she was being the perfect First Lady.

Arkansans didn't buy any part of Hillary's hypocrisy, and Billy lost the governor's office after only one term.

15

ONE MORE THING BEHIND THE GATES

In a previous chapter, I included a little ditty for the purpose of illustrating my childlike view of my early relationship with Billy Clinton, and I promised to return to it.

As I recall, the following incident took place at a party at the governor's mansion after the after-party following the premiere of the movie *Buck Rogers*. I'm iffy on the exact date, but it was definitely during the very early part of Billy and Hillary's first term of residence in government housing, probably in February or March 1979.

In a nutshell,

1. Gil Gerard starred in the movie *Buck Rogers*;

2. Gil Gerard is from Little Rock;

3. One of Gil's brothers grew up having special needs; (another of Gil's brothers was in my choir when I was directing the church

choir before I moved to Dallas to go to law school. I mention this as simply one more example of the small world we inhabit here in Arkansas;

4. Gil was a supporter of the AARC, the Arkansas Association for Retarded Children, which was later called Arkansas Association for Retarded Citizens, and is now simply "ARC"; (this is analogous to Kentucky Fried Chicken's changing its name to "KFC" after the word "fried" became somewhat politically incorrect;

5. Gil convinced the movie's producers (or whomever) to hold the premiere in Little Rock as a fund-raiser for ARC;

6. I was also a supporter of ARC due to the influence of my previously-mentioned friend Louise (who was my source in the section about Hillary, Chelsea, and Hillary's going back to work); Louise had a developmentally-challenged adult son who had spent his childhood after about age five at the Arkansas Children's Colony; Louise was very active in ARC affairs;

7. I had traveled from Dallas to Little Rock for the premiere of the *Buck Rogers* movie, as a supporter of ARC;

8. I happened to be in Billy's office (the governor's office at the state capitol) when Gil Girard stopped by to pay his respects to his friend Billy, the governor;

9. Gil did not have a date for the premiere;

10. Gil asked me to go to the premiere as his date that night; of course, I was married at the time, but this never bothered Billy and me, nor was it an issue with Gil because this was simply a public appearance and nothing personal. The handsome movie star invited me to be his date for the premiere in front of Billy, and it appeared to make the governor a tad jealous;

11. After Gil left, Billy invited me to an after-party at the mansion after the official, fund-raising, after-party after the premiere; I hope that's clear;

12. "It was a dark and stormy night," as Snoopy would write, and the after-after-party at the governor's mansion was a small one.

As I approached the west side of the governor's mansion that night, I flashed my bright lights on and off twice. Seconds later, the large wrought-iron gates swung open. I pulled in, stopped, and rolled down the power window as a uniformed Arkansas state trooper approached the car.

Billy had already assured me that the Warden would not be there all night, so I wasn't concerned about her. Billy did not say where she was. I don't know if he knew where Hillary was that night, nor any other time. He never seemed to care.

"The Governor is expecting you, Miss Kyle. You may park right over there." He pointed to a spot near the house. "Go in the kitchen door. I guess you know your away around."

As I walked through the kitchen door, I wished for the hundredth time that I knew what Billy was telling people about me, if anything. Sometimes I felt like an actor in a play where everyone else had a script and I was ad-libbing.

The kitchen was brightly lighted, but empty. I walked through the food preparation area and into the formal dining room, where the chandelier had been dimmed. Hearing muffled voices beyond, I paused a moment to listen, then followed the sound across the two-story entrance hall and into the front parlor, which was lighted by several lamps and the fireplace glow.

I paused again, and heard Billy among other voices in the next room. Billy had said there would be a few friends, and as usual I wished that I knew in advance who else would be there. I felt a twinge of annoyance that he had not met me at the kitchen door.

I walked around the plain, walnut-colored, baby grand piano to the keyboard side. I always thought that the governor's mansion should have a big Steinway, and I easily resisted the urge to try an arpeggio on it.

"I thought I felt your presence in the house."

Billy appeared in the doorway and held his arms open for an embrace. He held me only for a moment, kissed me lightly on the cheek, and said, "Come in here. We're playing Hearts."

I followed Billy into the wood-paneled game room where three men were seated at a poker table and another half-dozen guests were sitting around on sofas and chairs, drinking wine and talking politics. I was already beginning to be sorry I had come.

Ignoring the others, Billy introduced me to David Edwards, whom he described as his old roommate from Oxford. Again, I wished I knew what, if anything, Billy had told David about me. I would soon find out.

Billy pushed a chair up close to his and patted the back of it, motioning for me to sit down.

"Do you guys mind if Dolly helps me?" Billy asked. "I can't think of anyone who would make a better Hearts coach for me than Dolly. And you know I need help."

The guys chuckled and I felt a little uncomfortable. I would definitely have to talk to Billy about this recurring issue.

"I understand that you're a lawyer in Dallas," one of the guys said, breaking the ice.

"And the mother of three beautiful little girls," another added.

"And that you graduated in Billy's high school class," David chimed in, "although I find that a little hard to believe. You must be at least ten years younger than he is."

"Two years," Billy corrected. "She skipped two grades to be in my class. She's so G**damned smart, she always scared the daylights out of me. I dropped fourth-year Latin when I heard she was going to be in the class."

The guys all laughed as I sat in shock, hearing Billy so glibly admit to things I had never even imagined. The thought that I could scare Billy seemed absurd, but I had always wondered why he dropped fourth-year Latin after I told him I would be in Mrs. Buck's class with him.

He hadn't expected that because I had skipped the eleventh grade, so I missed being in the third-year Latin class. I would be going straight from second-year Latin to fourth, but I had never thought much about it. Did that really scare Billy? Could he be telling the truth for once in his life?

"She's a hell of a musician, too," Billy bragged. "I remember she won a first place in piano at the state band and orchestra competition when we were seniors. You'll never believe what she played."

I sat in stunned silence as the men proffered their guesses. Billy kept grinning and shaking his head.

"I'll have to tell you," he finally broke in, "because you'll never get it. My little fifteen-year-old Dolly Kyle played Beethoven's *Appassionata*. She played the hell out of it!"

"Wish I could believe you, ole buddy, but that's where I draw the line," David apologized.

"No offense," David said with a nod at me, "but our friend here has been known to stretch the truth from time to time."

They all laughed, including Billy. Then he turned to me and begged, "Help me out, Pretty Girl. Go hit a few licks to show these turkeys I'm not lying."

I forced a smile but didn't move. This evening was nothing like I had hoped. Billy stood up and took my hand.

"Come on. It's music time," he said, leading me back into the parlor. I didn't even look to see who might be following. Like a robot, I sat down at the piano and poised my hands above the keys, ready to play dutifully at Billy's request. Then, when I thought about the music's theme, I was captivated by it as always, and prepared mentally for the *pianissimo* opening.

The first three notes seemed to be an invocation wrung out in agony, as if I with Beethoven had exclaimed, "O my God!" A chill passed through my body as it always did with the opening notes. I continued the theme, mindful of the words of the Psalm, "from the depths I have cried unto thee; Lord, hear my prayer."

When I lifted my hands from the final chord, I took a deep breath and dropped my head forward, exhausted from the effort of playing that magnificent piece of music, forgetting for a moment that anyone else was in the room. Billy sat down on the bench beside me and encircled me with his arms. Everyone else broke into applause.

"I understand how you can play better now than you did in high school," Billy whispered in my ear, "but I don't understand how you can be even more beautiful."

"Well, Bill," David confessed as the applause died down. "I owe you an apology. That girl just played the hell out of the *Appassionata*. Damn!"

"I guess it would be an imposition to ask, would you play an encore?" someone else asked.

I looked around the room to gauge if the audience was interested or just being tolerant. They seemed interested and I spoke my first words of the evening.

"I write country-western music, and I've never played it for anyone except family. Would you like to hear some of it?"

Billy was the first to respond.

"Please, Dolly. We'd all love to hear it."

I played my "Hobo Song" and my "Daddy's Song" that I used to sing to my children at night after they were tucked in bed. The adults in the governor's parlor responded with great applause and calls for more. I sang another and then tried to beg off.

"One more, Dolly," Billy begged. "Just one more. These are wonderful songs!"

He was standing right by the piano, staring into my eyes, and I couldn't resist. I nodded and began singing what I had always considered to be a light-hearted, up-beat song—the kind that would make a good finale. I introduced this song earlier in this book with the first verses, and I'll repeat it now, as it occurred that night.

"The day that I first met you, I was just a little child,
But I still recall the feeling that you gave me when you smiled";

At that moment, Billy abruptly turned away from the piano and me. He walked over to the fireplace, clasped his hands behind his back, and stared into the glowing embers. For the dozenth time in that short evening, I was uncomfortable, but kept singing:

"Now the years have gone by, but I can still truly say,
That the feeling you gave to me has lasted to this day.

"And I knew, I always knew,
What that feeling was, but didn't know what to do,
And so I'd write down your initials,
And then six more letters, 'I - L - O - V - E - U.'

"The times we shared in high school were spent playing cat and mouse,
When I finally got a car, I drove each day right by your house,
When I dated your friends, I always acted so cool,
But when I was with you, I'm sure I acted like a fool.

"In my book, you wrote in blue,
'It's been fun to know you! Good luck . . . and God bless you!'
But what I wanted by your initials,
Was just six more letters, 'I - L - O - V - E - U.'

It was the third verse that would bring the song up to date in our adult life:

"Before it was too late, I should have learned just what to do,
Found some way to tell you how I felt; you surely felt it, too;
If I could go back, I would, to that innocent day,
But I'd know what to do and I would know just what to say.

"Oh, I knew, I always knew,
What that feeling was, but didn't know what to do;
Now I'd do more than write your initials,
I would let you know that 'I - L - O - V - E - U.'"

Though that was the end of the song and Billy still had his back to me, I spontaneously added a new section. I sang it very slowly, feeling my way along.

"And I think . . . you always knew, . . .

What that feeling was, . . . but didn't know what to do; . . .

Oh, did you ever . . . write my initials? . . .

And then six more letters, . . . 'I - L - O - V - E - U ?'"

Everyone except Billy applauded. David called to him.

"Hey, Bill, how'd you like that one?"

The governor didn't respond, but continued to stare intently into the fireplace, ignoring all of them. David wouldn't let it go.

"Come on, Bill. Didn't you like it?"

I shook my head at David, wanting him to back off, but he didn't seem to notice.

"Hey, Governor!" he insisted, "What'd you think of that?"

When Billy finally turned around to answer his friend, everyone in the room could clearly see big tears streaming down his cheeks.

"I thought it was beautiful," he said, with a catch in his voice. He walked over to the piano. "It was as beautiful as my Dolly."

Billy sat on the piano bench beside me, and silently encircled me in his arms. One by one, the guests said their awkward good-nights and drifted from the room.

David Edwards, who was staying overnight as a guest at the mansion, waited until all the others had gone before he said anything.

"It was truly a pleasure to meet you, Dolly. Now I understand why Bill talked about you all the time at school."

Then David turned to the governor, his brilliant former room-mate at Oxford, and whispered, "You, my Rhodes Scholar friend, are a f***ing idiot!"

* * *

Did Hillary know what happened that night at the governor's mansion? Where was the First Lady? What was she doing anyway? Did she have any friends at the party who would rat on Billy? So many questions may come to mind.

The important thing to know is that this was typical of Billy's behavior. He wanted what he wanted when he wanted it. I was usually amenable. We Americans would all find out later that many, many, many other women were not amenable to his sexual advances, but that would not stop Billy from forcing himself on them.

Hillary, the Other Woman and the Warden, tried to keep Billy in line, but she could not shadow him all the time, as his grandmother had done when he was an infant and young child. In many respects, Billy is still that hurt, confused young child and Hillary is still his grandmother.

Doesn't America need and deserve better than a tantrum-prone, emotional four-year-old like Billy Clinton back in the White House? Doesn't America need and deserve better than Billy's aging grandmother Hillary who is trying to control him while she tries to take control of the rest of the world?

16

WHEN THE WHEELS CAME OFF

Hillary Rodham was furious! Billy had lost the governorship after only one term! This rarely happened in Arkansas, with its short two-year terms (back then). Hillary took no responsibility for her part in *their* stunning defeat. She blamed Billy for every lost vote.

Hillary Rodham was furious because she was no longer the First Lady of Arkansas! Although she had hated the social requirements and the dressing-up-like-a-lady parts of the role, she was furious to have it snatched from her.

Hillary Rodham was furious that she had to move from the governor's mansion! To add insult to injury, the defeated political couple had to move into the tiny house in a less-than-stellar location that *she* could afford to buy on *her* salary.

Hillary Rodham was furious that Billy was unemployed! Although it was her part of their bargain to be the breadwinner and financial security for the political couple, she had not planned on an early setback like a political defeat this early in their coconspiratorial career.

Hillary Rodham was furious that Billy did *not* want to accept the position of chairman of the National Democratic Party! She saw that career move as her only hope of recovering from Billy's defeat as governor.

Hillary Rodham was furious that Billy wanted to stay home and spend time with baby Chelsea! Since Hillary apparently lacked whatever maternal instinct drives most women to want to spend time with their babies, she had no idea why Billy wanted to be a stay-at-home daddy to their infant daughter.

How do I know all this about Hillary Rodham?

Billy Clinton told me.

I admit that my source is not known for telling the truth, but I believe that Billy was being honest after his defeat in 1980. He was too dejected and depressed to be anything but honest with me at the time. Even the lines in the handwritten letters he sent me during that period sloped downward, which many experts regard as a sign of depression.

The loss of the governor's office in 1980 was nothing like Billy's failure to defeat the giant John Paul Hammerschmidt in his uphill bid for Congress in 1974. No. That was to be expected for a newcomer under the political circumstances.

In 1980, however, Billy was feeling personally hurt that the people of Arkansas wanted him out of office after his statewide victories to become their attorney general in 1976 and their governor in 1978.

It was a devastating loss, and it hit the political couple hard.

Although many people have speculated for decades about the viability of the "marriage" of Billy and Hillary, in my opinion, this was the only time that their "marriage" was in any real jeopardy.

There was also speculation about whether Billy was actually Chelsea's biological father. Many attribute her parentage to Webb Hubbell, who was Hillary's special friend at the Rose Law Firm.

This speculation seems to be based on the rumors that Hillary had an affair with Webb Hubbell in order to help secure her advancement to a partnership at the firm. The rumors were enhanced by the fact that both Chelsea and Webb have prominent lower lips. Very prominent.

Chelsea has now either outgrown the prominent lower lip or had it surgically altered. At any rate, I don't believe that Webb is Chelsea's biological father. I've had a couple of conversations with Robert Morrow about this issue. Robert cowrote with Roger Stone the 2015 book *The Clintons' War on Women*, which takes a firm stand saying that Webb is Chelsea's father. We agreed to disagree.

Take a look at early pictures of Billy's mother, Virginia Dell Cassidy Blythe Clinton Dwire Kelley, and see another prominent lower lip. Google an old photo of Hillary's own mother, Dorothy, with her very prominent lower lip. Chelsea looks almost exactly like her maternal grandmother. That does not necessarily rule out Webb, but I still don't believe it.

In any case, the most important issue is that Billy loved the baby Chelsea more than he ever expected to love any human being. It was obvious to people who saw them together. Not only was it obvious how much he loved that infant girl, but Billy told me that over and over. Yes, there is his ongoing issue with credibility, but I believe this. It was almost too weird not to be true.

One of the women with whom Billy had been having sexual relations in the late 1970s reportedly thought that he would divorce Hillary to marry her after losing the governorship in 1980. I never had any such thought about Billy and me, but later I heard that other women also had that same fantasy about marrying Billy. I can't imagine what he ever said or did to foster that notion.

No matter the truth of Chelsea's paternity, ironically, it was this baby girl who unknowingly kept her parents together. Billy talked to me about this at some length. Hillary was busy studying the exit polls and wondering if it might be time to find another coattail to clutch on her way to the White House.

Realizing the futility of finding someone else who could launch a political career for her (which was why she came to Arkansas in the first place), Hillary reached out to their political guru friend Dick Morris for help. Dick had worked on their successful 1978 gubernatorial race and had a good track record in politics.

Meanwhile, Billy took my very simple suggestions that gave him the best of both worlds: He took a job with a local law firm, and he requested the best paralegal in the firm to work for him, because he certainly didn't know how to practice law.

Taking a local job allowed Billy to avoid the need to travel that would have been required in the national job for the Democrats. He had plenty of time to spend with the infant Chelsea and this paid off later, especially during the Monica Lewinsky scandal.

Psychologically and emotionally, Chelsea was able to express her anger at her father during that difficult time because she was certain at the deepest level that he loved her.

On the other hand, Chelsea could not afford "emotionally" to be angry with her mother Hillary who had cultivated the environment that allowed the Lewinsky travesty to happen. At a deep level, Chelsea probably felt like the political pawn that her mother had conceived her to be. I don't say this to hurt Chelsea, but hoping she has healed or will heal from those early scars before she passes the dysfunctional script along to her own children.

* * *

Political guru Dick Morris rode to the rescue of the floundering couple and devised a plan for Billy to get back into the governor's office using two main campaign points:

Billy apologized profusely, frequently, and statewide for his arrogance and other sins during his first term as governor; and

Hillary Rodham became Hillary Clinton.

Billy and Hillary moved back into the governor's mansion in 1983 and resumed their quest for the White House, but isn't it obvious to everyone that Hillary is still furious?

17

DIGGING UP DIRT—
THE 1982 ELECTION AND BEYOND

It's hard to blame Hillary for hiring private investigators to tail her philandering husband. She didn't have any other way to get the information. Billy wasn't going to tell her the truth about his wide-ranging sexual escapades, and she didn't have any friends in Arkansas who would rat on him for her.

When it was time (in 1982), to take another run at the governor's race, Hillary enlisted the expert political advice of Dick Morris. In addition, and probably unknown to Dick, Hillary hired private investigators in an effort to contain and control Billy's uncontainable and uncontrollable sex addiction.

As far as common knowledge goes, 1982 was the first year in which Hillary hired private investigators to track the women who had sex with Billy. It would be another five years before Billy admitted to me that he was a sex addict. Later, we had an odd conversation when talking about pro basketball player Wilt Chamberlain's claim to have had sex with about twenty thousand women. Billy seemed almost undone by Chamberlain's stunning announcement.

"That's ten times more women than I've had!" he said.

There was disappointment, and admiration, in his voice.

Do the math. Billy's admitted sexual encounters were limited to two thousand—back then!

Despite the rampant epidemic of HIV, AIDS, and other sexually transmitted diseases, Billy (notorious for not using a condom) seemed to have no concern for the health implications of his acts. Hillary didn't seem concerned with the health implications of his outside sex conquests; I figured she wasn't worried because she wasn't having sex with him anyway.

No, Hillary was not at all worried about sexually transmitted diseases. Rather, she was obsessed with what effect Billy's philandering behavior could have on their political careers. Hillary had just spent two miserable years of living an ordinary existence and making ordinary mortgage payments on an ordinary house on an ordinary street. She had to get back on the political train that she had inadvertently derailed.

Hillary and Billy had weathered the storm of his 1980 defeat after only one term as governor of Arkansas, and they had decided to stay together in their politically based marriage. Chelsea provided a bit of bonding. Billy was the doting dad; Hillary was content to let him "parent" while she schemed.

Ivan Duda was Hillary's first private investigator, as I recall. She ordered Ivan to dig up dirt, and he said he didn't know why Hillary wanted the information on a dozen women who had been with her husband. Usually sleuthing like that is done to support a divorce, but that was not Hillary's plan. She had something more sinister and criminal in mind.

Women who had been with Billy started receiving anonymous phone calls and threats. Not coincidentally, those were the same types of intimidating experiences that Marla Crider, an attractive young coed at the University of Arkansas, suffered in Fayetteville when Hillary found out about her in 1974.

In 1974, Hillary slipped easily into playing the role demanded by Billy's dysfunctional attitude of "Let's you and her fight." That could have been his impetus for introducing Hillary and me that year, and it was most certainly evident in the conflict between Hillary Rodham and Marla Crider.

Marla Crider was an undergraduate student at the University of Arkansas when Billy was teaching in the law school there in Fayetteville, while running for Congress. Marla volunteered to work in his congressional campaign. The very attractive young woman soon became romantically involved with the articulate politician.

I believe that Marla was truly in love with Billy and she held visions of marriage. Marla was a beautiful person, both inside and out, and she could have made a wonderful "political wife."

Marla's battle back in 1974, however, was with a very mean woman who loved to fight if the battle psychologically replicated her early childhood drama. Like a boxer after years in the ring, Hillary visibly carries the scars of anger and fighting on her face.

Billy Clinton, on the other hand, wouldn't even step into the ring. He would sit back like a sissy (is that a politically incorrect word?) and let women fight over him. I knew that Billy was afraid to fight because of his confessed fear of being killed or wounded if he had to serve in the military. He was and is still afraid of his abusive stepfather, Roger Clinton, who died ages ago. There has been no healing for Billy . . . and I believe that his fear of assaults from his alcoholic, abusive stepfather is one of the many roots that spawned his sexual assaults on women.

Hillary discovered that Billy was having a relationship with Marla and began a campaign of threats and intimidation against Marla to secure her own place on his coattails. Billy finally explained to Marla that he needed to be with Hillary because "she kicks my butt and makes me do the things I have to do."

In the 1974 contest ostensibly between Hillary and me (and Marla Crider), the mean grandmother won; thus Billy's age-old psychological conflict seemed to have been resolved in a different way. Unfortunately, when Billy's fun-loving mother had beaten the mean grandmother in the original battle over him in the early 1950s, her Pyrrhic victory led to additional emotional casualties in the Clinton family. Hillary's victory over Marla *et al* in 1974 was destined to do the same.

Hillary's use of private investigators, along with threats and intimidation, would escalate over time as Billy's addiction and his risk-taking behavior escalated. This is a typical pattern of codependents and the addicts whom they try to control.

Although I'm familiar with the term "codependent" and its variations, it occurs to me that many people have heard the term, but have never thought much about it. People who have not been consciously involved with an addict (whether a sex addict, drug addict, alcoholic, gambler, or whatever) do not understand the dynamics and consequences of such an insidious bond between the addict and the codependent.

Billy's and Hillary's symbiotic dysfunctions are integral to their coming together and remaining a "couple," political or otherwise. One must understand a bit about codependency to understand the strong dynamic that operates between them.

Nothing has changed over the decades, except the escalation of their dysfunctional behaviors, much of which has been seen in public. Even some people in the mainstream media are beginning to notice these public displays and to use the terms "codependent" and "enabler" to describe Hillary. Since this is definitely an example of "past is prologue," I will take some time to elaborate.

The word *codependency* appears on its face to suggest that two people are mutually dependent upon each other. That's not it. Mutual dependence is *not* codependency; it is interdependency and it's a good thing. Interdependency is what develops when spouses support each other in a healthy way, with each one contributing for the benefit of the other.

In codependency, however, there is one person who is an addict of some sort (a sex addict in Billy Clinton's case) and that addict's life is *dependent* upon and revolves around getting whatever "fix" is needed.

There is a second person in the relationship whose life revolves around protecting and enabling or controlling the life of the addict. Hillary is the *codependent* because her life revolves around protecting, enabling *and* controlling Billy's sexual addiction

Admittedly, this could get a bit more complicated by the fact that Hillary is a power addict in her own right. Billy, however, is not codependently protecting Hillary in her power addiction; he does not try to control her because he doesn't care what she does. Billy is also addicted to power, and these power addictions work well together for two untreated, dysfunctional people who are known as a "power couple."

Not surprisingly, the roots of these addictions and codependent behaviors are found in the well-documented childhoods of Hillary Rodham and Billy Clinton.

Sometimes I feel sorry for Hillary.

Seriously.

Think about it.

She was raised by a drill-sergeant-type father; she competed with her mother for her father's attention; she competed with her brothers for her father's attention; and she has spent the past forty-something years competing with every woman in Billy Clinton's path for his attention. It's no wonder that Hillary as the other woman became angry and paranoid.

Then, my sympathy ends. No one grew up in a perfect home. No one escaped childhood without scars. If you believe the Bible stories at any level, even as allegory, you know that even Adam and Eve's kids had their own jealousy issues; brother Cain killed brother Abel.

Part of maturing is dealing with the issues that scarred us.

If we don't deal with the troublesome events in our past, we will keep approaching problems with the same childish, outdated, subconscious responses that didn't work for us in the first place. These unexamined, subconscious, and frequently destructive behaviors are not appropriate for any adult. Such behaviors are even less tolerable in a president of the United States of America, and equally unacceptable in a president's spouse, no matter which one is the co-president at the time.

For a clear explanation of the many ways that Billy Clinton's unresolved childhood issues negatively affected his years in political office, see Paul Fick's excellent and easy-to-understand book *The Dysfunctional President*. When I read it many years ago, I couldn't believe that a PhD psychologist who never treated Billy Clinton as a patient could have such clear insights into his sick behaviors that affected everything from foreign policy to sexcapades in the Oval Office, including sexual assaults. I'm hoping to see a companion book from Paul Fick sometime soon about *The Dysfunctional President's Dysfunctional Wife*.

Hillary Rodham and Billy Clinton are classic and public examples of what happens when abused children do not confront their own issues and thus never mature into reasoning, thinking adults. These are sad cases and I truly hope that people who read this book and have an "aha!" moment will be able to confront and heal their own issues. No one escapes without bearing some childhood scars. It is the open and growing person who will deal with them.

I'm not suggesting that we should encourage group therapy in the Oval Office. It's too late. Hillary has not dealt with her own demons, and she is nearly seventy years old. I don't think she's going to get any better, or any more truthful, or develop any integrity, or stop attacking the women (and men) who dare to confront her.

I would love to confront Hillary about her attacks on women, face-to-face, in a debate. I'm guessing she would have a headache that night and not show up.

18

BACK AND FORWARD—
PAST IS PROLOGUE

The way I see it, which is close up and personal, Hillary's and Billy's psychological and emotional dysfunctions were and are a great match. Hillary and Billy were and are together for political reasons. Their mutual goals to get to the White House were "outside" their marriage while paramount to it.

Even their decision to have a child was a calculated political maneuver to make them appear to be a normal couple. Having a child would also serve to take attention and Arkansas gossip away from what Billy described to me as Hillary's "lifestyle."

There is another important piece in my big picture of this very public couple. It is widely believed that men tend to marry someone like their mother. This has caused a good deal of discussion and speculation among professional therapists who had trouble seeing the similarities between Billy's mother, the fun-loving Virginia, and the woman he married, the less-than-fun Hillary.

Billy's biological mother was definitely Virginia, but Virginia left Billy at a very young age in the care of her parents at their home in Hope, Arkansas. For psychological purposes, Billy's early female caregiver, or mother figure, then, was actually his maternal grandmother.

While I didn't know either one of Billy's maternal grandparents personally, by reputation, Billy's grandfather was a great guy who ran a general store and was liked, if not loved, by all who met him. He was a gregarious man, and generous with extending credit even to the black people who were his regular customers. It is obvious that Billy picked up a lot of his grandfather's sociable traits and has used them to his advantage throughout his life and political career.

On the other hand, I have heard that Billy's grandmother was "the meanest woman in southwest Arkansas." This unkind assessment came from folks who I considered to be reliable sources. Billy's grandmother may, in fact, not have been the meanest woman in southwest Arkansas, but that sure is the impression that people had about her. And it would have been little Billy's impression of his grandmother at the deepest emotional level.

When Hillary came to Arkansas, she gave people that same mean impression. Without quibbling over the accuracy of those assessments, one can still draw the conclusion that both Billy's grandmother and Hillary Rodham said and did things which caused people around them to describe them as mean.

To Billy's untreated psyche, the subconscious attraction to the meanness in Hillary would be enormous.

Billy's grandmother was the disciplinarian in the family. She was the scheduler. She wanted everything to run like clockwork, including his sleeping, his eating and, by implication, his bowel movements. Sorry, but when one is analyzing the roots of later sexual dysfunction or inappropriate sexual responses, one must include a child's early associations with matters "below the belt."

Hillary was the disciplinarian in the "marriage" with Billy. Like Billy's grandmother, Hillary was the scheduler. She wanted everything to run like clockwork, especially their race to the White House. She was frequently, loudly, and famously frustrated that she could not control Billy below the belt.

Hillary, like Billy's grandmother, was always there to discipline him when he got out of line and to insert her tentacles into every possible aspect of controlling him. Like Billy's grandmother, Hillary has little tolerance for tardiness, for self-indulgence, and for "accidents" below the belt. She has the typical codependent's need to control.

It is clear that Billy Clinton, even (or especially) when he was the president of the United States, was still in rebellion against the attempts by his grandmother, or Hillary, to run his life.

If the infant and young boy Billy Clinton spent the first four years of his life in the care of the so-called meanest woman in southwest Arkansas, would he not be drawn to the meanness in Hillary Rodham like a moth drawn to a flame?

More importantly, wouldn't Billy be subconsciously projecting "meanness" onto other women? Wouldn't this deeply ingrained belief that women are mean affect the way he views women in general? Wouldn't this explain a lot about his assaults on so many women?

In the beginning of the public's budding awareness of Billy Clinton's sexual proclivity, there was general tolerance under the theme of "boys will be boys" and "sex is a private matter." There was even some male envy and some female attraction for the bad boy of politics.

Most of the mainstream media sycophants were all too happy to excuse or ignore Billy's sexual behavior. There was even a pervasive public debate in the 1992 presidential campaign: "Does character matter?" Most of the mainstream media concluded that character does not matter.

I believe that millenials are reaching a different conclusion. Somehow they seem to know that character is the one thing that really does matter because it affects every decision that a person makes.

Yes, character does matter, and thinking people are finally realizing that. Thinking people are also beginning to notice that Billy has grossly mistreated women, including rape and sexual assault. Thinking people are starting to see that Hillary, his coconspirator, is as guilty as he is. She goes around after him trying to clean up his "below the belt" messes, and she will do whatever is necessary to silence his victims.

Billy may be assaulting women in a subconscious retaliation for the meanness of his primary female caregiver in his early years. At the same time, he is retaliating against his own wife, who is the other mean woman in his life. Threatening and intimidating the untold numbers of women with whom he shared the most intimate of acts must be some kind of retaliation. And, being a serial sexual predator is not exactly a benevolent lifestyle.

While proclaiming himself to be the champion of women's rights, Billy Clinton has continually betrayed the woman he married, the girl he fathered, and the untold numbers of women he used for his sexual gratification.

Meanwhile, proclaiming herself to be the champion of women's rights, Hillary Clinton has been behind the threats and intimidation of the women her own husband abused and molested.

Is that mean, or what? As we all know now, the abused becomes the abuser.

First, Billy was emotionally abused by being emotionally abandoned by his natural mother and his biological father (whoever he was). Then, he was emotionally abused by his dominant, overly controlling, mean grandmother. The bright young Billy, at the age of four or five, already insecure from early abandonment by both of his biological parents, watched as the two most important women in his life "fought it out" over him. While he was still a preschooler, Billy Clinton was emotionally abused as his mother and grandmother got in a huge, prolonged fight over who would have custody of him when Virginia married Roger Clinton. Virginia, naturally, planned to take little Billy with her when she and Roger would settle in Hot Springs. Unbelievable as it would have been at the time in small-town Hope, Arkansas, they almost filed a custody suit in court. They also "fought it out" over their drastically different morals and lifestyles.

On the one hand was Billy's uptight grandmother and on the other hand was his very loose mother. Make no mistake about it—Virginia was not simply a harmless, fun-loving flirt any more than Billy is merely a charming rogue. He is a rapist and sexual predator whose sex addiction is out of control.

Billy's mother, Virginia Clinton, had a well-earned reputation in town for her out-of-control sexual behavior as well. And Billy's father, who sired the boy and then disappeared, was either the bigamist Virginia claimed to be married to or he was an unknown married man as the rumors in Arkansas have claimed for decades. Either way, not good.

For many years after that, throughout his teenage years, Billy would be subjected to the emotional incest of the relationship with his mother. As a teenager, I was aware of many of the things that Virginia did to Billy in the way of emotional incest, but did not realize the seriousness of that at the time. In addition to my own observations, many of these issues have been well-documented and confirmed by others:

Virginia's inappropriate conversations with Billy about adult matters;

the establishment of the "master bedroom" with its private bathroom as Billy's while he was only a young teenager;

Virginia's intense bonding with her older son Billy, while other men and stepfathers would come and go; and

Virginia's use of Billy as an escort at nightclubs and other venues.

And to make matters worse, Billy Clinton experienced the same issues throughout his teenage years with his abusive, bullying stepfather.

Several writers have documented those facts about Billy's childhood without drawing the obvious conclusion that there was emotional incest. Is Billy supposed to be able to love women after all that? Note that "love" here does not mean "to have sex" or "to rape" or "to have a one-night stand" or "to inflict a ten-second grope," all fueled by an uncontrolled sex addiction. None of that is "love."

Hillary Rodham has her own generational family script that she hasn't resolved in a healthy way. She has as much as admitted to experiencing the same type of emotional incest. She did not identify it with that terminology, probably because she didn't recognize it. Her mother was abandoned by her grandmother, and Hillary herself has done nothing (that I can tell) to stop the abandonment, and so it continues. Obviously, she has not healed from that unrealized emotional and psychological abuse because she is still reacting to the issues of public and private life from the stance of an untreated victim of abuse.

Hillary strikes out at everyone who she perceives to be a personal enemy, without ever recognizing that her most dangerous enemy resides within her own psyche. Many of Hillary's choices of attack are misdirected and subconsciously self-destructive, as one might expect from a person who is battling an unseen internal enemy. The childhood battles wage a constant war, with no peace in sight. This family dysfunction requires lying to face life. Later, of course, Hillary lied about dodging sniper fire when landing in Bosnia, and who can forget her lies about Benghazi. She lied to the American people. She lied to the families of the victims. What else could she do? She is not emotionally capable of accepting blame. She is not emotionally capable of dealing as an adult with the natural consequences of her own ill-conceived actions . . . or inactions, as the case was in Benghazi. She still can't grasp what she did wrong by sleeping through the massacre of our American ambassador and three other American citizens in Benghazi.

Even though Hillary Clinton as secretary of state had been forewarned of the danger in Benghazi, she did nothing. She was tired. She needed to sleep. She could not be bothered to answer a frantic phone call for the armed assistance that she could have sent.

Testifying before Congress about her inaction on behalf of the Benghazi victims that night, Hillary had the unmitigated gall and arrogance to ask: "What difference, after all this time, does it make?"

Four Americans, including an ambassador, were massacred, and American citizens rightfully want to know how this happened. Clearly, it does not make any difference to Hillary. It does make a difference to the families of the dead. It does make a difference to decent people everywhere.

As secretary of state, Hillary should have made a difference that night. She should have taken her share of the responsibility afterward. Hillary, however, is emotionally and psychologically incapable of facing that much truth all at one time. The abused child within her is running the show, but not taking credit for the production.

Hillary has proven that she could travel a million miles as secretary of state and still make no positive impact on behalf of the USA. She could not make any movement toward peace anywhere because it is a concept she cannot grasp psychologically or emotionally. Hillary's "life is war" mentality is the result of her untreated childhood issues.

Even her website as she runs for president is full of her "life is war" outlook. Count the number of times she uses the word *fight* on her website and in her speaking.

Ironically, although Hillary can threaten and intimidate her husband's victims, she is incapable of handling a real war because she is not a mature adult with the character and integrity to make important, substantive judgments. This failure is not acceptable for a commander in chief, or for the person with a finger on the nuclear trigger.

Like bullies everywhere, Hillary can attack defenseless women who were abused by her husband, but she cannot stand up with any moral authority to any real authority figure. She has no moral base, but only self-interest and an insatiable hunger for power. This is Hillary's recurring nightmare from being unable to stand up to her bullying father in her childhood.

In a nutshell, Hillary lies when she doesn't need to lie because it's a conditioned response. She will never feel "good enough" to meet her dead father's standards, and so she will continue to lie, to make up whoppers, to rewrite history as seen through the thick lens of her dysfunction. She will continue to attack any woman, or man, who has the nerve to contradict her.

Hillary met her perfect, emotionally and psychologically damaged match in Billy Clinton.

19

UPS AND DOWNS

The quiet hum of the airplane's single engine stopped. No sputter. No gasp. It just stopped.

From the seat behind the pilot, even in the darkened sky, I could see the propeller slowing to visible, and then countable, revolutions. Slower and slower the prop turned until it stopped, pointing straight up and down.

My next thought was a question and statement:

"So this is the way I'm going to die."

Instead of landing unannounced in Little Rock to have a private dinner with my sister without a hectic weekend of visiting friends, my arrival from Dallas was splashed on the local 10 o'clock news, which everyone watched back then.

It was September (or October) 1983, and it must have been a slow news weekend because the report was repeated on television and radio for the next two days, along with an article and photo in the statewide newspaper.

Billy Clinton, who was back in the governor's office thanks to the brilliant Dick-Morris-led 1982 campaign, called me at my sister's house the morning after the crash.

"You didn't tell me you were coming to Little Rock this weekend," Billy said in a pout. "The Warden's gone."

"I'm fine, thank you."

When would I ever learn?

Both Billy and Hillary were so self-absorbed that life was always about what they wanted, when they wanted it.

Who knows where Hillary "the Warden" Clinton was that day? Who knows what she was doing? Billy never mentioned any specifics about where she was, and he didn't seem to care. I do know that she was not at home with her family.

I also know that Hillary never took Chelsea to school. Billy enjoyed spending time with his daughter in the mornings and taking her to school. I heard that directly from Billy, and I also heard it from various state troopers who drove them in the Lincoln Town Car.

Billy's devotion to little Chelsea was one more reason the troopers liked Billy. Hillary's lack of devotion to Chelsea was one more reason that the troopers didn't like (or respect) her. I can't resist adding one more small-world Arkansas story.

Before Chelsea went to public school in Little Rock, which was a much-publicized and completely political decision made by Billy and Hillary, she went to Montessori. The school was on Markham Street, and it occupied three small houses on contiguous lots that I had purchased earlier as an investment.

I sold the three parcels on Markham to attorney Ben McMinn, whose then-wife Jyothi Rao connected the houses and operated the Montessori school there. Of all the properties in Little Rock, that's where Chelsea started school.

That reminds me of another ironic coincidence. My first home address, where my birth certificate was mailed, was 123 Clinton Street. I can't top that.

* * *

The following matters, on the other hand, are deadly serious and cannot be attributed to coincidence.

If Billy Clinton had been emotionally and psychologically capable of dealing with the terrorists who began attacking America on his watch in 1993, our country might have been able to avoid the tragic events of 9/11.

September 11, 2001, was the day that radical Islamic terrorists hijacked and flew airplanes into the twin towers of the World Trade Center in New York and into the Pentagon in Washington. The fourth hijacked plane was brought down by some courageous passengers and crashed into a field.

That date, September 11, 2001, is indelibly etched in the minds of those of us who saw the live television coverage. Our parents and grandparents had similar memories of where they were when they heard about the infamous bombing of Pearl Harbor by the Japanese on December 7, 1941.

After the Pearl Harbor attack in 1941, however, President Franklin Roosevelt was able to lead the United States of America into its valiant participation in World War II. Roosevelt had not lived his life in fear of a stepfather.

President Clinton was incapable of taking swift, targeted, decisive action against the Islamic terrorists who attacked America in 1993 and beyond. Billy was still cowering from his stepfather's attacks during his childhood and teenage years.

I should mention here that Billy has told some fantastic lies about confronting his abusive, alcoholic stepfather when he was fourteen years old. Lies and more lies. Roger Clinton ran roughshod over his family whenever he drank excessively, and the teenage Billy Clinton could or would do nothing about it.

How do I know Billy's "family hero" story is a lie?

When Roger Clinton, Sr., was on a rampage, Virginia would take Billy and Roger, Jr., to spend the night at the Holiday Inn on East Grand Avenue. If Virginia (a nurse-anesthetist who was on call 24/7 for several years) had to work that night, she would leave Billy and Roger alone at the motel.

When Virginia was working, Billy would call me from their motel room, and I would go visit. We would talk for hours while little Roger slept. This pattern continued through high school and beyond. Any tall tale about the teenage Billy's putting a stop to his stepfather's alcoholic, abusive behavior is as valuable as droppings on a newspaper in a birdcage.

I'm sorry that Billy has not dealt with his abuse issues, but it's time that the American people had some clue about the reasons behind his ineptitude and cowardice as commander in chief. Unfortunately, Billy's cowardice explains far too many of his decisions . . . or his failures to decide.

(Billy later declared under oath that he was AFRAID of what I might do at our thirtieth high school reunion . . . and he was protected by Secret Service agents at the time!)

Those who are too young to remember, or who were not paying attention to, the Clintons' copresidency should look up some of the earlier attacks on the United States:

1993: Islamic terrorists bombed the World Trade Center; six people died, and more than 1,000 were injured;

1995: Islamic terrorists attempted to crash an airplane into the White House;

1996: Islamic terrorists bombed the Khobar Towers, killing 19 United States military service members, and injuring another 500 people;

1998: Islamic terrorists exploded two massive bombs (nearly simultaneously) outside the U.S. embassies in Kenya and Tanzania; over 200 people were killed; another 5,000 people were wounded;

2000: Islamic terrorists attacked the U.S. Navy's guided-missile destroyer the USS *Cole* while it was harbored and being refueled in the Yemeni port of Aden; 17 U.S. servicemen were killed, and 39 were injured.

That is enough to make my point.

Billy Clinton, still terrified of his stepfather, did nothing.

Oh, wait, I almost forgot.

August 7, 1999: on the one-year anniversary of the Kenya and Tanzania embassy bombings that killed over 200 people and injured 5,000, Co-president Clinton reaffirmed his commitment to the victims of terrorism. He vowed publicly that he would "not rest until justice is done."

August 11, 1999: four days after vowing that justice would be meted to terrorists, while Congress was on its summer recess, the White House issued a quiet press release announcing that the president was granting clemency to 16 imprisoned members of FALN (Fuerzas Armadas de Liberación Nacional Puertorriqueña, the armed forces for national liberation of Puerto Rico).

The FALN were terrorists (not Islamic terrorists) who had been responsible for over a hundred bombing attacks on the United States in prior years. What message was the co-president sending to Islamic terrorists when he commuted the sentences of sixteen other terrorists serving prison time in the United States?

Who was upset about the co-president's pardoning of known terrorists on American soil? The U.S. Attorney, the FBI, and members of Congress were upset. Hillary, the co-president, didn't have a problem with it. Who did anything about it? Not the U.S. Attorney, not the FBI, and not Congress. This corporate failure to act illustrates one of the many reasons that informed Americans are getting sick and tired of "business as usual" in Washington.

There is one more critically important item to mention regarding the Clintons' failure to respond to terrorists:

1998: the Clintons failed to take action against the Islamic terrorist Osama bin Laden.

Bin Laden had formed and was the leader of the Islamic terrorist group al-Qaeda that took responsibility for the African (Kenya and Tanzania) embassy bombings. The Clintons shirked their responsibility to "take him out" when they had the opportunity. Three times bin Laden was in their sights. Three times the Clintons failed to stop him. Pitiful. Disgusting.

If Barack Hussein Obama could call an Islamic terrorist an Islamic terrorist, the United States of America would not be faced with such increasing and intolerable Islamic terrorist attacks. Everyone but Barack Hussein Obama can admit these Islamic terrorist attacks are escalating.

I'm not suggesting that Obama would have acted any differently. I believe he would have failed to address the same Islamic terrorist attacks on the USA that the Clintons ignored. I do suggest, however, that Obama's motivations for ignoring the Islamic terrorists' attacks would be different.

Hillary Clinton, Obama's secretary of state from 2009 to 2013, was no more emotionally and psychologically capable of dealing with terrorists in later years than she was as the co-president earlier. When Islamic terrorists were on the threshold of attacking America's embassy in Benghazi, Secretary of State Hillary Clinton was tired. She was self-absorbed.

Hillary said she was asleep during the Benghazi debacle. Then she lied. Then she lied again. Then she lied some more. She should have a permanent headache from trying to keep track of all her lies. Some of those lies will be uncovered in her emails, but that is another chapter.

The United States of America is now facing the potential acceptance of ten thousand Muslim "refugees" into our country. Obama is *not* going to stop or even question them. The pansies in Congress may or may not do anything about it. Hillary certainly wouldn't; after all, such a move against an entire ethnic group would be politically incorrect and would show her racism.

Muslim "refugees" have flooded Europe. Thanks to the leanings of the mainstream media, we see photos of sad women and children refugees from the Middle East. What we do not see in the photos from the mainstream media are the untold numbers of single, strong, able-bodied, military-age, Islamic males infiltrating those countries under the guise of being refugees.

In September 2015, the Greek coast guard intercepted an "aid for refugees" shipping container that was filled with weapons and ammunition. Disguised as furniture for Islamic refugees going to Europe, the container was found and confiscated.

Does anyone who is not brain-dead think that the Greek coast guard happened to find the one-and-only shipment of weapons and ammunition that was being sent to able-bodied, male, Islamic terrorists in Europe? Anyone?

Seven Islamic terrorists, who killed over 125 people in Paris and injured hundreds more in a coordinated attack in November 2015, had to get their weapons from somewhere. I suggest that their weapons and ammunition may have been in a "furniture" shipment that was not found by the Greek coast guard or by anyone else.

How many more "furniture" containers were shipped into Europe with weapons and ammunition? How many weapons are there now? How many "furniture" containers do we want coming into the United States of America with ten thousand undocumented refugees?

If the November 2015 coordinated terrorists attacks had been staged in Paris, Texas, rather than in the "gun-free" city of Paris, France, I'm quite confident that those seven terrorists would have been taken down quickly, and without such a horrific loss of life.

As the bouncer says to incoming patrons in an East Texas honky-tonk, "Got a gun on ya?"

If not, "then better go back to your truck and gitcha one."

Barack Hussein Obama wants to take away gun rights. Obama, who is half white by his mother and some part black due to an unidentified mix from his mixed-race father, is one of the most racially divisive presidents since Republican Abraham Lincoln decided that America should not have slaves.

Many people are afraid to criticize Obama for fear of being branded by the mainstream media as racist. Ironically, how racist is the view that is being perpetrated by the mainstream media? Doesn't it suggest that they believe Obama is president only because he claimed his black heritage? What kind of racism is that? What kind of racism suggests that an inept president can't handle criticism because he's partly black?

Do you remember the 2012 campaign counter-slogan?

"If you voted for Obama in 2008 to prove you were not a racist, vote against him in 2012 to prove you're not an idiot."

Hillary Clinton claims that she wants to walk in Barack Hussein Obama's dainty footsteps. Is it any wonder that middle-America is "up in arms" and looking for an outsider or any person of courage, conviction, and integrity to take the role of leader in America?

Hillary is *not* a leader. She is a coattail-clutcher who has a litany of jobs with no accomplishments. Hillary failed as co-president; she failed as senator (unless you are impressed with the bills she introduced to name a couple of post offices); she failed as secretary of state (and the half of that story has not been told yet); and she most certainly failed over the course of the past forty years as the defender of women and children that she claims to be.

Hillary says that she has "fought for" women for her entire career. She seems to be confused; she has "attacked" women.

Hillary apparently believes her own public relations spiels because she continually claims that she supports women's rights. Hillary knows (or has she forgotten?) that she was the instigator of the threats, intimidation, and other attacks on so many women (including me!) who had any kind of sexual encounters with her husband.

Pathological liars can sound convincing to people who don't know the truth. Pathological liars can often pass polygraph tests because they actually do believe their own tall tales. They can devise whatever excuses they need at the moment.

Like a child caught with her hand in the cookie jar, Hillary can conjure up a quick story and defend it, no matter how ridiculous it sounds to a person with the ability to think logically. She will defend her lies until forced to face the truth, and then what difference does it make?

Hillary can conjure up tears as quickly as lies, as she did when campaigning in New Hampshire in 2008. More recently, Hillary was able to maintain a straight face while she filmed a campaign ad saying that women who claim to have been raped or sexually assaulted should be believed. That blatant hypocrisy is truly amazing for a woman who has been married for forty years to a rapist and serial sexual abuser . . . without even mentioning again that *she* led the attacks against the women.

The latest series of Hillary's lies are nothing but campaign ploys. It's time for the American people—of all or no political persuasion—to take a good, informed look at the real persons behind the endless spewing of lies.

During Hillary's 2008 presidential campaign, my favorite feminist, Camille Paglia, wrote in Salon.com that Hillary "is a brittle, relentless manipulator with few stable core values who shuffles through useful personalities like a card shark."

I wish I had written that. Thanks, Camille.

20

WITNESS PROTECTION PROGRAM AND THE KKK

If there were a witness protection program for people who are afraid to tell what they know about the Clintons, there would be a groundswell of new information. As it stands now, however, the KKK (the Klinton Krime Kartel) is still able to operate at will because most people are afraid to speak against the mob in public.

Critics of the various books and articles about Hillary and the rest of the KKK point to the lack of *name* of credible witnesses. There are hundreds of true stories circulating about the KKK, about the KKK's ways of "doing business," and about the KKK's methods of silencing opponents.

In other words, the Klintons' lies, threats, assaults, and other forms of intimidation are still working to silence those who would tell the truth. The intimidation includes, especially, the public humiliation that is aided and abetted by ignorant and/or prejudiced "journalists" in the mainstream media.

When I was a student at Hot Springs High School, I wrote a paper about the other infamous KKK, the Ku Klux Klan. I talked to men who were members of the KKK, who didn't seem to mind telling a harmless teenage girl about the notorious exploits of the Klan in Arkansas.

I researched obscure newspaper references and all sorts of odd bits and pieces of credible reports that I could find about the Klan in Arkansas in the 1960s. I had a shoebox full of index cards with a different quote or incident on each one. It was certainly a lot harder to do this kind of research before the Internet!

Ultimately, I sorted, organized, and outlined my 3 x 5 cards, and then wrote what I (an "A" student since the first grade) thought would surely be an "A" paper. My teacher, however, gave me a great big "C-" at the top of the page, and added this comment:

"The Ku Klux Klan does not exist in Arkansas."

That was my first big slap in the face for telling the truth that someone didn't want to hear. In retrospect, I'm guessing that the teacher may have been a member of the Klan!

This brings to mind another interesting and relevant story. I recommend doing a little research if you don't already know about the Saint Valentine's Day Massacre that occurred in Chicago on February 14, 1929. In a nutshell, this was during Prohibition, and the notorious Al Capone's gang ambushed a rival gang for control of organized crime in Chicago.

When police officers arrived at the scene of the massacre, Capone's rival gang member Frank Gusenberg was still alive. This only surviving victim of the bold assault was rushed to a hospital where doctors were able to stabilize him for a little while.

The police questioned Gusenberg about who had attacked him and the gang. Gusenberg, who had fourteen bullet wounds in his body, responded, "No one shot me." He died a few hours later.

No one ever lived to rat on Al Capone or to be a witness, so the federal government was never able to make a case against Capone for his innumerable crimes ranging from bootlegging to extortion to murder. Finally, however, the dreaded IRS (Internal Revenue Service) took him down, and Alphonse Gabriel Capone served eleven years in prison for federal income tax evasion.

* * *

I haven't spent much face time with Hillary Rodham Clinton, but I've spent a lot of time with her husband and other members of his family. I've also visited with various Arkansas State Troopers and law enforcement personnel across the state who kept an eye on Billy and Hillary over the years.

Often when Billy and Hillary, usually separately, traveled to small towns around the state of Arkansas, the local police officers and even firefighters were called upon to beef up security for the governor and his wife. I could fill an entire book with their tales of Billy's notorious sexcapades and Hillary's imperious vexcapades.

All of us have our unique perspectives on Hillary Rodham Clinton, but not everyone is willing to tell the truth in public. I'm surely not expecting any small-town Arkansas law enforcement personnel to tell in public what they have whispered in private. That's still a good way to lose a job in Arkansas, or to be demoted or reassigned. I'm not going to violate anyone's trust in me by naming names, so I'm not able to tell all the juicy stories. Sorry.

I will simply say, after all these years, that some of the most fascinating and revealing comments are the unreported ones—fearfully told in quiet whispers behind Hillary's back.

Even people who carry guns for a living are afraid to let it be known what they know and what they really think about Hillary Clinton, as if she were the ruthless wife of a merciless dictator in a Third World country. They have all seen the "Clinton Death List" that is still circulating on the Internet, and they take it more seriously than most higher-up law enforcement officials seem to do.

I'll say this about the Clinton Death List. A lot of it is unsubstantiated baloney. I find it disgusting that the accidental deaths of many fine people in Arkansas have been added to this list by conspiracy theorists who jump on any tangential piece of information. Billy Clinton knew thousands of people in Arkansas, by name; it is statistically certain that a lot of them would die.

On the other hand, there are many ridiculously explained deaths in Arkansas (and beyond!) that would make spectacular topics for episodes of *Cold Case Files*.

Clinton operatives, knowing that the Death List is exaggerated, used it to intimidate people anyway. Linda Tripp comes to mind, as well as Monica Lewinsky. Both were threatened with that scary list.

What if you knew something terrible about your boss or about a higher-up in your organization? What if several people in your organization had lost their jobs or been transferred to the boonies after hinting that they "new something" about the boss?

How would you feel then if a Death List showed up on your office chair when you returned from lunch?

21

THE ME-FIRST LADY

One of the Clinton biographers called me several years ago to find out if Billy in real life called Hillary "the Warden."

Yes, he did. Before I would drive over for a visit, Billy would tell me to call Buddy Young, his longtime chief of security at the governor's mansion, to be sure that "the Warden" had left the premises.

Buddy Young and several of the other troopers whom I met at the governor's mansion picked up Billy's term "the Warden" and seemed to enjoy using it. I never heard any of them say anything complimentary about Hillary, though they seemed to enjoy working for and traveling with the affable Billy.

Any troopers who were appalled by Billy's outrageous sexual behavior didn't last long at the mansion. Any troopers who were uncomfortable with the governor's having his sexual needs met in the back seat of the car while they were driving would not be kept on his security detail.

Any troopers who objected and failed to get phone numbers from women whom the governor spotted in an audience somewhere, would be relieved of their plum positions on the governor's security detail. If they did stay at the mansion, it would be on the punishment detail of working for the Warden instead of Billy.

As a warden, Hillary did not do a very good job of keeping her "prisoner" under control. Too often, she was not at home. Her schedule as First Lady of Arkansas, as well as a practicing lawyer, seemed to be as erratic and unpredictable as Billy's.

They had a nanny to take care of their daughter, Chelsea, although Billy enjoyed spending time with her from her infancy. He was always a more involved and nurturing parent than Hillary ever appeared to be. It was rumored that Billy also carried on an affair with one of Chelsea's nannies, which is a completely plausible story, but I don't know about that.

I've noticed that many men who have affairs refer to their woman at home as "the wife" instead of the more personal "my wife." This verbal gambit distances them from the woman they are betraying and helps assuage their guilt, but it is also a true representation of the nature of their relationship.

Perhaps "the Warden" is the same—a true representation of the nature of their relationship. At least Billy didn't call Hillary "Granny" back then, even though she replicated many of his grandmother's controlling behaviors. It's just that the governor was no longer four years old (at least not chronologically), and he was more difficult to control. He was impossible to control. In fact, he couldn't control himself.

I've noticed that many people gloss over the reports about what I call Hillary's vexcapades, her screaming, cursing, and throwing fits usually as a result of Billy's sexcapades. Ordinary folks can easily understand how she would be upset with him for having sex with untold numbers of other women while "married" to Hillary. Many people think that her behavior was justified by his provocations, no matter what she said or did.

Another group of people believe that the stories about Hillary's verbal tirades and physically abusive assaults are simply idle, or even vicious, untrue gossip. I've heard both sides. I've heard troopers telling funny stories about Hillary that really weren't funny, such as slamming kitchen cabinets so hard that the doors came off the hinges, and throwing glassware across the room. I've also heard nice Arkansas people telling me that they simply couldn't believe such horrid tales about a woman, especially the First *Lady*, even though she was a Yankee.

The bottom line is that the egregious behavior of the Me-First Lady was so trailer trash that she was safe to indulge in it both in the Arkansas governor's mansion, and later in the White House. Hillary could get away with it as long as she didn't do it in public. If anyone ever reported her behavior, then that person was swiftly condemned in public as a liar.

I don't think that anyone realized Hillary was reacting based upon pent-up childhood abuses and traumas that had never been addressed. Her tantrums should be expected because she is a psychological and emotional volcano that is always on the brink of erupting.

Hillary's contemptuous, uncontrolled outbursts are so extreme that most people cannot wrap their minds around the possibility that a First Lady could act like that; therefore, they discount the reports. It is much easier for most people to swallow hook, line, and sinker the Hillary-bait that anyone reporting such incidents is a liar. Smells fishy to me.

Surely, people think, the First Lady of Arkansas, later the First Lady of the United States, could not be so crass and crude. Surely, people think, the First Lady of Arkansas, later the First Lady of the United States, does not curse like a sailor (with my apologies to sailors everywhere).

The same sense of disbelief holds true for Billy's outrageous sexual behavior. Surely, many people think, the governor of Arkansas, later *President* of the United States, could not be a rapist and a serial sexual predator.

Think again. There is more than one commonality that keeps those two "together."

* * *

There is a story about Hillary and the Easter egg hunt during one of her years as First Lady of Arkansas that people generally believe or disbelieve based upon their political affiliations. Maybe I'm too realistic, but I can believe both the bad and the good about people without regard to their (or my) political leanings.

It is traditional to hold an annual Easter egg hunt on the grounds of the governor's mansion. Hillary was the reluctant hostess every year while Billy was governor. There would be a hunt for the benefit of all the age-appropriate children who could run and pick up the eggs, and then there would be a special hunt for the children who were in some way developmentally challenged.

As I mentioned earlier, my friend Louise was a longtime advocate for what is now ARC (formerly Arkansas Association for Retarded Citizens), and Louise told me this story. I also heard the same story later from a lawyer whom I met at a different gathering at the governor's mansion; not surprisingly, he does not want to be named. The same story was told by a couple of the troopers who were present for this particular Easter Egg Hunt.

The children in the second group were naturally slower than those in the first group. The day was quite warm, as is common in Arkansas in the spring. Despite the heat, the children were having a wonderful time.

But they were having a v – e – r – y, v – e – r – y, v – e – r – y s – l – o – w time of finding and picking up the Easter eggs.

Hillary had enough. She stomped across the grass up to the shaded veranda on the back of the mansion (this was before the huge addition), and accosted one of the troopers. At this point, the story diverges a bit. Some people said that there was an open microphone; others said that Hillary could be heard across the yard because she was yelling. It's a toss-up in my mind, although I personally favor the "open mike" version, which is what Louise told me.

At any rate, the frustrated Me-First Lady demanded, "When are they going to get those f***ing ree-tards out of here?"

22

HILLARY CLINTON 1984 "MOTHER OF THE YEAR"

Hillary ("When are they going to get those f***ing ree-tards-out-of-here?") Clinton was named "Mother of the Year" in Arkansas in 1984. Based on that startling news, George Orwell might have been able to add another horrific chapter to his classic book *1984*.

I, on the other hand, even after all these years, remain speechless on this topic.

23

HILLARY AND HER MS. DEMEANORS

At home and on the road, Governor Bill Clinton was, like any untreated sex addict, always on the lookout for his next score, or fix. I never was deluded into believing that our relationship was exclusive, even before he "married" Hillary.

As my mother always said, "If he'll do it with you, he'll do it to you!" Hillary knew that too, or she wouldn't have sent her father and brother to spy on Billy as early as 1974, when we were all single.

I didn't realize until many years later, however, that Billy was a serial sexual predator and a rapist. It made me ill when I found out that he had raped Juanita Broaddrick. Before Juanita, there was a young woman at Oxford. It makes me nauseous to think about how many other women suffered sexual assaults by the predator Clinton over the decades.

Most of the women who were attacked by Billy are still terrified to talk about it in public. Hillary knew about Juanita long before I did. Hillary did a threatening number on Juanita, and then Billy kept trying to contact Juanita again—for what purposes we can only speculate.

I found it interesting that some of the media started to get excited about the possibility that Billy had fathered a child with a black prostitute while he was governor and Hillary was the Warden on watch. Much was made about the impending DNA test, which would have established his paternity.

When the DNA test was *reported* as negative, the media were happy to drop the matter altogether. Hillary knew about that too. Of course, she cursed the black prostitutes who would tell such "lies" about her political free ride.

Billy never denied the story of having an ongoing relationship with the black prostitute, and with her friends. Billy did deny having a black baby. Anyone, including Hillary, who is familiar with the special dialect known as Clintonese, realizes that this is a true statement.

Billy could not have had "a black baby" because Billy is not black. He could, however, have a half-black, half-white baby, but no one asked him about that.

Through ignorance, laziness, or prejudice, most "journalists" in the mainstream media don't ask the follow-up questions that would lead to a full disclosure (ha!) or at least a complete and dissectible lie. They didn't ask Billy the tough follow-up questions. They don't ask Hillary the tough follow-up questions.

For years, Robert "Say" McIntosh, one of the leading African-American activists in Little Rock, dogged Billy about his relationships with black prostitutes. "Say" McIntosh was one of the men whom Billy referred to as a "G**damned nigger"; Jesse Jackson was another.

No one in the media (as I recall) followed up on the activist when he suddenly lost interest in haranguing Billy. I suppose they figured he was too busy running his newest, well-capitalized, busine$$ venture to be interested in politic$ now. After all those years of speaking out and speaking up for his people, I guess he is just happy to be out of the spotlight. Surely, that must be it. (Someone else can delve into the prison-term pardon for "Say"'s son.)

Billy's trysts with numerous black women over the years were well discussed in Little Rock. A certain prominent black female newscaster in Little Rock used to brag openly around the television station about her relationship with the governor, although they were "only" indulging in oral sex. That same newscaster later worked in the national media; she could always count on having her consistently softball, friendly questions recognized and answered by Billy Clinton.

I don't recall any stories about Billy with Chinese women while he was governor of Arkansas, but there weren't too many Chinese people in Arkansas back then. Billy and Hillary have certainly made it clear that Chinese people are welcome around them now, especially if they have lots of money from their connections with the Chinese government.

While using and abusing women of all races and colors, both Hillary and Billy Clinton have professed to be the champion of women's rights. I mentioned this on a radio show in Chicago, where a bunch of the NOW (National Organization *for* Women) folk hang out.

I wondered aloud where all the defenders of Juanita Broaddrick and other abused-by-Clinton women were hiding. I challenged them to speak out on behalf of Juanita Broaddrick, an obviously credible woman, who was publicly calling the president of the United States a rapist. Silence from NOW.

The women of NOW didn't rally around Juanita Broaddrick. They didn't rally around Paula Corbin Jones who was assaulted by the governor and then trashed by Hillary.

The women of NOW didn't rally around Gennifer Flowers or Kathleen Willey or Linda Tripp or Monica Lewinsky or Sally Miller Perdue or Elizabeth Ward Gracen or Bobbie Ann Williams or Lencola Sullivan or Beth Coulson.

The women of NOW did not rally around the wives and the teenage daughters of prominent citizens and campaign contributors in Arkansas and other states where Billy went.

And the women of NOW sure as heck never gave me a call!

So, who exactly are the constituents of NOW? And, what women does Hillary support? Which women are they FOR?

Would that be the women who are abused by their boyfriends? Not according to the list above.

Would that be women who are abused in the workplace? Not according to that list.

Would it be women who are abused by men with money or power and then trashed when they get in his way? Not according to that list.

Perhaps it is women who want to have the right to kill their unborn babies? BINGO!

Okay, quickly, take a breath. I realize, although it is a scientific fact that a human being begins to grow and develop from the moment of conception, there are people who see anything less than a "fully emerged from the womb" baby as a blob of protoplasm to be destroyed at will.

In other words, if the baby isn't already fully out of its mother's body, it's okay to crush its skull and suck its brains out and call it partial-birth abortion. Who isn't gagging?

For the moment, however, I'll agree to disagree about the difference between killing babies and destroying protoplasm because my point is simply that the long-held, one-issue focus of NOW on what they call reproductive rights has done a grave disservice to women who need much more than that.

As NOW celebrates its fiftieth anniversary, there is a bit more diversity in its programs. I would like to see NOW support sexually abused women, even if the abuser was a former president—and even if his wife is now running for president.

Unfortunately, women and girls are still being raped, sexually abused, sexually harassed on the job, paid less than a man for the same work, expected to do much more than a man in order to occupy the same career path, and expected to do it all without complaining.

Women and girls are demeaned in a thousand subtle ways, but NOW remains focused on the "health issues" of women.

I suggest that health includes mental, emotional, and psychological factors. In this regard, Hillary and most of the *older women* of NOW are still failing to help. Hillary, of course, is still attacking women who dare to speak the truth about her husband, so that's worse than no help at all.

Hillary and most of the older women of NOW continue to support the ex-criminal-in-chief Clinton, pretending (as women who have been abused often do) that because he apologized (sort of) for some of it (not the rape, of course, because that would admit criminality), that he will never, never, ever do it again, and "there, there, now, honey, everything will be fine in the morning," and "Better put some ice on that." Those were Billy's parting words to Juanita Broaddrick after he forcefully incapacitated her by biting her lower lip before and during that vicious rape.

In the meantime, if Clinton or any other sexual predator knocks you up (as opposed to knocking you out), Hillary and NOW will be right there beside you supporting your right to kill the baby (or blob of protoplasm) that the big bad meanie gave you in a moment of passion, either sweet or violent.

After all, you have a right to choose, and the ex-criminal-in-chief and his coconspiratorial codependent spouse will support that right.

The older women of NOW, with a few, notable exceptions, are still standing behind an ex-criminal-in-chief whom none of them would want to have living next door.

None of them would want to allow their teenage daughters or granddaughters to fly to Orgy Island with him.

None of the older women of NOW would want to be trashed in the media for telling the truth about the Clintons.

None of them would want to be assaulted and threatened and intimidated by him and by his wife for revealing what they know.

And yet the older women of NOW continue to praise Billy and Hillary's stand on women's rights. Is that insane?

I'm gratified to see that younger women are beginning to recognize Hillary Clinton for who she is.

These younger women (many of the millennials) seem to have less tolerance for sexual abuse and harassment than their mothers did and still do.

These younger women have less tolerance for the "good ole boy" system that allows men to prey on women without serious consequences.

These younger, more savvy women are not amused when men think it's okay to "sow their wild oats" without concern for the women and girls whom they violate.

Why shouldn't Hillary and the older women of NOW continue to support the ex-president? The only right that William Jefferson Clinton would deny any woman is the right to speak the truth about him!

Hillary Clinton, on the other hand, would deny women a few other rights, such as equal pay for equal work. I have read, but cannot confirm, that the women on Hillary's senate staff earned less than 75 percent of what the men earned.

Both Billy and Hillary are delighted to receive laundered money via a Canadian "charity" to the Clinton Foundation from countries that allow unrestricted violations of women as a matter of national policy.

Still, Hillary's and Billy's most consistent stand on any political issue is that women do *not* have the right to speak the truth about them. Perhaps that will be their most lasting legacy.

* * *

By the way, how could a black, streetwalking prostitute afford to emigrate to Australia with her half-white/half-black baby?

24

DOWN HER NOSE / UP HIS NOSE

Hillary and Billy invited a few dozen people to a buffet supper at the governor's mansion before the 1985 inaugural ball. It turned out to be an odd evening.

The Warden always had trouble shifting into her First Lady role for affairs of state, and the night of Billy's third gubernatorial inauguration was no exception.

Hillary looked down her nose at most people at the mansion that night, probably because we were all Billy's friends and not hers. She must have felt like an unwelcome guest in her own home sometimes.

At one point after enjoying some of the *hors d'oeuvres* that filled the dining room table, I noticed that the photographer seemed to be taking an inordinate number of photos of me. I admit that I'm not always very observant when I'm hungry, so I wasn't sure when it started.

My first thought was that Hillary wanted to have some clear photos to be sure her "hit man" wouldn't get the wrong person when he came after me.

Then I thought that maybe Billy wanted to be sure to get a couple of good ones for his own collection.

Finally, I had to ask the photographer why he was taking so many photos of me. He shrugged his shoulders as if he didn't know the answer. Then he cocked his head toward Hillary and rolled his eyes. That was no help and I wondered about it for a while, but it would be many more years before I discovered a likely answer.

* * *

Later that evening at the Inaugural Ball, when Billy and I were dancing a slow dance and talking about nothing in particular, he said he wanted to ask a big favor of me.

"Of course. What do you need?"

"Roger will be going to prison in a few days and I'd like you to visit him."

Most people know that Billy's younger (by ten years) half-brother Roger Clinton, Jr., went to prison for dealing cocaine. Since Roger would be in the FCI (Federal Correctional Institution) in Fort Worth, Texas, and I lived in Dallas, about thirty-five miles east of there, Billy thought it wouldn't be too much trouble for me to visit him.

The FCI is a low-security United States federal prison for male inmates located inside the city of Fort Worth. It is operated by the Federal Bureau of Prisons, which is a division of the U.S. Department of Justice.

Within days of Billy's gubernatorial inauguration, I was filling out forms to get FCI security clearance. Then I began making frequent Sunday afternoon drives from Dallas to Fort Worth to visit Roger.

At first I was somewhat amused that the inmates and their visiting families at the FCI looked very much like the families I saw in church on Sunday mornings. Roger explained that FCI Fort Worth was a premier destination in the federal system, and that he was able to go there because it had the excellent drug rehabilitation program he needed.

It didn't seem to have occurred to Roger that his brother's being the governor of Arkansas may have been somewhat influential in his placement there.

The FCI is one of those federal country clubs (a "Club Fed") that we have all heard about, with tennis courts and numerous amenities for the benefit of the criminals who are incarcerated there. For some people, it was an upgrade from their home environment.

As far as I know, Hillary never visited her brother-in-law in the FCI, although the family was required to go for family counseling week. That week of family therapy, focusing on Roger's problems, was certainly not sufficient for putting that dysfunctional group on the right track.

Roger has been quoted as saying that Billy "had a nose like a vacuum cleaner" in reference to his older brother's cocaine use. I believe that Gennifer Flowers also made reference to Billy's partaking of drugs. Billy knew that I was adamantly antidrug and he never mentioned anything like that to me.

This is part of the dysfunctional family syndrome. No one ever gets all the truth because the addict and the family cannot face all the truth. They share appropriate bits and pieces of it with people who will not challenge them, but they never reveal all of it because they can't face all of it.

Roger never did fully acknowledge his drug problem. Like Billy, Roger could always find someone else to blame for anything that happened to him or around him. Hillary does the same thing, so she fit nicely into their dysfunctional structure. The Blame Game is a family favorite.

Roger and I exchanged letters frequently while he was in the FCI. He always put the date, as well as the number of days he had been there, at the top of each letter. I made sure he always had stamps; I guess that was a little silly, but that's what I did. I also allowed him to call me "collect" from the prison to my office in Dallas when he needed to talk.

Trivia buffs may be interested in knowing that Paul Vario, the consigliere of the Lucchese crime family in New York City was in FCI Fort Worth at the same time as Roger Clinton. Vario was portrayed by actor Paul Sorvino in the 1990 movie *Goodfellas*.

Jim McDougal, who was the financial partner with Billy and Hillary in their land deal in Arkansas known as "Whitewater," died in FCI Fort Worth in 1998 while serving a three-year term; that was long after Roger was paroled. Jim was convicted in 1997 of fraud and conspiracy; his wife, Susan, famously went to prison too, but not FCI. Many people in Arkansas probably remember seeing Susan photographed in an orange prison jumpsuit.

Another famous prisoner at FCI Fort Worth was Michael Fortier who was one of the accomplices in the 1995 Oklahoma City bombing. He testified against coconspirators Timothy McVeigh and Terry Nichols. Fortier was held at FCI Fort Worth during the court proceedings, and was released into the Federal Witness Protection Program in 2006.

Occasionally, I would ask Roger about some other inmate and what he had done to warrant a sentence there. Sometimes, Roger gave me a clear and straightforward answer; sometimes, he said, "You don't want to know."

Near his time for an early parole, Roger accepted a "break" in the lunch line from one of his friends, and he was punished with another couple of weeks (maybe months, but I think it was weeks) in the FCI.

Billy sent me a handwritten letter (dated December 12) telling me that Roger's release had been delayed and asking me to check on him. (That letter can be read online along with some of the other handwritten letters from Billy that were attached as exhibits to my sworn deposition testimony in the *Jones v. Clinton* lawsuit.)

I did check on Roger, and soon after that, I received a call from Billy. It turned out that none of his business and political "friends" who had promised to help Roger were going to do what they had offered earlier.

To be paroled, Roger had to have an "approved" place to live and a paying job. You guessed it. As requested by Billy, I wrote a letter to the parole board, promising that I would provide a place for Roger to live (in a guest room in our home) and a paying job in my office in Dallas.

I sent a copy of my parole-required letter to Billy and another one to Virginia; I kept one copy for my files.

The parole board approved the arrangement as proposed in my letter, and Roger was released. Virginia drove from Hot Springs to Fort Worth to pick up Roger at the FCI. Then she drove him straight to my office in Dallas.

Within hours, Roger received an approval for a transfer from Texas back to Arkansas, under the supervision of a parole officer there. However, I quickly learned that Billy had used me. He never planned on Roger's following the protocol of living in an approved location and having an approved paying job. Billy lied to me. He knew me well enough to know that I would never have written a fraudulent letter to the parole board! In addition to my own personal integrity, I had a Texas bar license that I would not have put in jeopardy.

The interesting follow-up to this little interlude occurred years later when I was visiting with Virginia at her lake house west of Hot Springs. She was showing me the scrapbooks that she kept while Roger was in prison.

Virginia had every letter that Roger had written to her, every newspaper clipping, every scrap of information that she had received from anyone. She even kept the notes of support and encouragement in her scrapbook.

What was missing from Virginia's scrapbook?

My letter to the parole board, without which Roger would not have been released. I know that Virginia had received it because she had mentioned it to me several times.

I don't actually care that my letter was not in the scrapbook. The fascinating piece of it to me is that it was not necessary to "remove" me from their version of history; no one but family members would ever see them. It's just another example of how they seem to truly believe their lies.

The Clintons, including Hillary, are always compelled to rewrite their history to look better in the public eye. This decades-long pattern of lying and deceit is what gave rise to the nickname that folks in Arkansas have given to the presidential center on the wrong side of the tracks (the freeway) in Little Rock. It's called the "Clinton Lie-berry."

* * *

Fast-forward another few years for my follow-up to the 1985 inauguration story about the photographs. At Billy's first presidential inaugural ball (in 1993), Hillary was wearing an Oscar de la Renta gown in a shade of purple. It had a high, round neckline on a long-sleeved lace bodice, with a draping floor-length skirt.

By coincidence, my 1985 inaugural ball selection was a Victor Costa gown in a shade of dark blue. It had a high, round neckline on a long-sleeved lace bodice, with a draping floor-length skirt.

Of course, I'm not suggesting that Oscar de la Renta himself would have copied a Victor Costa design. I'm just saying that it's another interesting coincidence from here in the land of coincidences.

Since I have always kept one favorite article of clothing each decade beginning in my teens, I still have that gown. It was definitely my favorite of the 1980s. In fact, it was such a favorite that I wore it again to Billy's first presidential inauguration in 1993.

Hillary and I did not have our pictures taken together that night, so the potential irony of it was lost to history. My photo would probably have been removed from the family scrapbook anyway.

25

GOVERNING AFFAIRS

Some people have asked, "How did you manage to have an affair with the governor of Arkansas? I mean, where did you meet and how did you keep it a secret?"

Other people asked, "If you had an affair with the governor of Arkansas, where is your proof?"

Now that it is a generally accepted fact that Billy Clinton is a blatant liar and an untreated sexual addict, I get fewer questions about my proof.

In any case, my response always was: "When people are having affairs, they try to maintain secrecy. They try to destroy any evidence of their affairs, and the smarter they are, the more likely it is that they will be successful in hiding the affair."

It's certainly counterproductive to save proof of an affair. Later, there was plenty of proof in my case, provided by Billy's own attorneys and through the investigation by the FBI and others during the impeachment proceedings.

Billy and I were both pretty smart in the matter of hiding our affair, although the Warden knew about it from the beginning. On the other hand, our affair fell into the "open secret" category. Everyone who was anyone in Arkansas knew about it, at some level. They just didn't discuss it that much, or maybe they did and I wasn't aware of it. Our affair went on (and off and on) for so long that it wasn't news anyway.

That first question, "How?" was probably asked by people who have not had affairs. They may not realize that the elements of an affair are similar in most cases, whether the participants are prominent or obscure.

Most people live their lives in a hurry, on a schedule, on a treadmill. They don't have any extra time for themselves. Yet, they can find time for an affair. That's the way it is, and I'm not the first person to realize it.

Concealing an affair usually takes the cooperation of third parties, either explicitly or implicitly. The classic example of this is the man whose secretary covers for him when his wife calls and he is out of the office spending the afternoon with his girlfriend.

Many secretaries do this as a matter of course, though their bosses have never said the words, "I am having an affair and I want you to cover for me."

The more successful the man is, the more likely his secretary (almost uniformly known as executive secretary or executive assistant or administrative assistant now) has risen to a level at which most instructions on any topic are sketchy, yet understood.

By now, most everyone in the United States, if not around the world, knows that Betty Currie facilitated the affair of her boss, the president of the United States, with Monica Lewinsky, a White House intern young enough to be his daughter.

I certainly find it difficult to believe that a woman who is smart enough to become the personal secretary of the president of the United States could be so oblivious that she didn't know what her boss was doing. I guess it could have happened.

Billy's secretaries during the years that he was the attorney general and then the governor of Arkansas certainly had some idea of what was going on between Billy and me. They knew that I called him on the private, unlisted phone number that bypassed both them and the switchboard. They knew that when he was out of town, I would call them on their direct lines to relay messages to him wherever he was.

They knew that when I called and he was down the hall or temporarily out of his office, he would immediately upon his return close the door between his office and theirs to call me. They knew that I was free to walk in and out of his office any time without an appointment. They probably knew that he kept a photo of me in his bottom right desk drawer. Yes, he is left-handed.

The secretaries knew my daughters. They knew the phone numbers of my mother and other family and friends who could locate me any time I was in Little Rock. They usually knew when I was in Little Rock, and they often knew when Billy was meeting me somewhere else. And they knew how Billy acted around me.

Did they talk about us?

Did they tell others what they knew?

I don't know. I never asked. If I ever really thought about it, I guess I just assumed that they would cover for us. After all, that's what good secretaries do. I've practiced law. I've had my own good secretaries.

I'm not trying to avoid answering the question of how Billy and I managed to have an affair. I suppose that what I am doing is trying to lay the predicate for explaining just how easy it was. For years.

After Billy became governor of Arkansas, there was another circle of people around him, specifically the troopers of the Arkansas State Police who had the job of safeguarding his life. In theory, this would be an insurmountable obstacle to carrying on an affair. Clearly, that was not the case.

The troopers, like the secretaries, knew what was going on. They could not help but observe. Did they talk about us? Did they tell others what they knew? I don't know. I did ask about them, though.

On several occasions, I asked Billy if he was concerned about the troopers and what they might say. He always insisted that they were no problem.

The troopers also traveled around the country with Billy, and some of that traveling was a nice perk for them. I met several different troopers in Dallas over the course of years when Billy was governor, and I would be surprised if they didn't know what was going on between Billy and me.

I'm sure that more than one of the troopers heard what I later realized was a standard line of Billy's. He would tell a hotel clerk that he was the governor of Arkansas, and was expecting a call from the president of the United States. He would charm them into providing a free room for a couple of hours so he could receive the call from the president in private.

Then he would go up to the room and wait for me, and probably dozens of other women over the years, to take another elevator up to meet him.

It was a great ploy. It was bold enough to be believable. It saved the taxpayers of Arkansas a lot of money. It left no paper trail, and it's unlikely that many of the hotel clerks who participated in this scam would step up to own their part in it now, after seeing what happens to witnesses against Billy.

We all know what happened when a couple of the troopers who had been assigned to take care of Billy at the governor's mansion (and elsewhere) told the story of his innumerable affairs and how they "pimped" for him:

The troopers were denounced as liars.

The troopers were maligned as opportunists.

The troopers were exhaustively investigated by the Clinton goon squad.

The troopers were discredited for some imperfections in their own lives.

In other words, the troopers were attacked.

If the troopers can be attacked, then surely any hotel personnel can be attacked. In fact, all the "enemies" of Billy and Hillary Clinton are attacked, eventually.

The message is: Don't cross Billy! And don't cross Hillary! This is somewhat akin to terrorism, when you think about it. The message is that everyone is supposed to be afraid. Most people got the message and kept quiet. Some talked and were attacked.

When the troopergate story came out in the *American Spectator* magazine, someone sent me a copy of it. I knew what was going to happen to the troopers if someone didn't step in quickly to vouch for them and for their story.

I knew that that someone to step up and defend them should be Buddy Young, the trooper who was head of security at the governor's mansion.

As I mentioned in an earlier chapter, I remember exactly when I first met Buddy Young, and I liked him instantly. He was an affable guy and we shared a great love of country music. Billy had given me Buddy's direct phone number at the mansion as another way that I could get in touch with him, and Buddy usually knew where he could find me.

Often, Buddy was the person Billy would call to relay the message to me that he would be late (surprise, surprise) in meeting me at the mansion, or elsewhere. This was before the days of cell phones.

Buddy would sometimes call to say that the Warden had not left town yet, or some other such message that would indicate that the coast wasn't clear for me to go to the mansion.

Buddy never came right out and said anything. Not every word has to be spoken to be understood. But Buddy Young was definitely in the communication loop.

One night shortly after the trooper story broke in the magazine, I heard that Buddy Young was going to be questioned on television about it. I was looking forward to hearing him, because I was troubled about the flack that the troopers were getting for telling the truth.

(There is another chapter that could be written about David Brock who told the truth on behalf of the troopers; he later lied in saying that he had lied about the trooper story. It's all convoluted and I never met David Brock, so I don't know what in the world is motivating him, but it is clearly not integrity and the love of truth.)

I called some friends and told them to watch the news that night to hear what Buddy would say. I assured my friends that my friend Buddy Young would set the record straight.

After all, when a fellow trooper is on the line, you back him up. Right?

Certainly you back up a fellow trooper when he's telling the truth. Right?

There is no way that an officer of the Arkansas State Police would flat-out lie to protect the governor from stories that everyone already knew were true. Right?

Wrong.

Buddy Young sat there, staring into the television camera, and flat-out lied through his teeth. I was astounded. Really, I was. Some people laugh at me for that, but it's the truth. I was speechless at what I was seeing and hearing.

Of course, I knew that Buddy Young had been promoted from his job as the gun-toting chief of security at the governor's mansion when Billy became president. Buddy was then comfortably ensconced in a nice government job as the head of FEMA, in Denton, Texas, just north of Dallas.

To be accurate, I must say that Buddy didn't get that FEMA job the very minute that Billy became president, nor was it during the initial transition period from the governor's mansion to the White House. I don't remember the exact date of Buddy's promotion, but I do remember that it was the day after Vince Foster's body was found in Fort Marcy Park.

So, there was my "friend" Buddy Young, lying to the entire world on television.

Perhaps I shouldn't be so judgmental to say that Buddy was flat-out lying. There remains the possibility that he was ignorant enough not to know what was going on with the governor, on his watch, at the mansion and beyond. It comes down to the fact, however, that Buddy either knew or he didn't know what Billy Clinton was doing.

Either he was flat-out lying, or my friend Buddy Young was actually the dumbest sumbitch ever put in charge of the life of a governor.

26

NO SIGNS OF A PROBLEM

Many writers have mentioned, almost in passing, that Billy Clinton grew up in a town that was known for its wide-open, though illegal, casino gambling. From that brief statement, the normal person who grew up in a more normal environment is expected to grasp the big picture.

Hillary Rodham grew up in Chicago, another town with a long history of infamous illegal activities in both politics and business.

I don't believe that it's easy, especially in an unexamined life, to understand the effect that an upbringing in a pervasive atmosphere of illegal activities could have on a person's life and perspectives. I don't believe that such socioeconomic, psychological influences are either simple or self-evident. Therefore, I'm going to take some time in this and the next couple of chapters to delve into the ways that these environmental elements affected Billy and me—and, by extension, Hillary.

As I wrote earlier, Billy Clinton moved to Hot Springs in 1953 when his mother married Roger Clinton. Billy entered the second grade at

St. John's Catholic School. The following year, he transferred to public school and I entered the first grade at St. John's. That same year, later in the fall, my parents and I attended St. John's annual school carnival for the first time.

I will never forget the look of shock on my Philadelphia momma's face as we climbed the steep steps from the parking lot to the church and were bombarded with the sights, sounds, and smells of the scene. The concreted, open area between the church and the old auditorium was packed with hundreds of people and all sorts of decorated booths.

What I most vividly recall was the overwhelming smell of something I did not recognize. I developed an instant, and so-far lifelong, aversion to the smell of what I later realized was beer.

My mother, who was raised in the protected environs of an exclusive, Main-Line Philadelphia, Catholic boarding school, was almost apoplectic at the sight of roulette wheels, blackjack tables, and other professional gambling equipment openly displayed within a dice throw of the church.

She walked over to a sign marked "INFORMATION" and demanded of the booth attendant, "Where is the pastor?"

The attendant pointed to a stocky man about thirty feet away.

"See that guy at the second roulette wheel? The one with the big cigar? That's the pastor."

My mother had a difficult time realizing that the kindly monsignor, whom she had seen only in church and wearing his priestly robes, was the 'guy at the roulette wheel—the one with the big cigar.'

My mother wanted to leave immediately, but my daddy convinced her that we should stay to support the school. I was glad they decided to do that, because I saw some of my new schoolmates there, and they were all having a good time. My daddy purchased a roll of tickets, gave me a generous handful of them, and I started exploring the area with my friends.

I quickly found my own lifelong favorite form of gambling: the cakewalk.

For one ticket, I could pick my place on one of the numbered squares permanently painted on the concrete patio behind the church. The music started and we all walked ahead one square at a time until the music stopped. A number was drawn, announced over the din of everything else that was going on, and I was the astonished winner of a dozen homemade chocolate cupcakes. I was hooked on the cakewalk. Completely hooked.

I soon discovered the most notorious of all the Catholic gambling games: bingo!

Need I say more? Surely anyone who has played thinks it's fun. It's especially fun to play with lots of bingo cards at once. It's fun to watch a friend have a good run of numbers, and then overtake them with a few lucky calls. I quickly became hooked on bingo too.

Not long after that, I discovered the slot machines at the country club. For gambling money, I would use the nickels that I had amassed by gathering cola bottles and redeeming them at the grocery store for two cents each. This was easy money, and though I had never heard the expression, "easy come, easy go," that was definitely my attitude about this form of income.

I would spend time swimming (and later, golfing) with my friends at the country club, but in the heat of the day, I found a nice, cool, dark place to recover from the relentless Arkansas sun. The bar at the country club was sparsely used during the middle of the day and no one ever suggested that the sign "NO MINORS" meant that a child under the age of ten shouldn't be in there.

I would watch one of the adults put nickel after nickel into a slot machine. Then, if he left after a long time without winning anything, I would go put a nickel into the same machine and pull the handle. Without knowing anything about statistics, I figured that there were so many nickels in the machine it was about time for some of them to come out.

I would limit myself to putting five nickels in the slot. If the machine didn't pay off by then, I left it too. It was amazing how many times it did pay, though. I can't say I got hooked on the slot machines as much as I liked guessing when they would pay. I could have just as much fun watching someone else do it. The more I learned, the more I just watched. By the end of the second grade, I had completely sworn off slot machines as a waste of my time and money.

When I was still very young, my mother took me to one of the most well-known Hot Springs nightclubs, the Vapors, to see Liberace. I had been taking piano lessons since I was six, and my mother always took me to the three community concerts that came to Hot Springs every year, to enhance my cultural education. My mother convinced herself that going to see and hear Liberace would be a sufficient substitute for a cultural experience.

The first time I went to see Liberace, I was expecting another plain piano concert. Was I in for a surprise! We had a wonderful dinner at the Vapors while watching couples dance on the parquet floor. At the appointed hour, the lights came on; the dancers gave up the floor; and an elevated stage about two feet high mechanically glided out over the dance floor, almost touching our table.

On the stage, there was a grand piano with candelabra. A nonde-script man came from behind the curtains to make a brief introduction. Then Liberace, the most glamorous and amazing curly-haired man I had ever seen, made his entrance. It was a magnificent entrance, with a flaring cape and a dazzling smile. Liberace beamed and nodded at everyone in the audience, and I thought he had a special smile for me, sitting right in front.

Then he sat at the piano, lifted his bejeweled hands, and began the most dazzling performance I had ever seen or heard. I was instantly hooked on Liberace. After the show, I asked him to sign my program. He took the time to ask me my name and if I might be taking piano lessons.

"Dolly is a very nice name," he said, as he signed the program for me, "and you're a very pretty girl. Keep practicing the piano."

For a while after that Liberace concert, I doubled the amount of time I spent practicing the piano. The next time I saw Liberace, I was surprised and flattered that he called me by name. From that experience alone, I understood why people were so taken with Billy Clinton for remembering their names. It's a marvelous ability.

When my mother and I went to the Vapors, I was only interested in dinner and Liberace. I didn't think about playing the slot machines because I had already sworn off them. We did go into the casino to watch other people play, though. I watched all sorts of games, and I particularly enjoyed watching the people themselves as they played the slot machines, roulette, and blackjack.

Of course, we paid no attention to the sign:

"MUST BE 21 TO ENTER THE CASINO."

Most of us who grew up in Hot Springs learned the subliminal message that signs didn't mean anything.

There was another commonly posted sign in restaurants:

"NO ALCOHOLIC BEVERAGES SERVED ON SUNDAY."

Everyone knew that didn't mean there would be no alcoholic beverages served on Sunday. It simply meant that on Sunday, one had to order Hot Springs Coffee and then specify a particular flavor such as Jack Daniels or Chivas Regal 25.

I didn't drink alcohol, but I was around adults who did. We would go to restaurants on Sunday evening, and the adults would order Hot Springs Coffee. I'm quite sure that I could have ordered it too, but I didn't like the smell of it, so I never was interested.

It didn't occur to me that all these signs around Hot Springs somehow represented laws that were being broken. After all, there were policemen everywhere to enforce laws.

I was much older when I realized that policemen were actually supposed to be enforcing laws. As a young child, I learned that policemen were there to protect us, to help us if we needed it, and generally were just the good guys who were easy to identify because they were wearing uniforms.

I knew the sheriff and the chief of police, and I knew a lot of policemen by name. To me, they were just friends of my daddy. They wore nifty uniforms and they carried guns. Their guns didn't impress me so much as their nice shiny badges and their big leather belts with all those bullets in leather loops.

I was glad to have policemen around because my mother had always tried to scare me about the Weirdos who came to Hot Springs every year for the racing season. The policemen and my common sense were to be my best protection against the Weirdos.

The Weirdos started arriving in December and their numbers swelled as the opening of the track neared. As I recall, the racing season itself roughly coincided with the six weeks of Lent, and ended on Holy Saturday, the day before Easter Sunday.

There were a lot of nice people who came to Hot Springs to enjoy the races, of course. My mother's aunt and her husband from New Jersey were regulars in Hot Springs. They were also regulars at Hialeah and other tracks around the country. It took me a long time to figure out that my great uncle might be addicted to the ponies.

The Weirdos, on the other hand, were those who arrived early with the horses to take care of them and to handle the thousands of menial tasks associated with setting up such a huge operation. They traveled around the country doing this type of work, and they ranked way below circus and theater people in my mother's social hierarchy.

I never met any of the Weirdos, so I don't know what they might have been like on a personal level. What I did know was that they (and the nice people who followed them) caused the restaurants in Hot Springs to be crowded, the streets to be jammed with traffic, and my childhood freedom to walk or ride my bike anywhere to be severely curtailed.

My mother's mantra during the racing season (and the months before it) was: "You'd better stay home. Something could happen to you while the Weirdos are in town."

My mother never gave a hint about what might happen to me, but her ominous tone was almost sufficient. To make matters even worse, though, our maid Nellie Mae agreed with my mother on this topic. That made it sound terrible to me because Nellie Mae (who had been raised in Chicago!) had seen a lot and, although she was superstitious, she generally didn't scare easily.

So, after my daddy died (having taught me to smile and introduce myself to strangers), his instructions were overridden during the racing season. I had to stay home more often and avoid the Weirdos when I did go out, although I had no idea what the Weirdos might look like.

I was in high school the first time I ventured to the racetrack. Oaklawn Park featured pari-mutuel betting on the horses, and had a nine-hole golf course in the center of the track. The sign at the entry stated: "MUST BE 16 TO ENTER WITH AN ADULT."

I was a sophomore in high school, fourteen years old, and going to the track with some of my friends, all of whom were under eighteen. We certainly were not adults and we didn't have an adult with us. Yes, we cut afternoon classes to go to the track; it was too crowded on Saturdays. No one batted an eye when I paid my two dollars and walked through the turnstile under the sign.

I should add that betting on the horses was legal in Hot Springs, although I didn't think about it at the time. Since I didn't realize that there was any illegal gambling (like the slot machines and roulette wheels), it wasn't an issue for me.

I got a scratch sheet and started reading about the horses. I went down to the paddock and looked at the beautiful animals. I watched the jockeys mount and watched the way they handled the horses. Then I decided which horse to bet on.

The lowest bet one could make was two dollars, and in those days of good thirty-five-cent hamburgers, that was too rich for my blood. The solution was to divide the bet among four friends and put up fifty cents apiece. That would still be enough to get the heart pumping and the adrenaline flowing as the horses bolted from the starting gate.

I would take the two-dollar bet, usually in the form of eight quarters, to one of the windows. There were three signs in green and white above the windows: "Win, Place and Show." The biggest challenge was to get my friends to go for the "Win." I liked the bigger payoff on a Win ticket, but we'd go for a Place or even a Show if the odds were very high and one of us "had a hunch." We only bet on about three races all afternoon, to keep our investment reasonable.

There I was, a fourteen-year-old standing in one of the fast-moving lines at one of the many windows and finally I would hand over my two dollars and take my ticket, right under the sign that read: MUST BE 21 TO PLACE WAGERS.

Billy Clinton grew up in this same environment, so he knew the signs didn't mean anything either. Billy went to a Baptist church, and Baptists "didn't believe in" drinking or gambling. They actually talked about drinking and gambling in church. They were "agin' it"—absolutely "agin' it."

The problem with that "agin' it" attitude is that Billy saw plenty of Baptists drinking and gambling. The state of Arkansas was primarily Baptist at the time. If they had all walked the walk instead of just talking the talk, Billy might have gotten the idea that the signs and the rules and the commandments might actually mean something.

At St. John's Catholic Church, there was no pretense of being against drinking. I've already mentioned that they served beer at the school carnival. There was also a pervasive smell of alcohol in the church on Sunday mornings when I arrived early to play the organ for the six o'clock Mass.

After the bars closed at 2:00 or 3:00 or 4:00 a.m., people (mostly men) would go drink coffee at the Pancake Shop. Then, they would go to church on an empty stomach so they were still "fasting from midnight" and thus approved to take Communion, under the old rules before Vatican II.

I distinctly remember the priests at St. John's talking about gambling in their sermons. They always reminded the churchgoing Catholic visitors to our fair resort city that they should give a percentage of their winnings to the church on Sunday. I'm sure the priests were praying for success at the track and in the casinos. Gambling provided almost as good an income for the church as it did for the restaurants and hotels.

Billy and I grew up knowing that good family people were involved in the gambling business. There were no obvious signs of anything sinister about it. My daddy and Billy's Uncle Raymond were friends of all the locals who ran the operations. We didn't consider them crooks or Weirdos.

One of the gambling kingpins in Hot Springs was the well-known, very likable Dane Harris. Although Dane was not a Catholic, he sent his two Episcopalian children to St. John's Catholic Elementary School because it was definitely the best school in Hot Springs. I was in the principal's office (for one of my usual, questions-about-religion and/or failure-to-respect-authority infractions) the morning that Dane's wife called to say that the children would not be in school that day. Their house had been bombed.

Fortunately, no one was injured in the bomb blast at the Harris home, but the family all stayed out of sight for a couple of days.

I heard later that the bombing was a warning, but I didn't know what such a warning could have been about. People in general seemed to have a "business as usual" attitude about it. Therefore, I learned in elementary school that having one's house bombed as a warning was something that could happen to anyone. After all, there was nothing unusual about the Harris family. At least, there were no signs of a problem.

27

THE GANGSTER ON THE CORNER

When my parents moved to Hot Springs in the late 1940s, one of the first things my daddy noticed was that the town lacked a city library. Having decided in 1948 that I was a smart little infant and would soon grow up to be a smart little girl, my father strongly believed that I would need access to a substantial library in addition to the many books we had at home.

He immediately embarked on a crusade to build a city library. He met and networked with all the right people.

The City Fathers in Hot Springs, however, had more on their post-war minds than making sure there were plenty of books for the baby boomers they had already begun to produce.

My daddy finally came to the conclusion that the city wasn't going to do anything about building a library.

Then my daddy started working on Q. Byrum Hurst, who was the county judge. Garland County was a fairly large and prestigious county in Arkansas, ninth by population at the time. It's easy to remember that because Arkansas license plates on cars back then started with the digit of the county and then a dash; we were 9.

The county judge carried a lot of clout, and he had a fairly substantial budget. My daddy and Byrum soon became, and remained, best friends.

I don't know exactly how it happened, but the Garland County Library was constructed. It opened in 1952. That was two years before I would enter the first grade, would learn to read, and would need that library.

My daddy never mentioned his pivotal role in having the Garland County Library built, but I'm sure he was pleased to see how much I used and enjoyed it. Byrum told me the library story many years later, while we were sitting alone at his lake home after the funeral of his oldest daughter, my friend Nancy. I was still in law school at the time, and Byrum was so pleased that I had cut classes for a couple of days to go to Hot Springs.

It's too bad that Q. Byrum Hurst died without writing his memoirs. Fantastic treasures of fascinating Hot Springs stories and Arkansas political folklore were buried with Byrum a few weeks before Christmas in 2006.

Byrum and my daddy and their accountant-friend Jimmy Dowds shared an office building across the street from the new Garland County Library, immediately south of the courthouse.

My almost-daily, after-school trek included a delightful stop at Byrum's, Jimmy's, and my daddy's office where the ever-gracious Natalie Martin always offered me a cup of chilled water. I was fascinated with the pointy-bottomed paper cups that I could pull from a chute all by myself (I was six!) and fill with cold Mountain Valley Mineral Water by pushing a button. That refreshing water was an especially wonderful treat on a hot summer morning or afternoon.

My daily trek to my daddy's office, and then to the Garland County Library across the street, always took me past a very nice, pristine, white frame house on the curving corner of West Grand and Hawthorne.

Everyone knew that the house belonged to the notorious gangster and contract killer Owney Madden. He had "retired" to Hot Springs after a violent past in New York City. As a teenager, he had killed a rival gang member in broad daylight in the street. Then he shouted, "I'm Owney Madden! Tenth Avenue." No witnesses came forward. He was not arrested.

Madden bought the famous Cotton Club in New York, bullied his way into part ownership of the exclusive Stork Club, and owned more than a dozen other glamorous speakeasies during Prohibition. He was known for his payoffs to City Hall, and was referred to as "the Killer."

Once, Owney was shot eleven times in a fight with a rival gang. He refused to identify any of his assailants to the police, but, one-by-one, the rival gang members were assassinated.

For another murder, Owney was sentenced to twenty years in Sing-Sing, the maximum security penitentiary, but served only nine. He retired to Hot Springs around 1932.

I heard many more blood-curdling tales of Owney's exploits up north. One might think he would be *persona non grata* in town with a history like that.

On the contrary, Owney Madden was treated locally as a kind of a folk hero, as was his former associate Al Capone.

Al Capone, Lucky Luciano, Bugsy Siegel, and other mobsters had been part of Hot Springs's lore for decades. They first came to town during the 1920s, attracted by the gambling and prostitution. They enjoyed the weather, the golfing, and the thermal baths, which provided a pleasant relief from Chicago and New York winters.

The fact that the locals rubbed elbows with such infamous, dangerous characters as Capone, Luciano, Siegel, and Madden without fear of them was partly a result of another piece of Hot Springs history. For some reason, Hot Springs has always been a sort of "no man's land" or "demilitarized zone."

From a young age, I heard stories about the various tribes of Indians coming to Hot Springs to enjoy the steaming hot waters in the Valley of the Vapors. Even if they were at war with each other, they had some great cosmic understanding that there would be no conflict in Hot Springs.

Whatever the reason, the most notorious gangsters and criminals in the United States carried on the demilitarized zone tradition. They came to Hot Springs to have a good time. I'm not saying they checked their guns at the city limits, but they did not carry on their turf wars in my hometown.

This condition of a permanent truce in the demilitarized zone probably brought with it a subconscious belief that things were not as they seemed. There were no consequences in Hot Springs for someone's bad behavior elsewhere.

I'm convinced that this "no consequences" societal attitude contributed subliminally to Billy Clinton's emerging style of misbehavior. He was Mister Nice Guy at home in Hot Springs. All the mothers, except mine, thought that he was the perfect gentleman who would never mistreat their girls or make sexual moves on them.

On the other hand, by reputation at least, Billy cut quite a swath through the state of Arkansas, even as a teenager. I can't prove he did that, and I can't prove my theory about his feeling immune from prosecution in Hot Springs for what he did on the road, but I believe it's true. It's a good possibility.

Whatever crimes that Owney Madden and Al Capone and Lucky Luciano and Bugsy Siegel committed elsewhere, there was no sign in Hot Springs that they would be punished, chastised, or even shunned by polite society. So, Owney Madden retired to Hot Springs National Park, Arkansas, to a white frame house—with a white picket fence! Schoolchildren walked safely by on the sidewalk daily. For a while, the chief of police lived next door to Owney, who had married the postmaster's daughter.

The older schoolchildren had heard stories about Owney, and they repeated them to me, perhaps embellished, but more likely sanitized due to ignorance of details. The kids swore, though, that there was a machine-gun nest in the dormer window upstairs over the garage attached to Owney's house.

One day, I expressed to a friend my interest in picking some of the huge orange flowers that we called tiger lilies that were growing between Owney's white picket fence and the sidewalk. I was probably seven or eight years old at the time and wasn't sure what the protocol might be for picking flowers that were outside the fence on a stranger's property.

Ever since I had entered first grade at St. John's Catholic Elementary School, I had pressed the limits of every rule.

I knew that this proposed taking of flowers approached the boundaries of "Thou shalt not steal" and "Thou shalt not covet thy neighbor's goods." Still, I was counting on an "outside the fence" loophole to get what I wanted. When I mentioned my idea about picking the flowers, my friend recoiled in horror.

"They'll *kill* you!" she whispered loudly.

"Seriously?"

"Yes, seriously. They will definitely *kill* you if you take any of those flowers."

"How do you know?" I asked. "There isn't even a sign!"

"Everybody knows there's a machine-gun nest up there."

My friend indicated the location of the dormer with a sly glance in that direction. She dared not point her finger.

"Don't do it! They'll kill you!"

She was so certain and so fearful that I took her advice to heart. I decided not pick any of Owney's flowers. Not just yet.

After that day, every time I walked by Owney Madden's house alone, I looked up at the machine-gun nest dormer, smiled at the unknown guard, and waved. I did that all year long, and the next time the tiger lilies were in bloom, I was still smiling and waving as I passed the house.

Finally, one day I couldn't stand it any longer. I was sure that I had "made friends" with the unseen guard in the machine-gun nest. I was alone and carrying eight books (the maximum of four on my card, and four on my little brother's card) home from the library.

I took a deep breath and balanced the books in the cradle of my left arm. I smiled, waved my wave toward the machine-gun-nested dormer, and snapped off one long-stemmed flower.

With the one flower in my right hand and eight books on my left arm, I tensed my whole body. For a long moment, I wondered what it might feel like to be shot by a machine gun.

Nothing happened.

Of course, nothing happened!

But I was a little kid, and I had no way of knowing what the guy in Owney Madden's dormer might do.

Emboldened by my success with the one flower, I soon decided to go for more. I repeated my smile, wave, and quick snap of a flower several times over the next few days.

Finally, one morning before school, I walked to Owney's house without books. I smiled and waved at my friend in the machine-gun nest. Then, I picked a dozen flowers all at once.

I took them to my teacher at school (which was practically across the street from Owney's house). I let my classmates know that I had taken the whole bouquet of flowers from Owney Madden's house in broad daylight.

That venture earned me some serious respect from my peers. It should have made them less fearful of the machine-gun nest too. Funny thing, though, even after that, the other kids still didn't pick any flowers near Owney Madden's fence.

I found out later that I could have had permission to pick all the flowers that I wanted. Owney Madden was a friend of my daddy's too.

For the past many years, people have asked me if I'm scared of Billy and Hillary Clinton because of their known threats, assaults, intimidation, and public humiliation of anyone who tells the truth about them.

First, I agree with Shakespeare that "A coward dies a thousand deaths," and I'm no coward.

Second, I rely on God's protection promises in Psalm 91.

Third, any kid who could take on Owney Madden's machine-gun nest isn't going to become an adult who cringes in fear from the threats of political bullies.

28

LET THE GAMES BEGIN— AND THE BAD GUYS WIN

In a nutshell in Hot Springs many of the people who operated outside the law were not seen as "the bad guys." Illegal casino gambling was everywhere. Organized crime was romanticized and glamorized.

Prostitution was a thriving business for the cheapest streetwalker and the highest-priced call girls available in the best hotels. Bribery and blackmail were part of doing business. Adultery was rampant, and high rollers were part of the redneck aristocracy.

County Judge Q. Byrum Hurst, Sr., (who we can thank for the Garland County Public Library and who should not be confused with Q. Byrum Hurst, Jr., who currently practices law in Hot Springs) was elected to the Arkansas State Senate in 1950. From then on, most people called him Senator and behind his back *the* Senator, and they always did. My daddy continued to call his best friend Byrum and so did I. We were already on a first-name basis when I was two years old.

Byrum was an extremely popular lawyer. I was amazed over the course of many decades to hear stories from dozens and dozens of people about wonderful things *the* Senator had done for them or for a family member or a friend.

In the early 1960s, Q. Byrum went to Washington to help defend his friend James "Jimmy" Hoffa before the McClellan Committee of the United States Senate. "McClellan" was, of course, United States Sen. John McClellan of Arkansas, and a good friend of Byrum.

Jimmy Hoffa was the (pick an adjective) famous, crooked, infamous, notorious president of the Teamsters Union. He had known (and, as far as I recall) undenied ties to organized crime.

Byrum's act of defending Jimmy Hoffa in Washington infuriated the young Robert "Bobby" Kennedy. Bobby had been appointed by his brother President John F. Kennedy to be the attorney general of the United States. Bobby Kennedy was trying to break up the connection between the Teamsters Union and organized crime. The attorney Q. Byrum Hurst of Hot Springs, Arkansas, was one of the many obstacles in the way of Attorney General Robert Kennedy.

After the hearings in Washington, Byrum Hurst and John McClellan and a bunch of the Hot Springs power brokers flew back home on the plane together, having a good old time.

Shortly after that, and unrelated to the prosecution of Hoffa, Senator McClellan's son was killed in a plane crash. Attorney General Bobby Kennedy came to Arkansas to represent his brother the president at the funeral; Byrum was an honorary pallbearer.

When Bobby Kennedy saw Byrum at the funeral, he told him point blank that he was going to "get" him for representing Jimmy Hoffa.

Not long after that threat, Byrum was audited by the IRS. (This may be a familiar theme to those who spoke publicly and were attacked by the IRS under the Clinton copresidency.) Subsequently, Byrum was indicted for income tax evasion. Apparently, Byrum's lavish lifestyle and stated net worth were more than the IRS thought he could have accumulated on his reported income.

I was in high school at the time of Byrum's indictment, and I remember well that Byrum's trial was the celebrity case of the decade in Arkansas. The judge was John E. Miller, who was a former United States senator from Arkansas.

We were all enthralled as the federal government presented its case—piece by piece and step by step—against Byrum. The local gossip was full of the details about everything that Byrum had bought, from his wonderful "Hazelhurst Farm" to the nice cars for himself, his wife, and his children. The Feds even knew how many Bibles that Byrum's wife owned.

People were amazed by the gossiped testimony that spread through town at the end of each day. Everyone heard that the four Hurst children did not have to ride in their nice cars all the way over to Dr. Kenneth David Stuart's house for their piano and violin lessons. Dr. Stuart would go to the Hurst home. I also took piano lessons from Dr. Stuart, but I had to walk to his house. Having a teacher make a house call sounded like the height of luxury in Hot Springs.

Although everyone loved Byrum (except those who hated him), the situation was not looking good for the small-town lawyer who often didn't charge his clients anything.

How had Byrum accumulated everything he had? His daddy was a preacher who never made much money, and his wife had been a schoolteacher when he met her.

Things were definitely not looking good for Byrum. The Feds and Bobby Kennedy were already tasting their vindictive victory over the Arkansas lawyer who had had the temerity to travel to Washington to defend the notorious Jimmy Hoffa.

Finally, Byrum had the opportunity to present his defense.

He called one witness.

Owney Madden walked into the courthouse, swore to tell the truth, took the stand, and declared under penalty of perjury that he had lent some enormous sum of money to his good friend, State Sen. Q. Byrum Hurst.

When asked how the senator was supposed to repay all that money he had allegedly borrowed, Owney replied, "That's between me and Byrum's daddy."

Byrum was acquitted.

The Feds left town angrier than when they arrived.

Owney Madden chalked up a public relations coup in the Valley of the Vapors.

* * *

Billy Clinton had been as interested in the details of the Hurst tax case as the rest of us. He had been fascinated to find out about all the things that the Hurst family owned. Even though his Uncle Raymond (who owned and operated the Buick dealership) was quite well-to-do, and Billy's family was not poor (because his mother had a great job), Billy was always on the outside looking in. Billy was so interested in money and power, he had no time for "losers," including his stepfather, Roger Clinton, and including his former mentor, Senator Fulbright, on the Democratic primary election night in 1974.

All of us cheered when Byrum Hurst, the Senator, beat the Feds at their own game. There was an "us against them" mentality that transcended law, ethics, and morality. That was the way it was and always had been in Hot Springs.

With that background, it was easy for me to understand how Hillary and Billy and his friends could cheer and gloat when he beat the impeachment rap in the early part of 1999. They didn't focus on the fact that their man in the White House had broken the law, or that the Republicans in Congress had been too cowardly to do their sworn duty. It was a repeat of IRS vs. the Senator, and the law be damned.

Bobby Kennedy didn't easily give up his quest to "get" the folks in Hot Springs who had protected the Senator.

The United States Attorney General convened a Grand Jury in Fayetteville, home of the University of Arkansas, in the very conservative northwest corner of the state. He started his assault on the Hot Springs infrastructure by calling local gambling kingpin Dane Harris to testify.

Kennedy came within one vote of getting a federal indictment against Dane from that Grand Jury.

I always figured there was some dirty money used on both sides of that one.

29

BLOOD TRAIL

It was initially and generally Hillary's job to make the money to provide the financial base from which she and Billy could maneuver their way to the White House.

As I mentioned earlier, Billy was quite comfortable with having the female be the breadwinner. That was exactly the case in his life as he was growing up. Billy's mother earned a good income from being a nurse anesthetist and it never mattered that his stepfathers did not provide the big bucks.

Hillary and Billy's political plan was on track in the early 1980s. They were back in the governor's mansion after the Dick-Morris-influenced, successful gubernatorial campaign of 1982. Hillary was making more money as a lawyer in the Rose Law Firm than Billy was making as the governor of Arkansas.

The Clintons always made it clear that they were looking for "good investments" although they had no money to invest. They had no shame about being on the lookout for additional income. It was no surprise then that Billy was presented with an easy way to make money "on the side."

I first heard about this particular deal when a couple of guys from Canada contacted me in Dallas to ask for my help.

The story from Canada was bizarre. In fact, it was almost unbelievable. The basis of it was certainly evil. Because I had grown up in Hot Springs, however, with its wildly fantastic but ultimately true stories of crime and cover-ups and bribery, I was able to detect a ring of authenticity in what I was hearing.

The Canadians had seen something about me in the media, and they knew that I had been brave (or foolhardy) enough to write a loosely autobiographical novel about my decades-long relationship with Billy Clinton.

I agreed to meet them at a resort on the lake outside Hot Springs the following weekend. I took precautions for my safety and that's all I'll say about that.

It was a covert operation from the beginning, and the participants in the meeting were terrified of the Clintons. The only reason that one of the characters was particularly bold was that this nice young man was going to die soon anyway. I'll call him Steve.

Steve was one of over two thousand Canadians who were infected with HIV, then commonly called the AIDS virus. The source of the HIV had been traced back to blood collected from prisoners in Arkansas and elsewhere.

Another thirty thousand Canadians had contracted Hepatitis C from the same source.

Here's the shortcut version:

Inmates in Arkansas prisons were paid $7.00 per pint for selling their blood. Billy's cronies then sold the prisoners' blood to some blood brokers for $50.00 per pint.

At some point, various people realized that the blood was tainted with diseases. The prisons instituted a "screening process" for prisoners who would give blood. A prison inmate acted as the "screening clerk" for blood donations. The screening clerk sold to other prisoners "the right to bleed." Infected prisoners continued to be paid for blood after bribing the screening clerk.

Some of the prisoners were paid with illegal drugs rather than scrip. More people discovered that tainted blood was coming from Arkansas prisons. Arkansas prisons were banned from selling prisoners' blood.

Infected inmates continued to sell blood, falsely labeled from a different source. Dummy corporations were set up in various states to purchase and resell the blood. The dummy corporations ultimately sold the infected blood in Canada.

Results of the tainted blood scandal in Canada:

It was Canada's worst-ever preventable public health disaster and resulted in years-long legal battles. A criminal investigation and a high-profile public inquiry was launched. Victims in Canada filed almost $10 billion in legal claims.

Between 8,000 and 10,000 of the victims in Canada have died or will die from the bad blood.

Results of the tainted blood scandal in Arkansas:

Mike Galster wrote the 1998 book *Blood Trail*, a loosely fictionalized novel of the Clinton blood scandal. When Mike Galster finally revealed that his real name was Mike Sullivan of Pine Bluff, his clinic was burglarized, the thieves stealing just his computers' hard drives, and then firebombed.

Little Rock journalist Suzi Parker wrote an exposé on Clinton's part in the infected blood scandal. When Parker began getting threatening phone calls in the middle of the night, she quit writing about Clinton's part in the infected blood scandal.

Steve died.

30

BLOOD MONEY TO DIRTY MONEY

Hillary and Billy Clinton continue to pooh-pooh the entire Whitewater scam every time someone has the temerity to mention it. Frankly, the Whitewater matter is too wide-ranging and too complex for most people's attention spans.

That's understandable. It's also a big pile of poo-poo that no one really wants to examine.

When considering the Whitewater crimes it is important to remember the business and political climate of Arkansas back then was one of corruption and cronyism to the extreme, especially through the reign of the Clintons. It is also critically important to remember that no politician in Arkansas welcomed the intrusion of investigators from Washington, DC, digging into the Clintons' business dealings because (1) they still didn't trust Yankees and (2) they knew they might be vulnerable too. Because of this "circle the wagons" attitude, the Whitewater investigators could only scratch the surface of the allegations and crimes. For example, no one told them who kept the books on Whitewater for the first two years of that big real estate fraud, so that person was never questioned.

From my perspective, the easiest way to understand Whitewater itself is to meet the cast and crew. Hillary and Billy were not only characters in the Whitewater play, but scriptwriters, directors, producers, set designers, stagehands, and the Greek Chorus.

JIM MCDOUGAL was the pivotal figure and public face of the Whitewater scandal. He was a brilliant guy, with a rapier wit. I liked Jim a lot, and I didn't know anyone who didn't like him, except those who hated him. The personable Jim died of a heart attack at the age of fifty-seven, after being held in solitary confinement in the Federal Correctional Institution in Fort Worth, Texas.

When he had the heart attack, Jim was not treated with the defibrillator that was on hand, nor was he taken to the nearest hospital. The failure to follow standard medical protocol, of course, led to speculation about Jim's early death.

Jim had been a professor of political science at Ouchita Baptist University, and briefly entered politics (unsuccessfully) on his own after being an aide to Sen. Bill Fulbright. Jim owned and presided over Madison Guaranty Savings and Loan. Madison was federally insured and its eventual $68,000,000 in losses were paid back by me and you and other millions of other taxpayers whether we wanted to pay or not, while Jim was convicted of eighteen felony charges, including fraud and conspiracy.

Billy and Hillary had expressed to Jim and his wife, Susan (and to a lot of other people in Arkansas), that they were always looking for "good investments." Thus, Jim and Susan partnered with Billy and Hillary in a ridiculously ill-conceived (to this real estate lawyer!) real estate development, to be called Whitewater, in the boonies in northwest Arkansas.

The Clinton-McDougal partnership borrowed nearly a quarter-million dollars from Madison S&L to buy a tract of land in the middle of nowhere to build vacation homes. The area had no decent roads, no infrastructure, no amenities, no shopping, and no chance to draw the kind of people who had money to buy a vacation home.

When the Whitewater "development" went belly-up, Jim tried to cover the losses with Madison S&L money. That's a no-no, and Jim was charged with fraud.

Jim hired the Rose Law Firm to defend him from the criminal fraud charges. Hillary was a partner in the Rose Firm. Yes, Hillary was a partner in the Rose Law Firm as well as a partner in the Whitewater deal that used the funny money from Madison S&L to fund the land development that led to criminal fraud charges that led to Jim's hiring the Rose Law Firm to defend him. Circle the wagons.

By the way, in a magnificent piece of political irony, the Whitewater project started while Billy Clinton was attorney general. It was one of Billy's main jobs to guard the people of Arkansas against consumer fraud!

Bonus information:

Jim held a fund-raiser to pay off Clinton's campaign debts. Of the $50,000 raised by Jim, $12,000 came from Madison cashier's checks. That's a no-no. It was also business as usual in Arkansas, especially with the Clintons. With them, follow the money only if you have a team of forensic accountants and only if the accountants are not afraid of the Clintons.

SUSAN MCDOUGAL was Jim McDougal's wife; they divorced. In case you were wondering, yes, she was about fifteen years younger than he was; they met when she was a student at Ouchita Baptist, and Jim was a fascinating professor there. Most people who remember Susan, if they remember her at all, have a vision of her in an orange prison jumpsuit and shackles. That was an unfortunate moment because she was an attractive woman who was photographed on her worst day ever.

Susan was sentenced to prison for criminal contempt and obstruction of justice because she refused to answer questions from a federal grand jury about Billy and Hillary Clinton. This was *after* Susan had been given immunity from prosecution in the Whitewater fraud matter. Therefore, it had nothing to do with covering her bases on her own fraud. Susan refused to answer questions about:

1. whether Billy Clinton had testified truthfully at Susan McDougal's criminal trial;

2. the nature of Hillary's legal work on behalf of the corrupt Madison S&L; and

3. Hillary and Billy's knowledge of an illegally financed real estate deal that was supposed to bail out their Whitewater partnership.

Surely, Susan's refusal to talk brings to your mind the previously told story of Frank Gusenberg. As he lay dying, with fourteen bullet wounds in his body after Al Capone's infamous St. Valentine's Day Massacre, Frank insisted: "No one shot me."

Susan McDougal kept her mouth shut about Hillary and Billy Clinton and spent twenty-two months in prison, still keeping her mouth shut. She received a full presidential pardon from Billy Clinton in the final hours of his presidency.

ROBERT B. FISKE, JR., was the original special counsel who began looking into the possible illegal activities of Billy and Hillary Clinton in their Whitewater partnership and their dealings with the federally insured Madison Guaranty Savings & Loan.

KENNETH STARR succeeded Robert Fiske as the independent counsel investigating Billy and Hillary Clinton's shady Whitewater and Madison S&L activities. According to Billy and Hillary, Kenneth Starr is the ultimate bad guy in the Whitewater matter, although no one ever suggested that Starr should go to prison.

Because Kenneth Starr had a broad directive and plenty of funds for the investigation, it eventually spread its tentacles. Ultimately, I was questioned by Starr's investigators when the matter expanded into different aspects of the Clintons' lies, perjuries, witness tampering, and obstruction of justice.

Anyone who understands what I have written about the old-style Clinton Arkansas business and politics should have no trouble realizing that Whitewater was the rock dropped into the pond. Its ripples spread statewide—and beyond. The half of it has not been told.

DAVID HALE was a former municipal judge in Little Rock who implicated Billy Clinton in another loan fraud. Hale was eventually indicted by Ken Starr for fleecing a loan company that he ran. The loan company, Capital Management Services, was supposed to help disadvantaged borrowers; those loans to disadvantaged borrowers were backed by the SBA (Small Business Administration). Yes, that's federal. That's our tax dollars at work. Eventually, we taxpayers paid $3,400,000 for this one.

David stated that Billy Clinton had pressured him to help Jim McDougal with a loan. David also said that Billy Clinton was at a meeting during which they discussed details about a $300,000 loan (the maximum allowable amount under the SBA guidelines) for McDougal. Billy denied making any such request on behalf of Jim McDougal and denied being at the meeting about the loan. (I'm sure David Hale kicked himself later for not making tape recordings, as Billy's paramour Gennifer Flowers did.)

David Hale did make the $300,000 loan—to Susan McDougal (despite the fact that the McDougals, at that time, had a stated net worth of over $2 million)! The loan "on paper" was supposed to finance a marketing company that she owned. Surprise, surprise, however, the $300,000 loan spread into other McDougal deals, including the purchase of more land on behalf of the Clinton-McDougal Whitewater partnership.

The SBA and the GAO (General Accounting Office) were "unable to analyze fully the transactions with McDougal because records were incomplete," according to a 1994 GAO report (GAO/OSI-94-23).

* * *

Remember that I'm describing only the high points and the main characters, but it should be enough to enlighten any thinking person to consider the extent of the crimes committed, the lies told, and the financial trails covered like poo-poo in a litter box.

The past is still prologue with the Klinton Krime Kartel, but so far it is only their accomplices who have gone to prison. With that in mind, I was as shocked as everyone else when in January 2016, during the fourth Democratic primary debate, Hillary tweeted: "There should be no bank too big to fail and no individual too big to jail."

It reminded me of Gary Hart's foolish challenge when he was running for president in 1987 and was accused of womanizing. He taunted the press to follow him to try to prove their allegations. The press did follow him, and caught him with his girlfriend Donna Rice. It was downhill for Gary Hart. Right. Gary Who?

After sending her challenging tweet, it would be poetic justice for Hillary to don an orange jumpsuit and eat her words on a going-away cake.

* * *

DAVID KENDALL served as one of the Clintons' lawyers in the Whitewater matter. Since I earned a 99 percent in ethics at SMU School of Law, I find his representation of the Clintons to be troublesome at best.

David Kendall "inherited" the Clintons as clients from another attorney in the Williams & Connolly law firm. The first attorney, Robert Barnett, withdrew from representing the Clintons because Barnett's wife, Rita Braver, was the CBS News correspondent who was covering the White House. Barnett (correctly, in my opinion) withdrew from representing the Clintons in order to avoid even the appearance of a conflict of interest.

The Code of Professional Responsibility requires lawyers to avoid conflicts of interest. A conflict of interest would be something like representing two or more family members who are fighting over an estate, or representing two or more criminal defendants who can point fingers at each other for the commission of a crime.

In addition, the Code of Professional Responsibility requires lawyers to avoid even the appearance of a conflict of interest. Therefore, Robert

Barnett properly withdrew from representing the Clintons because of his wife's position in the White House.

Here's what I don't understand. David Kendall agreed to represent the Clintons at the same time he was representing the *National Review* and *The National Enquirer*.

One week, early in the Whitewater matter, the *Enquirer*'s headline read: "Clinton: The Cheating, Lying, Dirty Phone Calls and Steamy Sex."

I'm still trying to figure out how Kendall didn't see that as a conflict of interest—or at the very least the appearance of a conflict of interest.

Although I made the 99 percent grade in ethics class, perhaps what I missed was the loophole in the Code of Professional Responsibility that the Clintons and Kendall saw.

WEB HUBBELL was a lawyer, managing partner of the Rose Law Firm in Little Rock, and a close friend of Billy and Hillary Clinton. He served on the Clinton transition team when they moved from the governor's mansion to the White House, and then he served as associate attorney general under Attorney General Janet Reno. In that position, he was the COO (chief operating officer) of a department of over 100,000 employees, with a budget of over $10 billion. Yes, billion.

As far as the Watergate connection goes, Webb Hubbell served a little time in FCI Cumberland (the Federal Correctional Institution in Cumberland, Maryland), but Webb's involvement in the Watergate investigation is one of the most complicated of all. Here is a very short-hand version, and you can find plenty of additional information on the Internet, if you want more.

Ken Starr had broad powers in the Watergate investigation, and he quickly realized that Webb Hubbell could be a shortcut to an indictment against the Clintons. Webb and Hillary practiced law together at the Rose Law Firm (more about the firm below) and Webb knew a lot about the Clintons' business and legal matters.

Yes, as a matter of fact, so did deputy White House counsel and former Rose Law Firm partner Vince Foster. Vince didn't live to be investigated and questioned.

Starr used a typical prosecutor's tactic of putting pressure on Webb Hubbell to try to squeeze information from him about the Clintons. Starr entered into an immunity agreement with Hubbell to get documents that he needed. Then, to put more pressure on Hubbell, Ken Starr used those same documents to indict Hubbell *and* his wife *and* his tax lawyer for various crimes including mail fraud, tax evasion, and conspiracy.

Webb Hubbell cried foul on all that!

I agree. Foul!

That tactic was definitely foul. It was an unfortunate error in judgment and integrity on the part of Ken Starr. The district judge agreed that it was foul, and he dismissed the charges against Hubbell and crew.

That district judge rightly concluded that Ken Starr had violated Hubbell's Fifth Amendment rights (the rights against self-incrimination) by using those documents that Starr had received based upon the immunity agreement.

Starr didn't give up with that. He filed an appeal. The Court of Appeals also agreed that the tactic was foul and affirmed the decision of the district judge.

Wouldn't you know? Ken Starr appealed the matter to the United States Supreme Court!

In a quick and completely proper decision, the Supremes (8-1) affirmed the lower courts' rulings, and found in favor of Webb Hubbell. This was a dark moment for investigator Kenneth Starr, but he kept going.

Finally, Ken Starr got another indictment against Webb Hubbell. I believe, and Webb Hubbell certainly knew, this indictment could nail him. It was based on Hubbell's alleged false testimony to the House Banking Committee and to federal banking regulators.

Hubbell quickly pled guilty to one charge in a plea deal with Starr. In exchange for that guilty plea, Starr dropped all charges against Hubbell's wife, his lawyer, his accountant, and his hunting dogs, and agreed never to file any charges against Hubbell. Ever. Ever wasn't a long time, since Ken Starr's job ended the next day.

It is important to note that Hubbell pled guilty to single counts of wire fraud and tax fraud, based on his illegal billing practices at the Rose Law Firm. I may mention later that Webb Hubbell's and Hillary Clinton's double-billing at the law firm most likely was approved by some of their clients and was a way of "legally" funneling money to them. Check out the name of James Riady from Indonesia for more about a single, typical example of that.

Webb Hubbell served his time in prison and in a halfway house. He never opened his mouth about the Clintons. He moved away from Little Rock, and he now writes books. He can also say, "No one shot me."

BRUCE LINDSEY was a lifelong friend of Billy Clinton and served as a senior White House aide. He also was Billy's treasurer in his 1990 gubernatorial campaign. Bruce was investigated by Ken Starr, but not charged, with making a large cash withdrawal from the campaign funds. It is generally believed in Arkansas that such cash money would be used, primarily in the black community, to pay pastors to "get out the vote." This was a time-honored tradition in Arkansas and not something that I'm using to disparage any ethnic group.

I suppose that Ken Starr decided not to get tangled in something so convoluted, so entrenched, and so lacking in tangible evidence as "get out the vote" money. It was difficult enough to follow financial trails on paper; it would have been impossible with cash.

Lindsey definitely knew, and still knows, a lot. He too can say, "No one shot me."

THE ROSE LAW FIRM is the oldest law firm in Arkansas, and it was the preeminent firm in Little Rock before Hillary Clinton caused the besmirching of its reputation.

Frankly, blaming the Rose Law Firm for all the illegalities of the Clintons and their cronies is like blaming a fine prep school for the delinquent acts of its teenage students over the summer break.

Webb Hubbell admitted to defrauding some of his clients at the

Rose Law Firm. I submit that some of those clients were complicit in that double-billing practice. I'm fairly sure, however, that the federal government as a client was not aware of the fraudulent bills, nor would it have approved them.

Hillary Clinton of the Rose Law Firm lied about her "minor" legal work for Jim McDougal and his troubled Madison Savings & Loan. She lied about doing other work for McDougal. Hundreds of pages of documents released by the House Banking and Financial Services Committee destroyed Hillary's credibility on the issue of her work for McDougal while at Rose. Who wants to read all that?

Hillary Clinton of the Rose Law Firm gave an "inaccurate" accounting of the Clintons' involvement in the Whitewater development with the McDougals. She and her husband also "made mistakes" on their federal income tax returns regarding their Whitewater investment. Don't blame the Rose Law Firm.

During the Whitewater investigation, when one of the old-timer partners at the Rose Law Firm was visiting with a group of friends at the CCLR (Country Club of Little Rock), he was asked what he thought about Hillary Clinton.

He answered, "That bitch is going to ruin my firm."

The partner who said that is dead now, and the very reliable person who told me the story does not want me to divulge his name. Normally, I wouldn't mention something that I am unwilling to "prove" by naming my source, but I think it's important to say that the ethical lawyers in the Rose Law Firm do not deserve to have their reputations trashed just because Hillary Clinton worked there.

Hillary Rodham was hired by the Rose Law Firm when her husband Billy Clinton was the attorney general of Arkansas. Hillary was named its first female partner when Billy became governor. Who couldn't see through that?

If either Susan McDougal or Webb Hubbell (or, especially, the deceased Vince Foster) had ever testified truthfully against their friends Billy and Hillary Clinton, the Whitewater Investigation would have had a much more dramatic ending.

Billy and Hillary could have spent many, many years in a different type of government housing. The Clintons' current international activities (such as laundering foreign money and influence peddling) with the Clinton Foundation may yet provide that opportunity.

Not to mention Hillary's emails that put American lives in danger.

31

RACISM AS PRACTICED BY THE CLINTONS

Hillary and Billy Clinton want people to believe that they are now, and have always been, supporters of racial equality. They would like everyone to ignore the fact that, behind his back, they refer to Jesse Jackson as "that G**damned nigger."

They would like to forget Hillary's famous outburst to the "f***ing Jew bastard."

The Clintons would like for everyone to forget about their history of supporting racial profiling in Arkansas.

So far, that seems to be working for them.

Once again, a bit of history is important to the understanding of Billy's and Hillary's political positions on racial matters when "they" were attorney general and governor.

Arkansas got its first big national black eye for race relations when the Democratic Governor Orval Faubus used the Arkansas National Guard to prevent the enrollment of nine black students at the all-white

Central High School in Little Rock in 1957.

The Republican President Dwight Eisenhower sent federal troops to support integration, which had been mandated by the landmark Supreme Court case "*Brown v. Board of Education (of Topeka, Kansas)*." Central High was closed for the school year, and most of the white students went to old and newly formed private schools in and outside the state of Arkansas.

Billy Clinton and I grew up with Jim Crow laws firmly in place. The term "Jim Crow" derived from an old song that was sung and made famous by a black-faced minstrel. These practices were in full force in Arkansas during the 1950s and into the 1960s.

In practical terms, we lived in a segregated society in Hot Springs. The white students went to the all-white Hot Springs High School; the black students went to Langston. (Through law school, I never attended any class with black students.)

In the movie theaters downtown, the black kids had to climb the stairs and watch the movie from the balcony. They were never allowed to sit near the white kids. Of course, they had separate bathrooms *and* separate water fountains.

Despite so many of the signs in Hot Springs that had no meaning (such as "MUST BE 21 TO PLACE A BET"), the signs that separated "WHITES" and "COLORED" were deadly serious and always enforced.

Although black people were allowed to shop at the Woolworth Five & Dime on Central Avenue downtown (somewhat the equivalent of today's dollar stores), no black person would ever be allowed to sit at the long lunch counter there to eat a sandwich.

"Colored" people couldn't even stand inside to eat. They could place a to-go order and eat outside. Black people were not allowed even to *enter* an all-white restaurant, except by the back door to work in the kitchen.

Public transportation, such as it was, was segregated as much as possible. Although I never got on a bus when I was a kid, I knew that, on both local and interstate buses, black people had to sit in the back. I never saw a black person on an airplane except to clean the galley.

When we traveled by train, there were black waiters in the dining car wearing crisp white uniforms, but I never saw any black people (other than the porters) in the sleeping cars. I know that there were some cars where black people could ride sitting up on bench seats because I saw pictures of those.

Everyone had to pay a poll tax to vote. The annual poll tax was $2.00. That may not sound like much, but it was a day's wage for black maids and janitors. If you're making $100 a day now, think about having to pay a $100 poll tax to be allowed to vote. That should put the poll tax in perspective.

In addition to producing a poll tax receipt, people had to provide some form of official identification in order to vote. Since most black people could not afford to own a car, they did not have driver's licenses.

With all the difficulties that faced a black person who wanted to vote, it was hardly worth the effort. The black vote was further diluted by the widespread practice of gerrymandering.

Named for the long-ago Governor Elbridge Gerry of Massachusetts, gerrymandering was the wide-spread practice of dividing electoral districts along racial lines to dilute the black vote. Picture a square, somewhat like the shape of Arkansas; it would seem reasonable and easy enough to divide it into equal parts.

Now, picture a city or county that grew along a highway or a railroad track or a waterway. The city or county would almost always have irregular lines.

In a gerrymandered district, those irregular outer lines would be convoluted on the interior as well. By encircling an all-white neighborhood with a tiny bit of the closest black neighborhood, the black votes would be diluted or undone by the white votes in the "winner take all" precinct or district.

Any time there was a big neighborhood of black people (which existed in most towns in the South), the voting district lines would be drawn to pull in tiny pieces of the black neighborhood into the closest white neighborhoods.

In a gerrymandered area (most of Arkansas), the white vote predominated every time. The white candidate won every time. In most races, however, there was no black candidate because there was no point in a black candidate's trying to win.

I have to digress a moment to say that none of the votes really mattered that much in many local elections, at least in Hot Springs back then. My mother was invited to be an "election monitor" in 1960. She sat at the most populous polling place all day, watching for any voting irregularities.

At the end of the voting day, she was invited to stay for barbecue and the auction. My mother did not like barbecue (she was, after all, from Philadelphia), and she had to ask about the auction. It seems that at 9:00 p.m., the individual precinct ballot boxes were sold to the highest bidder. Needless to say, there were never any black people bidding.

You don't have to believe that story to understand the rest of this chapter.

When Billy Clinton was governor and Hillary was his coconspiratorial First Lady in the 1980s, Billy was sued several times by groups of minorities (both blacks and Hispanics) for violations of the 1965 Voting Rights Act.

Billy lost every case.

He was reprimanded several times by the federal courts for violations of the 1965 Voting Rights Act.

All the detailed information about these (and other) lawsuits is available in public records, but you probably won't find many references to these cases against the racist Clintons in any mainstream media reports.

You won't find anything anti-Clinton in most new school textbooks, either, because the Clinton cronies have been busy rewriting history.

I'll give only a thumbnail sketch about the lawsuits here because I got tired of this kind of legal research in my first year of law school, and I'm not a fan of litigation. Real estate law is my interest, and I'll look at this somewhat from a real estate perspective.

The Delta area of Arkansas, for example, is both black and poor. It gets poorer every year. Property values, and thus the tax base, continue to deteriorate from both white flight and from desperate blacks moving from Helena to Pine Bluff in hopes of finding a job.

The unemployment rate among young black men in the Delta area is both sad and appalling. That doesn't count the number of young black men who are in prison; they don't even count in the unemployment statistics.

Despite the overwhelming black population in the Delta area of Arkansas, there had not been a single black person voted into the Arkansas legislature in hundreds and hundreds of elections (not years, but elections).

Black people sued Billy and other state officials. Blacks won. The district's lines were redrawn under court order to something more equitable so that blacks might have a chance to elect one of their own to serve in the Arkansas legislature.

In Crittenden County, which includes the Arkansas side of Memphis and runs along the Mississippi River north of the Delta area, Ben McGee (a black Democrat) was elected to the Arkansas state legislature in 1988.

It was actually only the Democratic primary, but it was tantamount to a win back then because Republicans rarely produced a candidate; whoever won the Democratic primary would win the election in November.

Billy Clinton (a Democrat) tried to replace Ben McGee with a candidate (a white Democrat) of his choice. The case went all the way to the United States Supreme Court. The Supremes ruled (8-0) against Billy and the other Arkansas officials who had challenged Ben's election.

Here's one more story to give some balance regarding the Hispanics who had started to move into Arkansas in greater numbers in the 1980s.

Three years after Billy's younger brother, Roger, went to prison for drug dealing, Billy instituted racial profiling against Hispanics. This was part of his much-politicized antidrug program.

Roger is white; Roger's drug suppliers were white; Roger's friends to whom he sold drugs were white, so it's not about revenge or retaliation for his brother's problems that clearly and most certainly were not caused by Hispanics.

For no good reason that I can imagine, Billy and Hillary decided to profile Hispanics as drug dealers.

Billy as governor gave state troopers the authority to stop and search any vehicle that looked like it *might* be carrying illegal drugs. Specifically, the troopers were to stop and search cars driven by Hispanics, especially those cars with Texas license plates.

Billy was sued in federal court for this Criminal Apprehension Program and, not surprisingly, the federal judge ruled that the program was unconstitutional.

That should have been the end of it, but Billy doesn't like to be told what he cannot do, whether it's his grandmother or Hillary or a federal judge.

Billy threw one of his infamous temper tantrums about the ban on his racial profiling of Hispanics and he threatened to renew the racial profiling program in spite of the court's ruling.

A few years later, without targeting Hispanics directly, Billy gave the Arkansas state troopers the right to stop and search *any* car at their discretion. Subtle, huh?

Years later, as co-presidents, the duplicitous (that's fancy writer talk for "lying dog") Billy and Hillary Clinton publicly criticized racial profiling as a "morally indefensible, deeply corrosive practice."

32

A TURNING POINT

In 1986, Hillary and Billy were in the governor's mansion and on track with their plans to get to the White House. Arkansas had just passed Amendment 63 which extended a governor's term from two years to four.

The Clintons were delighted with this fortuitous political development, and were running for reelection for the fourth time. (To recap: Billy was elected governor in 1978; lost the race in 1980, won in 1982, and won again in 1984.)

I was going to be in Arkansas over the Fourth of July weekend that year, and Billy invited me to join him for a party at a friend's house on Lake Hamilton. The house was past the race track, a few miles south of Hot Springs, off Highway 7.

Billy suggested that my daughters might want to join us for a while, via boat, since his friend's house was not far from the family lake house around the next peninsula.

I have no idea where Hillary was that weekend. As usual neither of us mentioned the other woman.

Billy was in his element that night, back in his own hometown, surrounded by friends, in a lovely home decorated with a patriotic theme. A welcome breeze off the water made the hot night bearable.

"I'm so glad you could be here, Pretty Girl," he whispered in my ear. "I've missed you for the past couple of months. You didn't even write to me after our morning in Dallas."

"I'll explain all that later," I promised. "Let's not talk here in front of everyone."

While Billy was talking to some other people at the lakeside party, I was thinking back to the last time we had been together. Billy had been in Dallas for some political gathering in late April, and had asked me to meet him at his downtown hotel toward the end of the event. As usual Billy was taking forever to break away from the big Texas crowd that night.

I had finally slipped him a note saying, "Sorry. Gotta go."

On that April night, I had left the hotel alone, disappointed that I wouldn't be able to visit with Billy privately on that trip. The next morning, he called me a little after seven.

He wanted me to join him for breakfast in his suite. I said it was impossible because I was to be the featured speaker at a real estate conference at nine o'clock.

"Just a glass of juice, then?" he asked. "I can't be in Dallas without seeing you."

"Okay, but just a glass of juice. I have a reputation for being punctual."

Billy had laughed at my oblique reference to his notorious tardiness.

I had stayed for more than a glass of juice that morning.

My reminiscing about April in Dallas was interrupted at the Fourth of July party by three pubescent girls. They wanted to meet the governor.

Billy was gracious to them. He stood there with his arm around me, and asked the girls questions about their school, their friends, and their goals in life.

"You're not his wife, are you?" one of the girls asked me.

I shook my head.

"No. I'm Dolly Kyle."

I smiled, but explained nothing.

"This is the girl I've been in love with since I was about your age," Billy told the three teenagers.

He was speaking openly, with his arm still around me.

"Then why didn't you marry her?" the bold one asked.

Billy paused for several seconds before answering, "I've asked myself that same question about a million times."

The girl looked at me again and inquired, "Are you married?"

Billy and I answered her simultaneously.

"Yes/No."

"What?" Billy exclaimed, looking into my eyes.

"What?" he repeated.

"I'm not married," I told the girl.

"Uh," Billy began, "uh, but, uh, if, if, uh,…"

Billy stammered. He couldn't get a complete sentence to come out of his mouth.

The girls looked at him as if he had lost his mind and then turned back to me.

"I'm divorced," I explained. "My divorce was final three days ago. I haven't had a chance to tell the governor yet."

Billy dropped his arm from my waist.

"Oh," the assertive girl said, grinning. "I see."

The girls giggled, and decided it was time to go get a soda.

"Why didn't you tell me?" Billy asked.

"I was going to tell you later, not here in front of all these people. I'm sorry it came out like that. We can talk about it all night if you want."

Billy had turned pale.

"I, uh, have to, uh, change our plans," he said. "I've got to get back to the Capitol tonight. Excuse me a minute while I say good-bye to our hosts. Meet me at the car."

I said good-bye to the hosts, strolled around the house to the parking area, passed by my own car, and struck up a conversation with the waiting state trooper. I figured that Billy would take at least thirty minutes to thank the hosts and shake hands with more people.

Amazingly, he was at his car in less than three minutes.

"It was nice to see you again, Dolly," he said casually.

Billy opened his own car door before the trooper realized he was ready to go.

"Good night. Have a safe trip back to Dallas."

Billy slid into the front passenger seat without another glance at me. The car sped down the driveway.

I stood watching the red taillights disappear into the night.

* * *

My oldest daughter had a serious water-skiing accident on Lake Hamilton that weekend, and it was a miracle that she didn't lose her leg. She was transported from Hot Springs to Little Rock by ambulance for surgery, and she lived with a long, stainless-steel pin in her right leg for over a year.

Billy sent her flowers while she was in the hospital, along with a handwritten note wishing her a speedy recovery. I, on the other hand, didn't hear from Billy until after his birthday the next month.

Despite Billy's cowardly disappearing act on me the night of the Fourth of July party, I sent him Woodrow Wilson's *History of the American People*—a first-edition, five-volume set of green hardback books for his fortieth birthday

Billy sent a typed, form-letter acknowledging the gift:

"You were good to think of me on my birthday, and I want you to know how pleased I am by your kindness. I am touched by your thoughtfulness and the special friendship which prompted your gesture."

It was signed:

"Sincerely, Bill."

Under that, Billy handwrote:

"Thanks. Sorry. I miss you."

Yes, the *"I miss you"* part was underlined.

With that little apology (*"Sorry"*), Billy and I were almost back to normal.

As usual.

* * *

I mentioned earlier in passing that for many years I was almost as "sick" as Billy was, but I arrived at a turning point in my life. My divorce that shocked Billy at the Fourth of July party also shocked me into asking myself some serious questions. It was my second divorce and I knew I needed to make some changes. I needed to do something.

I did some reading, realized that I was a codependent, contacted a counselor, and joined a codependency therapy group.

Billy was a sex addict; I was a codependent.

Fine. I began dealing with that.

Then I read more about sex addiction. I realized that Billy and I shared a similar problem. I was also a sex addict.

Not so fine. Not so easy to deal with that.

I started working a twelve-step program.

Not easy.

Not easy at all.

I shared with Billy many of the things I was discovering and experiencing in my twelve-step recovery process.

At some point, I realized that what I was writing as a therapeutic journal could be turned into a good novel. I told Billy what I was thinking about that.

Billy encouraged me to write a loosely autobiographical novel, as he had encouraged my song writing.

I argued that it might hurt him if I published something as obvious as a novel that was based on our decades-long story. He already was taking more chances than I thought were prudent, but he insisted that I should always write what was in my heart.

"You're a great writer," Billy said. "Promise me you won't ever censor anything you might want to write."

"That's crazy," I said. "Everyone will know it's about us."

I thought about all the songs I had written over the years.

Way too many of them were about Billy and me... from the "I-L-O-V-E-U" ditty that I had sung at the governor's mansion party one night to "It's A Good Thing He Can't Read My Mind," which is still one of my favorites.

Maybe I could have those songs published without drawing attention to my relationship with Billy, but I didn't think that would ever work with writing a novel.

"You're a great writer," he repeated. "Now, promise me."

I shook my head in complete disagreement with him.

"Pretty Girl, promise me you won't ever censor anything you might want to write," he insisted again. "You're a great writer, and you have to write what's in your heart."

I wondered why Billy would say such a thing, but I finally agreed. I promised him that I would write what was in my heart.

* * *

Silly, silly me. When would I ever learn?

33

LETTERS BETWEEN THE LINES

Although I promised Billy that I would not censor anything about us and that I would write what was in my heart, I was still very careful when writing letters to him.

I made my letters appear as innocuous as possible, in case the other woman or someone else might inadvertently (or otherwise) read one of them. My letters to Billy could not be fully appreciated without seeing them in the context of our previous letters—and our recent visits and our history—and so most of them appeared innocent on their face.

Billy was not that cautious with the letters he wrote to me, but none of them were steamy or scandalous. Taken all together, though, his letters painted a clear picture of a long-term relationship that was intimate on many levels.

I was always more concerned than Billy seemed to be about his behavior toward me when we were in public. I was apprehensive, especially in Billy's early years as governor, about what the ever-present state troopers knew and what they might say. Billy always insisted that they were no problem.

Over time, it became obvious to me that the troopers who remained on Billy's security detail liked him and were quite loyal to him. It also became obvious that they couldn't stand Hillary and held her in contempt.

I don't know if the state troopers told stories about Hillary to other people as well as to me, but I don't know why they wouldn't. Some of the tales were probably stretched a bit for comic effect, but, over the years and taken as a whole, they painted a clear picture of the temperament and temper of the foul-mouthed, arrogant, and imperious First Lady of Arkansas.

Hillary had alienated herself so much from the troopers (and from staff) that she would have to resort to hiring private investigators and thugs to shut the mouths of those who might endanger her coattail ride to the White House. I'm fairly sure that none of the troopers ever "ratted Billy out" to her.

Later, when the state troopers (or anyone else) dared to tell the truth about what they had seen, heard, and known about the Clintons, they would be trashed by Hillary's attack machine. I think that Billy always trusted the troopers' loyalty to keep his stories private; I know that Billy was shocked and hurt when some of the troopers did tell a few tales in later years.

There was an Arkansas state trooper traveling with Billy (the governor) the night of May 17, 1987, when we met at the Airport Marina Hotel-East at DFW Airport.

I didn't actually see the officer, but Billy said that he was staying in a nearby (not adjoining) room. It was an unexpected stop in Dallas because their plane from Washington had been diverted on the leg from Atlanta to Little Rock; at least, that's what Billy told me when he called me to meet him. He had no luggage which explained why he was wearing only a hotel towel when he opened the door to his room for me.

We got comfortable in the window-side bed in the bland hotel room. We watched the tail end of a movie; we ate grapes and cheese; then we talked.

Billy was very interested in my latest insights from working my twelve-step recovery program. After being involved in "family week" at the federal prison in Fort Worth when his brother was there, Billy had some familiarity with the twelve steps.

"I'm worried about Roger," Billy said.

I bit my tongue to keep from saying that it's much easier to worry about your little brother than it is to look at your own issues.

"He's so angry. Even after all this time, Roger still wants to blame everybody else for his problems. I just don't understand it. Maybe this twelve-step thing will work for him."

"The problem isn't just with Roger. Since I've been in therapy, I see these things much differently. These are known as family of origin issues. Everyone in the family is somehow involved in the development and support of an addict."

I wasn't sure that Billy wanted to hear this, but he nodded some encouragement, so I continued.

"This is generally not a conscious act by people in the addict's family, but it's important to realize that an alcoholic or a drug addict or a sex addict isn't formed in a vacuum. It's a family matter."

Billy nodded absently, turned off the television, and pulled me closer to him. Over the next hour or so, he asked me more and more questions about what I had learned regarding sex addiction.

Finally, after we informally went through the check-list of sex addiction questions, Billy admitted that his sexual behavior was out of control.

If Billy had taken what I said to heart, if he had moved forward instead of backward after our intense and candid talk, if he had done anything at all to get some therapy and change his behavior, I would not be telling this now.

Unfortunately, Billy didn't get help.

He didn't change his behavior for the better. He continued in his escalating sexual addiction, and I ended up testifying truthfully under oath about this particular night in my deposition in the *Jones v. Clinton* lawsuit.

"But I haven't slept with another woman since I-don't-know-when," Billy protested.

I did laugh out loud when he said that.

"'I haven't slept with another woman since I-don't-know when,' quoth the noble governor, lying naked in a hotel room with his arms wrapped around a nude blonde. Really, Billy? How does that sound?"

He looked surprised, and even hurt.

"This is different," he said. "This is you."

Billy's response led to reminiscing about our relationship, about the day we met, about how intertwined our lives and families had been, which came back around to the emotional and psychological issues.

Then Billy confessed that talking about the family dynamic made him worry about how all this would affect his daughter, Chelsea.

"I want to be a good daddy for her," he whispered. "That's really important to me."

His voice trailed off, and then returned.

"I never knew my father. I want to do this right, but sometimes I'm not sure how. What should I be doing?"

I didn't answer him.

"What should I do?" Billy repeated. "I know you've learned a lot in your therapy. Tell me what I can do for Chelsea to save her from this kind of hurt."

"What I learned is that the most important thing a man can do for his daughter is to love and honor her mother."

There was a very long, very uncomfortable silence.

* * *

Despite our conversation that lasted most of the night at the Airport Marina Hotel in mid-May, Billy didn't want to admit to himself that his sexual addiction could cause an immediate disaster in his political life.

Billy had an incredible, lifelong sense of immunity. It seems that he never had to experience the negative consequences of his actions. I think that he picked up much of that attitude from the pervasive societal "norm" of illegality in Hot Springs as we were growing up there.

No, not everyone growing up in Hot Springs absorbed that sense of immunity from negative consequences. Billy had the double-whammy of an extremely dysfunctional home life too.

Billy was obviously in deep denial about the extent of his sexual addiction. He did not believe me when I said that what was happening to fellow Democratic politician Sen. Gary Hart could possibly happen to him. The strongest part of Billy's character seemed to be his defense mechanisms.

Gary Hart, who had appeared to be a shoo-in for the Democratic nomination for president in 1988, had just dropped out of the race because he had been caught at his townhome in Washington with a twenty-nine-year-old model-actress named Donna Rice. The married Senator Hart of Colorado had previously been questioned about rumors of infidelity during his twenty-eight-year marriage.

Hart denied the charges of philandering. He even defied and dared the press to follow him to prove he was doing nothing wrong. Yet, it was no secret in Miami that the senator had recently traveled via yacht from Miami to Bimini in the company of friends and a gorgeous, much-younger woman.

From everything I have heard, Donna Rice seemed to have been genuinely smitten with the politician, although she didn't even know who he was when they had been introduced in Aspen several months earlier.

After the Gary Hart–Donna Rice affair became intimate, the apparently naïve young woman talked and talked and talked to numerous friends about Gary. When she met him, she thought he was single and available. He certainly acted single and available.

The similarities between Gary Hart's hubris and Billy Clinton's arrogance scared me. The only thing Billy could see at the time was that Gary Hart's dropping out of the presidential race left a potential opening for him in 1988.

I begged Billy to get help for his sexual addiction, and I warned him repeatedly that running for president before he got his act together would spell certain disaster.

I thought I had made my point.

Hillary, of course, was chomping at the bit to get Billy into the presidential race in 1988. She planned all along to become the first female president after Billy would win and serve two terms in the White House.

They had already been in the governor's mansion for several years, and Hillary was ready for "moving on up."

I knew I had to do something to make an impact with Billy, or I would have to kick myself later for my silence if he did something as foolish as entering the presidential fray.

I handwrote him a letter, dated "Saturday, June 6, 1987, Very early in the morning." I made a copy of it, as I frequently did with correspondence that I thought was important. That copy is also included in the exhibits to my deposition in the *Jones v. Clinton* lawsuit. I wrote:

> I woke up this morning with a feeling of *déjà vu* and recalled the time after you lost to Frank White when you were considering whether or not to head the national party. Your mind seemed ready to do it because your intellect thought it was the best thing to do at the time, but you admitted that in your gut you wanted to stay home with Chelsea and, thank God, that's what you did.
>
> Now you've developed yourself well – intellectually, socially, and politically – yet you know there are other parts of <u>you</u> that are less strong and mature. I've always believed that God wants you to be a great leader someday. I'd hate to see you settle for being a great politician.
>
> Get quiet. Look inside yourself. Feel. Forget about the polls, the political 'facts,' the supporters who have their own reasons for wanting you to run. Do what you did when Chelsea was a baby: Listen to your gut. Trust it. Are you ready to be a great leader? Is your own house in order? . . .
>
> I was praying for guidance for you and my eyes fell upon 1 Corinthians 14:8 – 'for if the trumpet give an uncertain sound, who shall prepare himself to the battle?'

Whatever you do, I support you. Just remember that I care about you as a human being, not a human doing.

Love, Dolly

A week later, I received Billy's handwritten reply on his governor's stationery. It was dated June 12, and it is also a part of the subpoenaed letters that are attached as exhibits to my deposition in the *Jones v. Clinton* lawsuit:

Dear Dolly –

Thanks for your letter – It's good advice and you sound good in it –

I'm in a quandary and exhausted. We're about to take a few days off so that I can quietly "feel" what I should do –

Best, Bill

Thanks for coming by the office too – Let me know when you're here again –

Your letter was on target –

You know me.

Since a word to the wise is sufficient and since Billy is a fairly smart guy, I thought that would be the end of that.

But, no.

On Friday, the tenth of July, as I was preparing to leave the country on a vacation, I heard that media personnel from one coast to the other were making plans to travel to Arkansas. Governor Clinton had called a press conference to be held the following Wednesday in Little Rock.

There would be only one reason for Billy to call a national press conference in Little Rock. I was terribly upset that he was about to do something as stupid as getting into a presidential race prematurely.

I quickly sat down at the desk in my sunroom and pulled a piece of my gray executive-sized stationery from its fancy little box. I stared at my name DOLLY KYLE engraved in block letters at the top of the page. I couldn't think of a thing to say.

I addressed an envelope to Billy, added my return address, and put a stamp on it. I still couldn't think of anything to say. My car to the airport would be arriving in a few minutes, and I needed to tuck a few more items into my suitcase.

I folded the single piece of stationery, put it in the envelope, and stashed it in my purse. I would think of something brilliant to say on the way to the airport.

Nothing came to me on the way to the airport. I checked my bags with American Airlines at the curb and headed for the mailbox. I still had no idea what to say.

What could I say that would make a difference after all this time? I had tried, hadn't I?

We had talked and talked and talked. I had already written my thoughts about his running for president in a letter. Billy had said he was going to *feel* what he should do.

I had forgotten to take into account that Hillary had been pushing, pushing, and pushing some more to get Billy into the 1988 presidential race. Her political clock was ticking.

My vacation clock was ticking too. My flight would be boarding soon.

I pulled the single personalized page of stationery from its addressed envelope and I stared at it. I'm never at a loss for words. I still couldn't think of anything to say.

Finally, without writing a single word on the page, I refolded it and stuck it in the envelope. I licked the envelope to seal it, dropped it in the mailbox, and headed for my departure gate.

When Billy received my unwritten little gray "letter" on Tuesday, July 14, 1987, he immediately drafted and sent a press release to the world.

He announced in his press release that at his press conference the following day, he was going to announce that he was not going to run for president.

Political pundits have been wondering and speculating for decades about Billy's very strange communication that day.

Now you know what happened.

34

THE SEX CHAPTER

Throughout this book, I have used the terms "sex addict" and "sexual addiction" as if everyone understands the meanings of those words and their variations. I should not have made such an assumption.

Even the well-read and intelligent Billy Clinton didn't understand the meaning and impact of those terms when I first mentioned them to him.

In the 1980s, when I encountered the notion of sexual addiction, there was not a lot of information readily available. I did find and read an enormously helpful book *Out of the Shadows: Understanding Sexual Addiction* by Patrick Carnes. I'm glad to see that it is still in print, following its original publication in 1983. I highly recommend it.

There are plenty of online resources available now, and many of those sites offer free and anonymous questionnaires to help people do a self-assessment in the area of sexual addiction. There are also many types of groups providing support in the format of twelve-step programs.

I think that AA (Alcoholics Anonymous) is probably still the world's premier twelve-step group, at least in terms of name recognition and membership. Numerous groups (in addition to AA for drinking problems) exist to help people with addictions including, but not limited to: drugs, gambling, overeating, overspending, and sex.

Sexual addiction, much like an eating disorder, is a bit trickier than many other types of addictions. It is easy to say "stop drinking" or "stop gambling," but "stop eating" presents a real problem. The issue of sex addiction is even more complicated by the various religious, societal, and family norms that can enter into the equation.

I'm not going to do a dissertation on sex addiction here, but it's important to understand some of the basics in order to grasp the extent of Billy Clinton's addiction problems. His sexual addiction has not only affected his life, and his family's life, but, by virtue of his political status, it has affected the entire country.

Hillary Clinton is Billy Clinton's chief enabler and coconspirator. I don't think she has faced the underlying issues that drive her own behavior, especially in relationship to the addict who is her husband.

Over the past couple of decades, Hillary and Billy have lived separate lives, in separate homes, frequently in separate countries. As they are forced to spend more and more time together during the campaign season, some of their old, unresolved issues will emerge again.

Like a codependent family, the United States of America will be dragged into their dysfunctions unless we send them "home" to heal in private.

As Hillary campaigns we see a new spate of attacks against anyone who raises the voice of truth against them, especially in regard to the women who have been raped or sexually assaulted by Billy Clinton over the past decades. Such women will again be called liars by the Clinton sycophants in the mainstream media.

Attacks will also be launched as needed against the hundreds (or thousands, if using the estimate that Billy gave me) of women who had consensual and nonconsensual sexual encounters of any sort with Billy

Clinton—from his years at Oxford to his years in political offices in Arkansas to his years in the White House and thereafter.

When Billy and I talked about sexual addiction and he admitted his problem to me, we focused on a few of the self-assessment questions that were then the basis of membership in Sex Addicts Anonymous, which I had joined in Dallas. I had the questions memorized.

Some of these issues were raised by Billy Clinton's lawyer in his attempted contradiction of my sworn "sex addiction" testimony during my deposition in the *Jones v. Clinton* lawsuit.

Billy's lawyer seemed unfamiliar with the self-assessment nature of all the twelve-step programs, and his main argument seemed to be that neither Billy nor I were "experts" in the study of sexual addiction and, therefore, could not know we were addicts.

I invite you to read through the self-assessment questions below and decide for yourself if an untrained person could determine from the answers whether or not he or she might have a sex addiction problem.

You will recognize the way these sex addiction issues apply to Billy Clinton's life and political career if you remember or have read anything much about him. I'll add my comments in brackets for those who are too young to remember, or were in denial with Billy back then when more of this was in the news . . . or at least being whispered.

The sex addiction questions [with my comments in brackets] after each one:

1. Have your desires driven you to have sex in places you would not normally choose? [The Oval Office of the White House, perhaps? The backseat of a state-owned car with a state trooper driving? A bathroom in the governor's mansion while a party was in progress in the next room?]

2. Have your desires driven you to have sex with people you would not normally choose? [A young government employee such as Paula Jones or an intern like Monica Lewinsky . . . or a rock-band groupie like Connie Hamzy?]

3. Do you frequently want to get away from a partner after having sex? [Allowing your wife to attack your sexual partners indicates that you are not interested in staying with them, but that you really do want to get away and forget about it. Denial is a special type of forgetting.]

4. Do you feel remorse, shame, or guilt after a sexual encounter? [I only know this about Billy Clinton because he admitted it to me. He certainly didn't express remorse, shame, or guilt for his known sexual encounters publicly, although he was quite remorseful about getting caught in so many of them.]

5. Does your pursuit of sex or sexual fantasy conflict with your moral standards? [Billy was raised in the Baptist Church so he certainly heard about moral standards, whether he adopted any moral standards or not.]

6. Do your sexual activities involve force or violence? [There are plenty of women who have attested to being raped or sexually assaulted by Billy Clinton, including, but not at all limited to Juanita Broaddrick and Kathleen Willey, both of whom are credible witnesses by any objective standard. If you haven't seen the NBC/Lisa Myers interview with Juanita, you should try to find it online.]

7. Do you keep secrets about your sexual behavior from those who are important to you? [I submit that American voters are the most important people in Billy Clinton's life, and he certainly hasn't been forthcoming with all of us: "I did not have sexual relations with that woman, Miss Lewinsky." Not to mention the secrets he tried to keep from Hillary and Chelsea Clinton.]

8. Do you lead a double life sexually? [Billy Clinton probably leads the most blatant double life of anyone I have ever known . . . except Hillary.]

9. Do you need greater variety, increased frequency, or more extreme sexual activities to achieve the same level of excitement or relief? [I'll just mention again that when Billy heard the basketball star Wilt Chamberlain brag about having sex with 20,000 women, Billy said that was 10 times more than he had had. That would leave Billy with "only" 2,000 sexual encounters, by his own admission. I'd say that Billy's sex fixes would have to be frequent to get a number that high.]

10. Have your sexual activities jeopardized your significant relationships or employment? [We all know by now that Hillary isn't going to leave Billy, no matter what, at least until she finishes her coattail-riding. But employment? As president? Impeached! That was almost being fired from your job, wouldn't you say?]

11. Have your sexual activities caused you legal problems? [It was lucky for Billy that Juanita Broaddrick didn't file rape charges against him while he was attorney general of Arkansas! It was lucky for Hillary too, since she could have been charged with being an accessory after the fact for her intimidation of the victim. The *Jones v. Clinton* lawsuit and the IMPEACHMENT were certainly legal problems. I must say here that the good people of Arkansas who started a legal defense fund for Billy Clinton could not have had any idea of the extent of his sexual crimes, or they would not have supported him. I should count my own federal lawsuit against Billy too, since that can be traced back to sexual activities.]

12. Have your sexual activities involved the threat of disease? [Sorry, Connie Hamzy. Having unprotected sex with a self-confessed rock-band groupie would not have been smart. I know that Connie's sexual tryst in a broom closet with Billy Clinton was not consummated, but it really wasn't a good idea in the first place. Billy was known in Arkansas for not wearing condoms, with his black, streetwalker prostitutes or with anyone else. It's a miracle if Billy is still disease free. I do believe in miracles.]

13. Have your sexual activities jeopardized your life goals? [That's enough.]

Some of the sex addiction groups suggest that experiencing even *one* of these issues in a serious degree is a sign of sexual addiction. Let's say, for the sake of argument, that one strike is an extreme standard.

How about three strikes? How about half of these issues?

Is it extreme to self-diagnose sexual addiction if half of these problems apply?

Again, for the sake of argument, let's say that having as many as half of these issues is still too extreme a standard.

When a person scores 100 percent on the above sex-addiction questionnaire, however, that person is definitely a sex addict. Billy Clinton is definitely a sex addict. Untreated.

The list above shows some of the ways that his addiction has affected his life and his career, not to mention his family. Hillary is as complicit as a spouse has ever been in supporting a sexual addiction, and she is worse than most because she was and continues to be in a position to attack his victims.

Frankly, I'm concerned that if Hillary gets access to FBI files again and uses the IRS to attack her perceived enemies, again—as she did the last time she was in the White House—it's going to get even uglier than it has been for those of us who will be perceived as her enemies.

Sex addiction and codependency need to be treated in private. How about this idea? Let's all agree to give the dysfunctional duo of Hillary and Billy Clinton the privacy they need to start their healing process. And let's all pray that they will do it.

In private.

Not in the White House.

35

THANK GOD FOR MISSISSIPPI!

If Hillary Rodham had grown up in Arkansas, she might have been more understanding and more tolerant of Arkansas people. Hillary, however, grew up in a middle-class suburb in Illinois and she never let people forget it—unless she was campaigning in New York and telling everyone there that she had been a lifelong Yankees fan!

Hillary looked down her nose at Arkansas people because she considered them to be ignorant hillbillies. What she failed to appreciate is that, while many Arkansans may be a bit behind her in book learning, we are no fools. For example, when she repeatedly told the story that she had been named for Sir Edmund Hillary after his historic climb of Mt. Everest, many Arkansas people questioned the tale because their instincts told them not to trust Hillary in the first place.

It turned out to be a lie, of course, since the historic climb occurred when Hillary was five or six years old. People in Arkansas weren't surprised when her lie became so well known that Hillary had to admit it in public. There is a kind of country wisdom here in Arkansas along with the ability to spot lies and hypocrisy that city slickers rarely appreciate.

Even in Hot Springs, where nothing was as it seemed and the criminal elements had control for decades, a man (or woman) is only as good as his word. The expression "honor among thieves" comes to mind to describe it. In other words, even though a guy like Owney Madden had been a contract killer and who knows what else in New York, when Owney promised to do something for you in Hot Springs, you could be sure that he would do it. The worst of the worst in Hot Springs adhered to a generally understood and well-accepted "moral" code of conduct.

My daddy, who was in the real estate business, always told me that he'd rather have the handshake of a man with integrity than an eighty-page contract with a snake. That lesson served me well even after law school when I was giving real estate advice. The best way to avoid being bitten by a bad deal is to avoid doing business with a snake.

"It's not what you know, it's who you know."

My clients and I walked away from many potential snake deals; I'm happy to say that I was occasionally blessed to see what happened to those who were greedy enough to stay.

I often wondered why Billy Clinton failed to adopt the moral lessons that he had learned in the Baptist Church in Hot Springs, or even to adopt the loyalty code of the blatantly disreputable and unethical leaders in Hot Springs. Billy's lack of loyalty is one of the worst of his character flaws, and I believe now that it stems from his being an outsider in his own hometown.

By "outsider in his own hometown," I mean that Billy felt isolated from others by the incredible dysfunction in his family at home. He could not be honest with his friends about the psychological and emotional traumas he was experiencing as a child and teenager. Since he could not be honest at a gut level, he could not expect his friends to be honest with him. Therefore, he was not able to bond with them in a way that would engender real loyalty.

I remember when Billy turned on his childhood friend Mack McLarty. They had been in kindergarten together in Hope, Arkansas, before Virginia married Roger Clinton and moved to Hot Springs. Billy and Mack remained friends over a lifetime, and Billy named Mack to be his chief of staff in the White House when he took office in 1993. Some people around Billy expressed concern that Mack was too much of a "nice guy" to serve in that office, but Mack was unquestionably loyal to his old friend Billy, the new president.

Mack's loyalty was not reciprocated by Billy, however. In short order, he summarily removed Mack from his position and let it be leaked that Mack was an ineffectual chief of staff. One might be tempted to believe that "ineffectual" assessment unless one knew that Mack McLarty served quite competently as the chairman and CEO of Arkla Gas/Arkla Inc., a Fortune 500 company.

One of my favorite quotes of the Clinton presidency came from Mack. A reporter asked him how it felt to be removed from his position of honor by someone who was supposed to be his loyal friend.

Mack replied, "A friend is someone who will stab you in the chest."

(Mack was referring, of course, to the famous death of Julius Caesar at the hand of the Roman senators and his dear friend Brutus. Being stabbed in the chest is preferable to being stabbed in the back, I suppose. Hillary and Billy both seem to prefer to stab in the back—figuratively speaking, of course.)

The other reason that Billy failed to adopt the "honor among thieves" loyalty that was common in Hot Springs is that Billy felt like an outsider from the powers that be.

Uncle Raymond was a financial, social, and political bigwig in Hot Springs, but he did not include Billy, his nephew by marriage, in his social and business interactions as my father had done for me. Instead, Billy was stuck with the erratic and abusive behavior of his alcoholic stepfather, Roger Clinton, Uncle Raymond's ne'er-do-well little brother.

Billy saw what was happening around him in Hot Springs, but he was always on the outside looking in. He never felt part of the in-crowd.

Even in high school, he felt one down by being in the band instead of being a football jock. He has admitted this publicly without ever grasping its psychological and emotional significance.

When Hillary moved to Arkansas, she was obsessed right away with covering the tracks of her sex-addicted husband, who was her only hope for a political career. Hillary was so busy with those codependent, coconspiratorial activities, as well as providing the financial support of the sex addict, that she never was able to recognize and relax into the joys of Arkansas life.

When the Clintons' daughter, Chelsea, was a young child, Hillary conceived a game that was designed to toughen the little girl about the *lies* that the people of Arkansas would tell about her daddy the governor.

Night after night, when her parents were at home, Chelsea was subjected to the psychologically and emotionally sick game that was played at the dining room table. Little Chelsea would cry and cry when Hillary pelted her with the many lies that the people of Arkansas would tell about her daddy the governor.

Naturally, while the child was being brainwashed at the dinner table, she never considered the notion that her mother, the First Lady of Arkansas, was the biggest liar of all. Chelsea was being brainwashed to believe what her lying parents told her instead of learning to discern the difference between truth and a lie.

Meanwhile, over a meager dinner in the poorest hovel in the Arkansas hills, parents were instilling in their children the simple rural principles of honesty and integrity and telling the truth that had been passed down to them from their parents and grandparents.

Hillary saw the people of Arkansas as nothing but potential votes. After her White House years as First Lady, she wouldn't even think about moving back to Arkansas. Even though it was Arkansas people who had provided the launching pad for Billy's political career, Hillary had no regard for that.

Instead, Hillary turned her back on Arkansas as a place to live because there were not enough potential votes in the state to help her move up politically. Besides, she didn't like it here anyway.

When I was growing up in Hot Springs, there was a popular saying that we heard and repeated any time we read about national test scores, or national income levels, or any other national statistic that represented the American ideal of success: "Thank God for Mississippi!"

Of course, I remember when there were only forty-eight states. Back then, in the early 1950s, Arkansas would generally rank as number forty-seven in whatever was being counted, and we could count on our neighboring state of Mississippi to be number forty-eight.

After the additions of Alaska and Hawaii to the USA, Arkansas would generally rank number forty-nine and Mississippi would bottom out at fifty. Hillary never caught on to the local and state pride that we had in the face of such numbers.

The catch is that Arkansans aren't numbers.

We are people. We are neighbors. We are friendly. We are helpful. We are creative and resourceful and hardworking, and we are nice. Where are the statistics for these qualities and traits that bind us together in a beautiful, geographically diverse little state with a fascinating history?

Yes, there are problems in Arkansas. It's part of the world, and there are problems in this world. There are no perfect people and there are no perfect solutions.

What we have here in Arkansas, though, are people who love the land and their neighbors. We also have a long history of wanting to handle our own issues without government intervention. We would rather help our neighbors raise a barn than raise the taxes to have the government build the barn.

Hillary never caught on to the Arkansas way of life. She thinks that government (known derisively here as "gummet") rather than individuals should make decisions for people about their schools, their health care, their retirement, their you-name-it. It appears that, in Hillary's view, individuals are too ignorant and lazy to take care of these matters for themselves and for their families.

To support all her grand "gummet" ideas, Hillary believes that the answer lies in more taxes and in the distribution of wealth. I don't see her offering to part with any of her multimillions of dollars that she earned "on the side" while working as a gummet employee. Hillary hasn't offered to help equalize the financial situation in the country by sharing her own money, but maybe she intends to do that real soon.

Meanwhile, it's the poorest of the people in Arkansas who are still disproportionately bearing tax burdens that should have been the first taxes to be lifted. It wasn't until I moved to Dallas to go to law school that I even thought about the tax on groceries. There is no tax on groceries in Texas. Arkansas has finally started to reduce such taxes, although our neighboring state immediately to the east across Ol' Man River has not made such a move. Therefore, as usual, we can say, "Thank God for Mississippi!"

Although Hillary Rodham Clinton never learned to "Thank God for Mississippi," there is one thing she did learn during her years in Little Rock. You can hear it in her speeches when she is in South Carolina or Georgia or Alabama or anywhere in the Deep South.

Listen for it, *y'all.*

36

HILLARY THE HUNTER

If only Hillary Rodham Clinton could be trusted to tell the truth, it would be a lot easier for me to write this chapter! On second thought, if she told the truth and acted with integrity, I wouldn't have felt compelled to write this book.

I'll do the best I can with what I know about this topic. The issue of gun control is prominently on the table in the 2016 presidential race, so it's important to mention a few things.

Hillary, who claimed to be a lifelong Yankees fan when she was campaigning for the Senate in New York, has also claimed to be a hunter. This was a convenient line to use in Arkansas, and is equally appealing across the Deep South, in the Rockies, and in the Midwest. It could prove problematic to her in other parts of the country where more of the antigun voters congregate.

Hillary has said that her father taught her to hunt. Frankly, that's not what I would consider evidence of the fact. She has lied too often to be believed. In my mind, Hillary is like the little boy who cried wolf. She has lied so often on so many different topics on so many diverse occasions that I'm not naïve enough to believe her on much of anything.

The issue of gun control is certainly problematic, as was the issue of alcohol control during Prohibition. "Those who do not learn from history are doomed to repeat it."

It would be wonderful if we could prevent people from becoming alcoholics by banning alcohol, but anyone living in a dry county knows that we can't.

It would be wonderful if we could prevent psychos from buying guns, but we can't. We don't usually know who the psychos are until they do something psychotic, such as killing dozens of their fellow students.

It would be wonderful if we could prevent family members from shooting each other during domestic disputes at home, but we can't. People who shoot and kill a parent, spouse, or other family member usually have no prior history of violence. Something happened one day, and they snapped. Without a gun, they could have used a candlestick, a knife, a lead pipe, a rope, or a monkey wrench.

It would be wonderful if we could prevent armed robberies of persons and stores after dark, but we can't. Desperate people (and career criminals) will do what they need to do to get what they need to get.

Does anyone believe that Al Capone and his gang would have been without guns if there had been a gun-control law? Take a look at the number of illegal aliens entering the United States every day. Consider the amount of illegal drugs entering the United States every day.

An unprotected border that includes thousands of miles of coastlines is just as open to the illegal importation of guns and ammunition as it is to illegal aliens and drugs.

Don't forget about the shipping container marked "furniture" that was being sent to Muslim refugees in Europe. It was examined by the Greek coast guard and found to be filled with guns and ammunition.

We are being naïve if we think we can stop gun violence by taking guns away from American citizens. Our Founding Fathers put the "right to keep and bear arms" at the top of the Bill of Rights for some very good reasons.

Our Founding Fathers had learned about tyranny firsthand under the reign of King George of England. They pledged their lives, their fortunes, and their sacred honor to form a more perfect union. They were wise and forward thinking. Not perfect, but wise and forward thinking. The right to keep and bear arms is just as important today as it was over two hundred years ago.

Now, many of the gun-control advocates are counting on Hillary Clinton to save us all from gun violence. It will be interesting to watch and listen to her shifting stance on the issue as she travels from state to state around the country.

Billy Clinton was Hillary's model and mentor with this issue. In one of his gubernatorial campaigns, Billy staged a scene in which he was striding manfully across a field with a rifle or shotgun over his shoulder to appeal to the hunters in the state.

Meanwhile, I have a few lingering questions about Hillary the Hunter. One of the first questions is about whether she actually did go duck hunting once in Arkansas, as she claimed. Hillary did tell a fairly elaborate story about it. She claimed that she actually shot and killed a duck. Perhaps some of the men who were on that hunt will step forward to corroborate her report. We all know by now that just because Hillary tells an elaborate story about something doesn't mean it's true.

If Hillary did go hunting and if she did have a license and if she did kill a duck, what is she going to tell PETA? And I don't mean Arkansas's PETA, People Eating Tasty Animals.

There is a pioneer tradition, not only in the South but across this country, of hunting and fishing to put food on the table. The AGFC (Arkansas Game and Fish Commission) establishes hunting seasons and dozens of other regulations. One of the AGFC objectives is for hunters to thin the herds of deer to keep them from dying of starvation, which many deer would otherwise do because of the influx of "civilization" into their habitats.

The AGFC has extensive authority to "search and seize," and it strictly enforces its regulations. If Hillary had gone duck hunting without a license and got caught doing it, she would have had much bigger trouble than she faced for some of her other transgressions.

Remember the stupendous whopper of a lie that Hillary told about dodging sniper fire when she was landing in Bosnia? Remember that she told it repeatedly, but unnecessarily, and with different embellishments?

The sniper fire in Bosnia story was an outlandish, completely fabricated episode that Hillary irrationally insisted was true and accurate. She continued to lie about it until someone finally produced the photographs that forced her to admit that it never happened.

When Hillary is asked by gun-control advocates or PETA supporters about her alleged duck hunt or duck killing in Arkansas, she can assure all of them:

"I had to do it. The duck shot at me first."

37

THE RACE . . . THE PROMISE . . . THE RACE

In 1989, Billy and Hillary had been in the governor's mansion for a total of eight years. He was getting tired of the routine, the hassle, and the frustrations of being the governor of a small Southern state. Billy did not want to run for reelection in 1990.

From time to time, he still expressed his recurring anger at me for "causing" him not to run for president in 1988 when Gary Hart had dropped out of the race. Billy's anger was a result of his usual pattern of finding someone else to blame for everything. I was the bad guy, as far as he was concerned.

The still-young governor of Arkansas was marking time until he could make his move to the White House, but he wanted and needed some time off. Hillary decided that, if Billy didn't run for reelection in 1990, she would run for governor in his place. They conducted a poll, as they generally did before making decisions.

The notable exception to their poll-taking, of course, was Billy's last-minute decision not to enter the presidential race in 1988. His sudden change of plans surprised and infuriated Hillary at the time. Billy was angry too—at me. Yes, I was the bad guy, but I doubt if Billy ever told Hillary about my letter that precipitated his veering off her chosen path.

Much to Hillary's chagrin, she realized from the statewide political poll they took in 1989 that she didn't have a snowball's chance in hell of being elected governor of Arkansas. Despite Hillary's clinging to the coattails of the popular governor and her legal career that was based on his position, she was still disliked by most of the people in the state.

Many people in Arkansas wondered aloud why the handsome and charismatic politician had ever put up with his very unpleasant wife in the first place. Then, as now, people scratched their heads about the Clinton marital situation. Apparently, they never scratched the surface of understanding the dysfunctional dynamics that glued Billy and Hillary together.

The codependent political couple faced a real political dilemma in 1989. The governor's term had been extended by law from its traditional two years to four years. If Billy ran for governor in 1990, his four-year-term would overlap with the 1992 presidential election cycle.

Both Billy and Hillary wanted to get into that presidential race in 1992.

Knowing that Hillary could not be elected governor, they discussed Billy's "sitting out" the 1990 election and taking a couple of years to regroup and prepare for the 1992 presidential race. Of course, they took another poll to make that decision.

This time, rather than polling the people of Arkansas, Billy questioned other governors and politicians around the country. The general consensus was that if he were not in office continually, he would be forgotten and would not be considered a viable candidate for national office.

Therefore, Billy and Hillary announced a reelection bid and dove into the 1990 gubernatorial election with a *promise* to the people of Arkansas: If elected governor in 1990, he promised not to run for president in 1992. They promised to stay in Arkansas and serve the full four-year term.

I knew he was lying.

When Billy announced that he would run for president in 1992, after insisting that the people of Arkansas had "released" him from his promise, news journalist Meredith Oakley of *The Arkansas Democrat* wrote: "His word is dirt."

Well said, Meredith. That goes for Hillary too.

Her word is dirt.

38

WE WILL DESTROY YOU!

It was late January of 1992. I was at a real estate law seminar in San Antonio, Texas. With no premonition of anything unusual, I called home to retrieve my voice messages.

A very British male voice stated that he had researched and prepared a story about my "long-term relationship with Governor Clinton." He left a Dallas callback number.

I was stunned. I almost went into a panic.

Immediately, I phoned Billy's secretary at his state capitol office in Little Rock. She said that Billy left his luncheon meeting in San Antonio and was en route to Houston. After that, he would be flying back to New Hampshire to resume his presidential primary campaign work there.

Billy's secretary asked me what I had told the reporter.

"Nothing. I didn't return his phone call. I have no intention of talking to him, nor to any other reporter, but I want to talk to Billy about it. I didn't ask for this. I don't want to get dragged into it. I certainly don't want to see our story in a tabloid magazine."

I was picturing the recent press conference and tabloid headlines featuring Gennifer (with a *G*) Flowers. I'm sure that Billy's secretary was thinking the same thing. Billy, the teetering presidential candidate, could not withstand another scandal like that.

Gennifer was an attractive blond singer who claimed to have had a twelve-year-long adulterous relationship with Billy Clinton. I knew from the reports that Gennifer lived in a high-rise condominium within easy jogging distance of the governor's mansion. I had no reason to disbelieve her story. It certainly fit with what I knew about Billy's sex addiction.

Billy didn't call me back while I was in San Antonio.

I flew to Dallas and stayed inside, apprehensive that the tabloid reporter might be lurking. A neighbor confirmed my suspicions about that, telling me she had talked to a man with a British accent and that he had spoken to several people on my block. She assured me that she had not told him anything, and I wasn't worried about her anyway because she did not know me very well.

Billy didn't call me back at all. Instead, he passed that chore along to my brother Walter, who was working with him on the campaign in New Hampshire.

Walter is a lawyer (and an engineer) and a pilot who had been helping Billy in his campaigns since the first one when he ran for US Congress in 1974 against the incumbent Republican John Paul Hammerschmidt. Walter had borrowed planes for him and had flown him around the district. He did all he could to help our family friend Billy Clinton from Hot Springs.

Even though he lost the 1974 race, it had been a good start for Billy's public life, and it provided some sound bites that have come back to haunt him:

William Jefferson Clinton on President Nixon:

> Yes, the president should resign. He has lied to the American people, time and time again, and betrayed their trust. He is no longer an effective leader. Since he has admitted guilt,

there is no reason to put the American people through an impeachment. He will serve absolutely no purpose in finishing out his term; the only possible solution is for the President to save some dignity and resign. . . .

No question that an admission of making false statements to government officials and interfering with the FBI is an impeachable offense.... If a President of the United States ever lied to the American people, he should resign.

* * *

As the hours passed with calls only from my brother and not from Billy, it became obvious that the fearless public campaigner was afraid to talk to me. I was upset that Walter was "on the other side."

"I told you I want to talk to Billy!"

"We don't think he should talk on the phone with you. Your line could be tapped."

"You've called enough to satisfy anyone who might have tapped the phones."

"Billy says you've got to deny the story."

"You tell that coward to call me!"

"I'll call you back."

"I bet you will!"

The phone rang a minute later. I picked up the receiver when I heard my brother on the answering machine. One of the male voices in the background was Billy's.

"Billy wants you to deny the story. If you don't deny it, we'll have to destroy you."

"Are you telling me that Billy is threatening to destroy me? Destroy *me*?"

"Listen, Dolly, you have to understand."

"I don't have to understand anything! I'm not running for president! I warned Billy years ago that something like this would happen if he didn't get his act together!"

"Get this," Walter said. "If you cooperate with the media, we *will* destroy you."

Shocked and furious, I slammed down the receiver.

The phone rang ten seconds later, and I grabbed it without screening the call.

"What!?!" I yelled.

A very refined British accent greeted me.

"Is this Ms. Dolly Kyle?"

"Yes. Sorry. I thought you were someone else."

"Thankfully. I have been waiting for your call, Ms. Kyle."

"I was out of town. I didn't intend to talk to you anyway."

"I quite understand, but, Ms. Kyle, I have researched and written a very interesting story concerning your relationship with Governor Clinton. I thought you would like to have the opportunity to confirm or deny it before it is published next week."

I said a silent prayer that I would say the right thing. This polite man with the nice British accent had the power to destroy Billy—and me as well.

I knew that my true story would be credible, and Billy's shaky candidacy could not withstand such publicity. I also didn't want my life and likeness smeared across every newspaper in the country.

"Would it be better to call you at another time? I would prefer to visit in person."

"I don't think that would be a good idea," I said.

"Very well, then, we can speak by telephone."

"All I am prepared to tell you is that Billy Clinton and I have been friends since we were children, and I don't talk to the media about my friends."

"I quite understand, Ms. Kyle. I would simply ask you to consider listening to what I have discovered and help me to make it as accurate as possible. To that end, I shall call you back on the morrow, if I may."

"It won't do you any good. I have nothing to say."

"Nevertheless, I shall call again. Good-bye, Ms. Kyle, and thank you for your time."

I hung up the phone.

Walter kept calling back.

Billy's threats didn't change.

I quit answering the phone.

Shortly after one o'clock in the morning, the phone rang again. I picked up the receiver when I recognized the voice of Billy's younger half-brother, Roger Clinton, on the answering machine.

"What are you doing?" he asked.

"Sleeping. It's what I usually try to do in the middle of the night. Where are you?"

"In Los Angeles, at my place. So, what's new with you?"

"A tabloid finding out about me, as if you didn't know!"

"What are you talking about? Gennifer Flowers?"

"No, Roger. I'm talking about Dolly Kyle."

"I'm sorry, I don't get it. Some Dolly Kyle thing?"

"The story about Billy and me."

"What? Dolly, are you trying to say that you had an affair with my brother Bill?"

I realized that Roger was reading from a script.

"No, Roger, I'm not trying to say anything. *They* are planning to publish the story."

"How could they publish a story? You never had an affair with my brother, Bill!"

"Roger, what are you talking about? Why would you say such a thing?"

"The question is why you would make up a story like that about having an affair with my brother, Bill."

At that point, I was sure that he was recording the call and reading a script. He had never referred to Billy as "my brother, Bill." Roger always called him Big Brother.

"Roger, you have known that Billy and I were in love from the first day we met on the golf course. You were there when we met, and we talked about it more than once. You remember all those conversations in the prison yard on Sundays at the FCI in Fort Worth, don't you?"

"I don't know what you're talking about, Dolly."

I decided that I would have to hit lower.

"Listen, Roger, I realize that you had a $5,000-a-week cocaine habit and dealt drugs to support it, but I thought that at some point in the past ten years you were coherent enough to know what was going on and to remember it. If not, I am truly sorry for you."

"That isn't nice, Dolly."

"And it isn't nice to call me in the middle of the night, trying to make it sound like I'm concocting a story. Do you think I'm an idiot? I know you're recording this. You tell Billy to quit sending little brothers to do his dirty work. You tell him to call me."

"My brother Bill is very busy these days, Dolly. He is running an important campaign to help assure a better future for all American citizens. As much as he would like to have a chance to talk to all the people who remember him from Hot Springs, it's just not possible."

That final script was so aggravating that I hung up the phone and turned off the answering machine. I slept soundly until eight. The British reporter called at ten.

"Ms. Kyle, I realize that you probably think I am a sleaze because I am working for a tabloid magazine. I assure you that I am a responsible, professional, freelance journalist. I have been researching your story for the better part of the past month in Little Rock, Hot Springs, and Dallas. Frankly, I am fascinated with the story of your life."

I figured he would say anything to get a quote, but I said nothing. With seeming embarrassment, he offered a huge sum of money, but, in his next breath, he added that he knew the money would have no bearing on my decision to cooperate.

He had learned enough about me to know that I would not sell out my integrity for any amount of money. He was so correct and polite, and his voice was so compelling that I couldn't hang up.

"Of course, I began my research because of the candidacy of Governor Clinton, but I must say, Ms. Kyle, that you should write a book. Your life story is infinitely more varied and unusual than his. And there is one thing about you that truly amazes me."

"Okay, I'll bite on that one. What truly amazes you?"

"Not one person with whom I spoke had anything negative to say about you other than your inexplicable attraction and devotion to Mr. Clinton."

"Surely my ex-husband had something negative to say."

"Allow me to check my notes for a moment. Ah, yes, here it is. He said that his ex-wife is the most beautiful, intelligent, talented, and interesting woman he has ever known. She is a devoted mother, an excellent lawyer, a concerned citizen, and a loyal friend."

"He said all that?"

"Yes, quite enthusiastically, I must say. But, he added some things which in my gut I did not believe."

"Such as?"

"He said that Governor Clinton broke up your marriage."

I smiled to myself. Surely, he didn't think I would take that bait. I remained silent. After a moment, he continued.

"I have enough corroboration to print that in the story. My gut feeling, however, is that it is not accurate. Could you help me on that one, Ms. Kyle?"

I laughed out loud.

"I told you yesterday that I wouldn't comment on your story. However, I will say that, as a general rule, I believe people should go with their gut feelings."

"Thank you, Ms. Kyle. Would you like to hear the rest of the story I have written?"

I couldn't help myself. Curiosity prevailed.

"You may tell me what you have, but I will not comment either way."

"Very well then, here's what I have,"

I listened in quiet astonishment. When he finished his report, I had to bite my tongue to keep from saying, 'Damn! You're good!'

"Would you care to confirm or deny any parts of the story as I have reported it, Ms. Kyle?"

He should be calling me 'Dolly," I thought. He knows me better than most people.

"As I said earlier, Billy and I have been friends since we were children, and I don't talk to the media about my friends."

"I do understand, Ms. Kyle, and I thank you for your time. I also hope that someday you will write the whole story from your perspective. It would be fascinating."

After hanging up the phone, I contemplated the reporter's story. I knew I would be targeted by Billy and his cronies for cooperating with the media when I had not done any such thing.

Billy was needlessly afraid that I would tape record our conversation. He was foolishly afraid that I would cooperate with the media. He was irrationally afraid that I would try to destroy him.

The man who would someday have his finger on the nuclear trigger was so full of fear that he overlooked or distorted some very important facts:

1. I had maintained our open secret for decades;

2. I had called Billy simply to warn him, not threaten him; and

3. I would continue to avoid the media, as I always had (though not just for him).

This situation was a microcosm of the problems arising from the faulty judgment that the whole world would someday see in this man. Perhaps, if the fearful draft-dodging Billy Clinton had spent time in the military, he would have been equipped to choose the right weapons. In this case, a telephone conversation would have worked well.

But, no.

What was the presidential-candidate-soon-to-be-the-most-powerful-man-in-the-world's best solution to a perceived obstacle to his ambition? It was not a personal phone call to his friend-lover-confidante of the past thirty-two years.

Instead, Billy set the tone for the future by having my own brother call me to convey his threat:

"If you cooperate with the media, we will destroy you."

39

HILLARY THE HUCKSTER

Hillary was furious, and with good reason this time. The tabloid story about Billy's affair with Gennifer Flowers was starting to get some traction with the mainstream media. Hillary frantically worked on a plan to save their presidential campaign. Her White House hopes were hanging by a thread.

Billy still hadn't called me directly and my brother finally gave up because I wasn't answering his repeated attempts to talk to me again.

I should not have been surprised when my sister called.

As usual, she went straight to the point.

"This tabloid mess with Gennifer Flowers is getting out of hand. Billy needs your help."

"The last thing I heard from Billy was that they were going to destroy me."

"Not if you help. Hillary has come up with a plan."

"What's the plan?" I asked, although I really didn't want to know.

"She has arranged to have an interview on the television show *60 Minutes,* and she wants you to be on there with her—and Billy."

"What? Are y'all crazy?"

"No. Here's Hillary's plan, and they're on the other line to answer any questions you might have. The three of you go on television together and explain that you have been friends for decades. Say that you and Billy were girlfriend-boyfriend in high school, and that your close relationship continued as adults."

"Wait a minute! What about Gennifer Flowers?" I asked. "I thought *she* was the problem."

"They will deny everything about Gennifer Flowers, and then they will turn the focus on Billy's relationship with you. It will get all the attention after that, and everyone will forget about Gennifer Flowers. Billy says that yours is the only relationship he ever had that made any sense."

"Did Hillary hear him say that?"

"I don't think Hillary cares what he says, just so they get out of this mess without losing the election. There is so much good stuff about you, all the years you've been around, the family connections, tons of pictures from parties and stuff with both families. The media will go into a feeding frenzy over all that."

"I don't like the idea of being part of a feeding frenzy!"

"Just listen. It won't be that bad. Hillary will say that she knew about your affair with Billy, that all is confessed, all is forgiven, and y'all are still friends. Okay, the show is set for Sunday night. Will you do it?"

"No, I won't do it! They want *me* to be the scapegoat for everything? After they threatened to destroy me? No! No, I'm not going to do it."

"Listen to me, Dolly. Please. Do the *60 Minutes* show with them. Otherwise, if that tabloid publishes the truth about you and Billy, then there won't be any option. Hillary and Billy will have to destroy you."

* * *

I was very upset with my brother and sister. My sister redeemed herself rather quickly, though. It's somewhat amusing now, after all this time, to think that Billy was so concerned about *my* taping his phone calls. I guess it never occurred to him that my little sister, who is also a lawyer, would tape every call he made to her.

My sister cleverly used those tapes as a peace offering to me, and all was forgiven. We talk nearly every day now. I don't know if she's still recording.

* * *

Hillary and Billy made their big fake appearance together on *60 Minutes*, both lying through their teeth about Gennifer Flowers and the other women. The interviewer didn't seem to believe them, but he didn't have any proof, so all he could do was keep repeating questions about marital infidelities.

My name was not mentioned by any of them on the *60 Minutes* interview, and, fortunately, the tabloid guy didn't run the truth that he had uncovered about Billy and me.

Hillary and Billy's later attempts to destroy me ran the gamut from planting false stories in national publications to pretending that I didn't exist. Billy would later lie about me under oath in a federal lawsuit, and he would suborn perjury to get another person to lie about me too.

Some of those lies and attacks formed the basis for Billy's impeachment charges, but I'm getting ahead of myself again.

Despite my decades-long relationship with Billy Clinton, I did not deserve to be the scapegoat for every consensual sexual affair he ever had. I did not deserve to be the scapegoat and a diversion from every nonconsensual sexual attack that Billy perpetrated on women and girls. (At that point in 1992, I still did not know that Billy was a rapist, a serial sexual abuser, and that he would become an enthusiastic and regular visitor to "Orgy Island" in the company of underage girls.)

Hillary knew exactly what she was doing. She could not have cared less what sort of impact her devious plan might have on me, not to mention on Gennifer Flowers, who was the original target for this particular attack. I'm not sure I ever discovered the full extent of Hillary's attacks on me because she used various publications to do her dirty work of discrediting me. There appears to be no limit to what Hillary will do to destroy her perceived enemies. I wonder how long it will take her female supporters to realize that they are not her "longtime friends" any more than I was. They are votes for her, pure and simple.

In her speeches and on her website, without giving any evidence of what she has done, Hillary states that she has been *fighting for* women for over forty years. She is confused again. She has been *attacking* women for over forty years.

Try to confront Hillary, or ask her nicely, about how she has attacked the women who had sex with her husband. See if she ever invites you over for tea and cookies after that.

40

PERUSING PEROT

I lived for thirty years in relative proximity to Ross Perot in the sprawling metroplex of Dallas, Texas. However, the billionaire and I visited only at our nearby yogurt stop when we happened to indulge in a frozen treat at the same time—usually in mid-afternoon. Our occasional talks were casual and shallow, as you would expect from people standing in line waiting for a double-chocolate yogurt in a cup with strawberries on top and a long spoon, please.

On the other hand, I have a friend who was deeply involved in the 1992 presidential campaign. He has shared with me some of his up-close and personal observations of the "eccentric billionaire," as the media insisted on describing Perot. Yogi Berra, the iconic baseball catcher, might have said of the 2016 presidential race: "It's *déjà vu* all over again."

The mainstream media have shown a blatant bias toward candidates of the Democratic Party for as long as I can remember. I was somewhat surprised, therefore, that the mainstream media used every opportunity to denigrate Ross Perot who entered the 1992 race as an independent.

It appeared to me that most of the potential Perot support would be pulled away from the Republican Party and its nominee, the incumbent President George H. W. Bush. Thus, a Perot candidacy would be good for the Democratic Party at the final tally.

I would never accuse the mainstream media of thinking logically, however. Therefore, as a whole, they may not have analyzed their knee-jerk reaction to a non-Democratic candidate.

In 2015, when Donald Trump announced his candidacy for the Republican presidential nomination, the billionaire was not taken very seriously by the media and regular folks across the country—including me. To say that Trump was denounced by the media as eccentric is to put it mildly. Granted, in all fairness, Trump is a larger-than-life character with amazing name recognition due to his television shows.

Donald Trump is bombastic and in-your-face and highly opinionated. The word *eccentric* fits him quite well, but not necessarily in the negative way that it was used for Ross Perot.

Ross was a little guy, with big ears, and a nasally voice that reminded me of a fake Texas accent in a cheaply made cowboy movie. Perot was attacked by the media for his lack of integrity—an amazing paradox as the media ignored every piece of evidence pointing to Billy and Hillary Clintons' lack of integrity.

Billy Clinton ended up winning the 1992 presidential election, with his and Hillary's "two for the price of one" campaign. After his inauguration, Billy and his "co-president" Hillary proceeded to act with the same type of dictatorial arrogance that they displayed in his first term as governor of Arkansas in 1979. Billy and Hillary based their arrogance on their self-proclaimed "mandate" from the people that put him into office.

The numbers, which I have rounded slightly for ease of illustration, tell a different story about the votes:

BILL CLINTON   45,000,000

GEORGE BUSH   40,000,000

ROSS PEROT   20,000,000

If those numbers look like a Clinton "mandate" to you, I respectfully suggest that you take another look at a junior high math book.

* * *

I have to admit that I did go to Billy's inauguration in January 1993. I can't really say for sure if I would have traveled to Washington solely for the inauguration, but I was going to be in the capital for a housing seminar anyway, and I decided to stay for the festivities.

Some of you may be interested to know that I wore my still-favorite navy-blue evening gown that I had worn to Billy's 1985 gubernatorial inaugural ball. I was quite surprised to see its similarity to Hillary's 1993 inaugural gown. I wondered why the photographer had taken so many pictures of me at Hillary's bidding at the governor's mansion that night in 1985.

There were about a dozen different inaugural balls, and I attended several of them, as many people did. I avoided a face-to-face encounter with Hillary and Billy that night, although I did run into Virginia quite unexpectedly at one of the balls.

Virginia was having an uproariously good time "dancing" with Dr. Ruth. The tiny (less than five feet tall) sex therapist Dr. Ruth Westheimer was the 1980s version of today's Dr. Phil or Dr. Oz. She was a hoot.

Roger Clinton sang a newly composed song (I think it was at that same ball where I saw Virginia and Dr. Ruth) that was billed as a tribute to his mother. It was something about having sons who were now the president and a "rock star." Although Big Brother had been inaugurated as president, Roger never did quite become a rock star.

In retrospect, I'm glad I went to the inauguration. It was fun to run into old friends from Arkansas who seemed to have taken over the capitol that week. More importantly, I still had tender feelings for the little boy I had met on the golf course in Hot Springs in 1959. It is always good to see people whom we know succeed at something important to them. I think it gives us all a kind of hope and encouragement that anything is possible.

41

CHANGING OF THE GUARD

Every four years in the United States, a president takes the oath of office and begins a new term at noon on January 20. Billy and Hillary Clinton did arrive on time for the swearing-in ceremony, but they had been nearly a half hour late for their official entry into the White House a couple of hours earlier.

The outgoing President George H. W. Bush and First Lady Barbara Bush had been waiting on the North Portico of the White House for twenty-seven minutes beyond their scheduled meeting at 10:00 a.m. when the Clintons finally arrived.

It was one thing for Billy to be late for our "after-date dates" in high school. It was bad enough for him to have me hold that plane for him when he was running for Congress in 1974, not caring about how much he might be inconveniencing the other passengers and the crew.

It was another thing entirely for Billy and Hillary to be late for the formal ritual of the changing of the guard between the families leaving and entering the White House. This very public show of tardiness was only the first of thousands of times that both of the Clintons showed their disrespect for the people's house as well as for any people who did not appear ready to provide some immediate benefit to them.

The Clintons saw Washington as a place of intrigue and calculation where powerful people would maneuver for position and would worry endlessly about who is in and who is out, who is up and who is down, forgetting the people whose toil and sweat sends them there and pays their way.

Where did I hear such negative and pessimistic ideas held by the Clintons about the seat of our federal government? All that is in Billy Clinton's First Inaugural Address.

A new administration always brings some kind of change, but there is also a process of comforting continuity in the United States government. Much of that comforting continuity is provided by those behind-the-scenes people who serve in the White House and in numerous other government offices from one administration to the next. The butlers, the cooks, the housekeepers, the clerks, the service people in the White House perform their necessary but unsung roles without fanfare year after year after year, regardless of politics.

People working in the White House do serve "at the pleasure of the president," but it has always been understood that their jobs are secure. People who work in the White House may personally like one president and his family more than another one, but their jobs are not political positions. They are career professionals, performing their jobs well. From what I can tell, they serve loyally and have a strong sense of pride in their work as well as respect for the positions that they hold.

I have heard it said that if a corporate CEO takes off for two weeks, it doesn't matter much around the office. If the janitor takes off for two weeks, there will be problems. Try to imagine the chaos that would ensue if every staff position in Washington changed every four years!

When Billy Dale arrived at work in the White House on May 19, 1993, he wasn't expecting anything unusual. President Bill and First

Lady Hillary Clinton had been living in the White House for less than six months; Billy Dale had been working there for over thirty years.

If the Clintons had wanted Billy Dale to leave, they could have simply requested his resignation. It would have been unusual to do such a thing, but it was allowed because Billy Dale and his staff of six were, as always, serving "at the pleasure of the president."

Billy Dale, however, happened to be in the wrong place at the wrong time.

Hillary Clinton wanted to give his job to Clinton friend Harry Thomason. Harry was a nice guy from Little Rock, a former high school football coach who had decided that he wanted to go into the movie business. Harry had checked out a book from the library to find out how to do it, and he proceeded to follow his dream. Within a few years, Harry was succeeding in the film industry.

Harry Thomason had a few interesting financial issues along the way to his Hollywood success, including a lawsuit filed against him by Federal Express for unpaid invoices. I don't know how or why Harry was able to get the money to produce movies but couldn't afford the FedEx fees to distribute the films, but that's what happened.

The judgment against Harry that was awarded to Federal Express resulted in garnishments on those involved in his coproduced miniseries *The Blue and The Gray*. That was a minor skirmish, however, compared to the controversy that would come later.

Harry married Linda Bloodworth from Missouri and went into business with her. In addition to film and television, Harry and his partner and friend Darnell Martens had an air charter service. In the 1992 presidential campaign, the partners not only flew the Clintons around the country, but acted as image consultants for them as well.

Hillary made no secret in Arkansas of her annoyance at the Hollywood types who were always trying to change her looks.

One of Harry's biggest contributions was producing an adulatory biographical film about Billy Clinton's life titled *The Man from Hope*. That film, by the way, is what confused a lot of people about where Billy grew up. As a reminder, he was born in Hope, Arkansas, but moved to Hot Springs when his mother married Roger Clinton, Sr. Billy was educated from the second grade through high school in Hot Springs. The film was shown as an introduction for Billy at the Democratic National Convention in 1992.

After the election, Harry served on the inaugural committee and made himself generally helpful to his friends the Clintons. Harry asked Hillary to return the favors by letting his air charter service take over the business of the White House travel office. Harry was also looking at procuring some other government contracts.

The details became murky, as frequently happens around the Clintons. Catherine Cornelius, one of Billy Clinton's distant "cousins" related to his putative "father" Bill Blythe, wanted to take over the White House Travel Office.

Hillary Clinton circumvented all the normal procedures for the firing of White House personnel. She didn't even contact the Justice Department, which would have been the standard procedure to use if any irregularities were suspected.

Instead, Hillary instigated an FBI investigation of Billy Dale and his handling of the travel office, after his thirty years on the job. On May 19, 1993, Billy and his staff were fired.

The firing of Billy Dale and the staff was not enough for Hillary, who prefers to destroy her perceived enemies. Billy Dale was removed from the White House like a common criminal. He was taken outside and made to sit on the floor of an FBI paneled van that had no seats in the back.

That was still not enough to satisfy Hillary. Eighteen months later, Billy Dale was indicted on embezzlement charges. Hillary wanted to make sure that he was disgraced forever so that no one would question her original motives.

Hillary didn't count on the fact that Billy Dale would file a lawsuit to protest his unfair treatment and the false accusations made by Hillary, so that Harry Thomason could take over the White House travel office. After lengthy proceedings five of the former employees were reinstated in government jobs and transferred to other departments in the executive branch; Billy and another senior staffer were allowed to retire.

For simplicity, here's what happened with the criminal charges against Billy Dale:

Jury trial: 13 days.

Jury deliberation: 2 hours.

Jury verdict: Not guilty.

It was nearly two years from the date of the firing until the acquittal of Billy Dale by a jury. In the meantime, Billy Dale and the other fired employees from his staff had incurred substantial attorney fees and costs.

House Report 104-484, accompanying H.R. 2937, printed by the U.S. Government Publishing Office, sets forth the circumstances of the firings of Billy Dale and his staff, the reimbursement of fees and costs for the terminated employees, etc.

In part:

"After the May 19, 1993, firings, several months of independent review and oversight hearings uncovered the actual motivation for this action. Certain individuals, wishing to advance their own personal agendas and financial self-interest, attempted to destroy the reputations of these employees by accusations of kickbacks and wrongdoing. White House staff and volunteers apparently misused their authority and initiated an F.B.I. investigation using unorthodox methods. The investigation was based on accusations made by persons with a direct interest in Travel Office employment or Travel Office business."

Reimbursement for former White House Travel Office employee Billy Dale: $425,991.76.

Thus, Hillary's attempt to pay back Harry Thomason for his favors (by giving him what would have been a lucrative White House Travel Office contract) backfired terribly. I don't know if Hillary knew that Billy Clinton was also beholden to Harry for a very personal favor.

According to talk in Arkansas, when it came to light that former Miss America Elizabeth Ward Gracen had accused Billy Clinton of raping her, she was whisked off to Canada via the air charter services of Harry Thomason. Elizabeth later changed her story to say that her sexual encounter with Billy Clinton was consensual. (Of course, most of the women who were threatened by Hillary and her goons changed their stories over time.)

The typically uncreative mainstream media called this disruption of the lives of loyal government employees Travelgate. The mainstream media pooh-poohed it as some little tempest in a teapot, as the Clintons still do to this day.

If you were fired from your job and had to spend nearly a half-million dollars in legal fees to defend yourself from false accusations of fraud and mismanagement, I hope you would set off your own tempest in a teapot. I hope you could find a lawyer to help you. I hope that your life would eventually get back to normal. I hope that you never have to suffer from a "transparently political prosecution," as the *L.A. Times* called the action that Hillary initiated against Billy Dale and his staff.

After all that, in an irony that would fit quite nicely in a Harry Thomason film, the White House Travel Office was temporarily run by Federal Express Travel Services.

42

JUST ANOTHER SUICIDE

In earlier chapters I wrote about growing up in Hot Springs and about some of the abnormal happenings there, at least as compared to daily events on Main Street, USA. There is no doubt that the nothing-is-quite-as-it-seems background that Billy Clinton and I shared had a great influence on us as we grew from children to teenagers to adults.

I remember hearing some wild stories about the Garland County coroner when I was very young. I don't remember his name and I don't know if the stories are true or not. The truth is not so important in this instance as the fact that stories like this became folklore; as folklore, these tales can add some understanding of the cultural milieu in which we were raised.

Such reports may not be any truer than "the bogeyman will get you," but the effect on the audience is what matters. I was part of the audience back then. These things are what we heard—and believed.

Reminder: Gambling in Hot Springs (other than pari-mutuel

betting on horses at the track) was illegal, but casinos were wide open. Everyone from the local police to the governor of the state was "on the take" to maintain the status quo.

In addition to the casinos, there were also private, high-stakes poker games attended by both locals and well-connected out-of-towners. The big games frequently took place in the rooms above the popular clubs all over town.

I had often heard that there were "ladies of the night" upstairs above the various clubs too, but it was a long time before I had any idea what that phrase meant.

Then as now, the Garland County coroner had to be notified of all deaths that are not from natural causes and all deaths from natural causes that are not attended by a physician.

As the story goes, one Saturday night, the coroner was called to the Southern Club to take a look at the body of a guy who had been found dead in an upstairs room above the casino. The Southern Club, by the way, was across the street from the Arlington Hotel, where Al Capone always stayed, but this was after the Capone era.

Anyway, the coroner and his assistant clomped up the stairs to the designated room above the Southern Club's casino. The coroner had some guys with a stretcher who were there to carry the body downstairs and take it to the morgue after he made his ruling. The coroner took one look at the face-down body of a fully-clothed man sprawled on the wood floor, and announced: "Death by natural causes."

The coroner told his guys to take out the body. When they lifted the dead man and turned him over to put him on the stretcher, one of the attendants asked the coroner, "What do you want me to do with this knife in the guy's gut?"

"You can keep it," the coroner answered. "I have plenty."

The other story that I heard about that same coroner had to do with a similar dead body found above another club at another time. The guy was found face up with a small caliber pistol in his right hand.

"Suicide" was the coroner's immediate ruling.

It was the men preparing the body at the funeral home who found two bullet wounds in the guy's back. The coroner was never interested in revising his original opinions. True or not, that's a Hot Springs story.

You know where this chapter is going, but it's critical to understand more about the background in Arkansas if you care to look at it from my perspective—and from the perspective of many other Arkansans.

The state sport of Arkansas when I was a kid was Razorback football. Weddings, birthday parties, and even funerals in the fall were planned around Razorback game days.

The other pastime was gossip.

I'm not saying that Arkansans could outdo all the other Southerners in the speed of spreading the latest rumors, but they could certainly hold their own. I'm talking about the olden days before we all had cell phones.

Two examples will suffice to set up my ultimate point.

I mentioned previously that Billy Clinton and I were single and were seeing each other in 1974 while he was running for Congress and I was preparing to move to Dallas with my children to go to law school at SMU.

At the end of January, the required time had elapsed for my divorce to become final in Pulaski County. I went to my lawyer's office in downtown Little Rock. I signed the papers, picked up the cashier's check that represented a property settlement agreement, walked across the street, and opened an account in one of the largest banks in Arkansas. I thought that would provide the best chance of maintaining confidentiality. I opened my new bank account with the cashier's check and drove home.

My phone was ringing as I walked in the door.

"You settled too cheap!" exclaimed a friend who had already heard the amount.

The other incident that I will mention to make my point about Arkansas gossip occurred several years later, starting in Dallas. I was involved in a Texas legal matter with a lawyer, and he understood that it was extremely confidential.

That said, I gave him permission to tell a lawyer in Little Rock who would need to be involved later. I left my lawyer's office, drove home, and answered a phone call from my irate younger sister in Little Rock.

"I can't believe what I just heard!" She berated me for not telling her the news first.

Turns out my lawyer in Dallas had called the lawyer in Little Rock. The lawyer in Little Rock, who should have maintained total confidentiality, told another lawyer who was heading to the courthouse. That lawyer ran into another member of his firm at the courthouse and told him about it. Their conversation was overheard by a judge who knew my sister, so he called her at her law firm, and she called me.

Elapsed time from the confidential conversation in Dallas to the irate phone call from my sister in Little Rock? Under thirty minutes.

* * *

Vince Foster died on July 20, 1993.

Vince was the deputy White House counsel at the time.

A childhood friend of Billy Clinton and a former partner of Hillary Clinton at the Rose Law Firm in Little Rock, Vince Foster knew the facts about Hillary's double-billing practices that had enabled her to receive questionable foreign money with strings attached.

Vince Foster knew all about Whitewater and the Clinton partnership with the McDougals.

Vince Foster knew all about Hillary's ordering the firing of the White House Travel Office staff and her vicious attacks on Billy Dale, using the FBI to do her dirty work.

Vince Foster knew about FBI files that had been taken illegally for illegal purposes and would later be found with Hillary's fingerprints on them.

Vince Foster was painfully involved in the Branch Davidian Massacre in Waco, Texas. Hillary had pushed Vince to end the fifty-day standoff there because it was giving the co-presidents a lot of bad national publicity. Rather than starve them out, Hillary wanted something done about the situation immediately.

As a direct result of Hillary's political maneuvering, seventy-four men, women, and children died violently at the hands of the US government. Hillary was unfazed by the deaths there; she had achieved what she wanted, and she counted on Americans to forget about it as old news after a month or two.

Vince Foster, on the other hand, was devastated when he heard about the enormity of the conflagration—and the children burned alive—on his watch.

I believe that Vince Foster was a man of integrity, despite his friendship with Billy and Hillary Clinton. I believe that Vince was about to resign because of what he had seen in his first six months of the Clinton copresidency. I believe that his resignation would have raised a lot of probing questions.

Vince Foster spent the weekend before his death at the home of big-time Democratic operative Nathan Landow.

Kathleen Willey would be taken to that same home of Nathan Landow over a weekend to be pressured into silence after she reported that Billy Clinton had sexually assaulted her in the Oval Office. Kathleen had enough to deal with in her life after the death of her husband; she was not going to continue talking about Clinton's assault on her.

Vince, on the other hand, more than likely responded to the weekend pressure by giving voice to his concerns about ethics and morality and the right thing to do. That would not have been comforting to the co-presidents when they heard Landow's report about the weekend meeting with Vince, who died two days later.

Hillary Clinton's White House assistants removed boxes of files from Vince Foster's office before the possible crime scene could be examined by those investigating his death.

Vince Foster's office safe was opened and emptied by Hillary's people.

Vince Foster's death was ruled to be a suicide.

No, I do not believe that Vince Foster committed suicide.

You don't have to believe what I believe, but know this. The news of Vince Foster's death was being talked about in beauty shops here in Little Rock before his dead body was found in Fort Marcy Park.

43

CLINTONS AND THE PLANTATION MENTALITY

The "plantation mentality" is not limited to a particular ethnic heritage or skin color. The term derives from the situation in the American South after the War between the States (aka the Civil War), but it now affects people of all colors.

It's necessary to understand something about history to understand the origin of the term "plantation mentality." After the African slaves in America were "freed" by the Emancipation Proclamation in 1863, most of them left the plantations where they had been working in the homes and in the cotton fields for nothing more than food, clothing, and shelter in slaves' quarters.

Their plight, of course, soon became obvious. Most of them had nowhere to go, no jobs, no connections, no ability to make a fresh start. The notion of giving the freed slaves "forty acres and a mule" would come a couple of years later, after the war ended.

Those free forty-acre plots were to come from four hundred

thousand acres of land to be confiscated from plantation owners. Here is the big catch: that land was to be located in swamps and backwaters from South Carolina to Florida *and* it was to be occupied and governed *only* by freed slaves and their families. Has anyone noticed the parallel with the Indian reservations provided to Native American tribes?

After coming to grips with their plight, some of the freed slaves moved to the North, but many of them went back to the plantations that they knew—and, in many cases, loved. Whites and blacks in the South had to face a complete restructuring of their lives in the aftermath of the War. They had to work together just to survive.

The freed slaves still looked to the plantation owners for food, clothing, and shelter because the plantation owners had been the managers of everything. Raising cotton was a big business that involved seeding, growing, harvesting, shipping, warehousing, and exporting to other countries. Plantations were businesses, not just places to sip mint juleps on the porch, as you might see in the movies.

Freed slaves and former owners banded together to get back to business. It's impossible to say what might have transpired if the reconstruction process had not been sabotaged by carpetbaggers from the North who invaded the conquered Southern territory to make their own fortunes.

It is not surprising that Hillary Rodham Clinton from Chicago has been called a carpetbagger by more than one cynical observer in Arkansas.

* * *

If you are a person of any color who believes that the government owes you a place to live and food to eat and a monthly stipend to buy clothing, electronics, and cars, then you have adopted a plantation mentality.

The missing piece is that the freed slaves who went back to the plantations actually worked for their upkeep. They looked to the owner of the plantation for management, for guidance, for establishing the business plan, for protecting them from outside harm, and for whatever other needs might arise, but they did work. When they got old and sick, the better plantation owners took care of them.

It has been over 150 years since the slaves were freed. There are untold numbers of inspirational stories about what the freed slaves and many of their descendants did with their lives. They made valuable contributions to science, art, literature, music, education, business, philosophy, politics, and to the economy of the country. In the process of doing that, they had to shed the plantation mentality—and they did.

Unfortunately, the plantation mentality was adopted by other groups and it persists to this day. It is a cyclical, self-defeating attitude that destroys the potential of hundreds of thousands of people of every race and ethnicity who are born into it and accept it without question.

Some politicians (go ahead and call them carpetbaggers) continue to foster and support this plantation mentality by promising, and sometimes providing, the handouts that keep dependent people dependent. They provide no plan to help the recipients mature into contributing members of society.

Such politicians want only the votes that dependent people will give them; the only way to keep the votes is to keep the people dependent.

Yes, there are people in dire straits who do need help and should receive it, but I am now addressing the issue of the able-bodied people who need to receive what has become a cliché: a hand up, and not a handout.

Before you accuse me of being selfish or of not understanding the situation, please know that I worked for nearly ten years in the area of low-income housing in Dallas and across the state of Texas, as well as presenting my ideas at national conferences. Billy Clinton, when he was president (admittedly, with some ulterior motives), asked me to take my model program Lawyers for Affordable Housing (LAH) to Washington and incorporate the concepts into HUD (the Department of Housing and Urban Development).

As the founder (and the first-year funder) of Lawyers for Affordable Housing, I recruited over 350 volunteer real estate lawyers, including every African-American and every Hispanic real estate lawyer in Dallas, to provide *pro bono* housing services for low-income people.

The minority lawyers also served as role models and mentors for people of their own ethnicities. LAH provided much-needed education in the low-income communities about the rights and responsibilities of home ownership, and provided free Wills Clinics to ensure a legally-proper but inexpensive transfer of title at death.

For low-income persons living in housing with governmental rent assistance, we worked to instill an understanding that it was a temporary place to stay while getting life in order. It should not be a lifelong confinement to quarters under a plantation mentality.

* * *

Hillary and Billy Clinton have fostered and exploited a plantation mentality focused on African-Americans. Since their first days in politics, the Clintons have been very successful in their big con of this large group of people because, frankly, they are extraordinarily good liars.

The Clintons campaigned for the presidency in 1992 with several slogans that those of us who were around then can remember quite well. The following quotes are the ones that had the greatest negative impact on African-Americans:

CLINTON QUOTATION #1
"Two for the price of one."

FOLLOW-UP #1
Billy and Hillary Clinton billed themselves as an inseparable team, assuring us that the combination would be a great benefit to the American people. Their "two for the price of one" campaign slogan did not include an estimate of the ultimate cost of that big discount!

Remember that nothing on sale is a bargain if you don't need it. As a result of this "two-fer" campaign, Hillary considered herself to be the co-president from 1993 to 2000. Remember her famous statement, "We *are* the president"? Could we argue that she has already had her eight years?

Hillary the co-president parlayed her First Lady years in the White House into a Senate seat and then the office of secretary of state. The American people are still paying for this bargain deal, and many are beginning to wonder if Hillary ever had any positive accomplishments of her own.

Hillary didn't have a snowball's chance in hell of being elected governor of Arkansas. She would not have been elected to the Senate without Billy's coattails. I have not seen any evidence of anything positive that she has contributed on her own, especially to African-Americans.

As the 2016 presidential race gets more heated and as Hillary becomes more desperate to hang on to the undeserved support from African-Americans, she will probably talk about making reparations for slavery.

Reparations for slavery is a completely degrading notion to black people, 150 years after the War and slavery ended! If Hillary wants to insult African-Americans any more than she already has by talking about them as nothing but votes and implying that they are too pitiful to make it on their own after 150 years of freedom in America, then let her pay those reparations from her own pocket.

CLINTON QUOTATION #2
"We will end welfare as we know it."

FOLLOW-UP #2
This campaign promise was the Clintonese version of, "Don't worry, white folks. I'm going to protect you from those bad African-American ghetto-dwellers who scam your tax dollars for their welfare checks."

Yes, yes, I know about welfare statistics. As Mark Twain said, "There are lies, damn lies, and statistics." The Clintons have used lies, damn lies, *and* statistics to con Americans of all ethnicities and every socio-economic status.

The Clintons have waged a subterranean race war while accusing others of racism. They are extraordinarily good at this particular con game, and they will call *me* a racist for pointing out the facts about *their* racism.

The Clinton welfare reform policy had a devastating effect on African-Americans throughout the country, especially when individual states adopted versions of the federal bill. Clinton's punitive welfare reform had the net effect of causing more poverty and more hunger for American children, and there was no Clinton plan to give their families a "hand up" to improve their lives.

African-Americans might realize the truth of this deception by the Clintons if it were taught in schools, or reported by the mainstream media, or preached from the pulpits in their churches on Sundays. Instead, most black preachers are mindlessly supporting the Clintons and following the divisive example of people like the "Reverend" Jesse Jackson, whom the Clintons refer to in private as "that G**damned nigger."

CLINTON QUOTATION #3
"Three strikes and you're out."

FOLLOW-UP #3
The co-president Clinton's crime bill added dozens of new categories of death-penalty crimes. That was no surprise to anyone from Arkansas. We knew that Billy Clinton, the presidential candidate in 1992, had flown back to Arkansas right before the pivotal New Hampshire primary to sanction the execution of Ricky Ray Rector.

Ricky Ray Rector was a black man who was so mentally challenged that he didn't have a clue what was happening to him. Allegorically, Ricky Ray could have been one of the slower kids at the Easter Egg Hunt at the governor's mansion when First Lady Hillary Clinton demanded, "When are they going to get those f***ing ree-tards out of here?"

Ricky Ray enjoyed his last meal before his execution. Since he was in the habit of eating dessert right before bed, he politely asked that his dessert might be saved for later.

After Ricky Ray Rector was executed without his dessert, Billy

Clinton proudly announced, "No one can say I'm soft on crime."

The "three strikes" law that the Clintons loved so much caused the near lifelong incarceration of multiple thousands of African-American males. There are over 2.5 million people in prison now, although the Clintons have avoided jail time so far.

More than 150,000 inmates are serving life sentences largely because of the Clinton "three strikes" rule. It did not matter if the crimes were petty ones such as drug possession or major felonies like armed robbery.

"Three strikes and you're out" meant a life in prison for the third offense, whatever it was. When a defendant was white and wealthy and could afford competent legal counsel, there would hardly ever be a third strike. There would rarely be even a second strike for the white kid.

The good statistic that the Clintons found in their "lock 'em up and throw away the key" solution to crime was that, on the economic side, they could claim credit for less unemployment. That's right.

The Clintons claimed economic progress because there was less unemployment in America. Employment was up! The unemployment numbers actually did go down, but that was partly because the young black males in prison were no longer counted as unemployed. In fact, by the Clintons, those young black males were no longer counted for anything at all.

CLINTON QUOTATION #4

"America is in trouble. Our people are hurting. The rich keep getting richer and the politicians seem to be taking care of themselves."

FOLLOW-UP #4

When the Clintons left the White House in 2000, Hillary stated that they were "dead broke." Fifteen years later, the Clintons had a net worth (estimated by *Forbes*) of $80 million.

From zero to $80 million in fifteen years is quite impressive. It would be nice if the Clintons shared information about how to make such individual economic progress with the people who are still picking cotton for a living—or doing time in prison without any real hope for a better life when they leave their government-provided housing.

When the Clintons left their government housing, they stole over $200,000 in furnishings from the White House. Those furnishings belonged to the people of the United States.

If the Clintons had stolen furniture and accoutrements like that in my neighborhood, had loaded their loot in a truck, and had been caught due to the security cameras around here, they would definitely have served prison time.

Ask the Clintons about that particular $200,000 crime now. They will tell you it's old news.

I wonder how many African-American males are serving life sentences for three crimes of stealing that did not total even 10 percent of what the Clintons stole on their way out of the White House.

CLINTON QUOTATION #5:

The unspoken promises: Some of the 1992 Clinton-Gore campaign buttons had a background of the Confederate flag, which is not surprising for candidates from Arkansas and Tennessee.

FOLLOW-UP #5:

What was the unspoken promise that the Clintons were making to white folks? What was the pandering message to black people when Billy put on sunglasses and acted "cool" on television?

As amazing as it seems, Billy's playing of the saxophone on the *Arsenio Hall Show* was enough to convince most African-Americans that he was one of them. Still, without thinking about it and without media reporting about the consequences of Clinton policies, most African-Americans still support the Clintons.

Those African-Americans who don't support the Clintons or, worse, who speak the truth about them, will still be branded by the Clinton supporters as Uncle Toms. More racism.

I can't improve on the follow-up quotation delivered by none other than one of the Clintons' chief fawning sycophants. George Stephanopoulos was an advisor and consultant to the Clintons before moving into his more powerful position with ABC television, so he was in a position to know about the Clintons.

George Stephanopoulos said: "President Clinton has kept all the promises he intended to keep."

* * *

Finally, if you have read this far, you are not stupid. Stupid connotes a lack of intelligence, and it is a condition that cannot be fixed. Ignorance, on the other hand, is a lack of knowledge, and it is a condition that can be fixed through education, awareness, and the consideration of new ideas.

If you have been ignorant about the lies of the Clintons and if you have been lulled by rhetoric or government support into living with a "plantation mentality," it is not too late to change your life. A positive change starts in your mind with a willingness to learn and do something different.

If the idea of making positive changes excites you even a little bit, then you can take the next step. Educate yourself. Read about both sides of an issue. Think.

If you have a closed-minded reaction that I am lying and the Clintons are telling the truth, then you may not be ready to change your plantation mentality. Think about that.

44

ANNIVERSARY SEX AND OTHER SERVICES

As I said in an earlier chapter, Hillary never attended our Hot Springs High School Class of 1964 reunions. Never. There were several reasons for her absence every five years. First, Billy didn't want her there. Second, Hillary didn't want to be there. Third, no one else wanted her to be there either.

Some people have asked about my high school class status, so I will clarify. I started school in 1954 at the age of six with the Class of 1966, so I go to reunions with the Class of 1966. Then I skipped a grade and became friends with kids in my new Class of 1965, so I go to reunions with the Class of 1965. Finally, I skipped another grade, and graduated with the Class of 1964, so I attend those reunions too.

If Hillary had owned a crystal ball, she would have attended the thirtieth reunion of the Hot Springs High School Class of 1964 to keep tabs on Billy. She didn't go, and there were long-term consequences—all the way to the impeachment of the other co-president.

For weeks before the thirtieth reunion, I debated about going. I knew that Billy would be there.

In a nutshell, I had not talked to Billy Clinton since before the "We will destroy you" threat that he conveyed to me during the 1992 election. I had no intention of talking to him at the reunion in 1994. Billy pursued me all evening and, at one point, he got close enough to ask me, in a very condescending "I feel your pain" tone of voice, "How *are* you?"

I responded, "You are such an asshole, I can't believe you'd bother to ask."

When I said the word *asshole*, a secret service agent reached out to grab me, and Billy blocked him with his arm. He said, "We need to talk."

Ultimately, Billy and I sat down together, away from, but in full view of, everyone else. We had a long conversation that no one could have overheard. According to witnesses, Billy and I sat together on side-by-side chairs and talked for between thirty minutes and an hour. I didn't look at my watch.

At some point during our conversation, a blonde female version of a Secret Service type approached us and told Billy that they were closing the bar and that the party was ending. Without looking at her, he told her to keep the bar open.

When she asked who would pay for it, he said, "We will."

I learned later that the woman was Marsha Scott.

* * *

What's such a big deal about what Billy and I did at the high school reunion? As a writer, I found it to be the perfect ending for the loosely autobiographical novel that I had started writing nearly ten years earlier as a therapeutic journal. I could not have imagined such a fitting conclusion… full circle after our innocent years in high school… followed by decades of adult intimacies… back to high school…. THE END.

Billy saw it in a completely different light. The fact that he sat and talked to me so intensely (yes, with tears) for such a long time in front of our old classmates reinforced the common knowledge that we had experienced a very long, very intimate relationship.

It became necessary for Billy and Hillary, over the next few years, to follow through on the earlier threat to destroy me. The reunion scene had to be re-written to serve that purpose.

I suppose I should be grateful that Billy and Hillary did not choose to destroy me in the same way they had destroyed others—emotionally, psychologically, financially, and publicly.

I was not beaten to within an inch of my life as happened to Gennifer Flowers's neighbor who had witnessed and videotaped Billy's comings and goings at her condo. Nor was I threatened with a dead cat on my porch as Kathleen Willey was.

No one threatened to break my knees, as they did to Sally Miller. No one put the Clinton Death List on my desk chair as they did to Linda Tripp. No stranger came up to me while I was jogging and asked about my children by name. Of course, I don't jog.

No. I, the writer, had to be destroyed by being annihilated. I, the writer, had to be painted as a fabricator of fiction. I, the writer, could not be allowed to have a credible, public voice. Hillary knows that the pen is mightier than the sword. The pen of this writer had to be silenced.

Unbeknownst to me at the time, Billy wrote a page-and-a-half-tall tale about his version of what happened at our thirtieth reunion. He then had Marsha Scott write a half-page confirmation of what he had written.

This was all in Billy's handwriting and Marsha's. I will explain more about that, but first I'll introduce Marsha Scott.

Billy and Marsha had known each other since the 1970s in Arkansas, and she went to Washington with him to work in the White House, as an aide. At some point, Marsha Scott reportedly told her boyfriend Danny Dwyer that she and Billy Clinton had had sex every Christmas for the past thirty years.

"It's my annual Christmas present to him," she supposedly said.

That made sense to me because Billy can be sentimental in an odd sort of way. I remember that he called me after seeing the movie *Same Time Next Year* with Ellen Burstyn and Alan Alda. Billy said that it reminded him of us. Of course, we did not limit ourselves to one visit per year, but I got the point, as you do.

Marsha Scott and Billy Clinton had their sentimental Christmas anniversary sex every year, and she continued to aid him in whatever else he needed in the White House. Lying didn't seem to bother either one of them.

In his lying-notes version of our high school reunion, Billy made it clear that he and I had never had a sexual relationship, although I had pursued him in high school and beyond.

Billy wrote, "I tried to be nice to her."

Those notes eventually became more important than anyone could have imagined at the time.

The thirtieth high school reunion turned out to be a very important event in 1994, Billy and Hillary's second year in the presidency.

45

THE DEAL AND THE FILES

Although Billy Clinton and I had talked about my loosely autobiographical, therapeutic-journal-turned-novel many times in previous years, he was surprised when I said I had finished writing it. Billy wanted to know if he was still a main character in the story.

Of course, he was. I revealed all this to him during our very public conversation in 1994 at our HSHS thirtieth reunion.

I have no idea what Billy told Hillary about my novel and its impending marketing and publication. Since Hillary had long ago assumed the role of destroyer of women in their codependent, coconspiratorial relationship, I presume she knew what I was doing. Certainly, she had always known about me.

In any case, a month after the reunion, Billy's childhood friend Bruce Lindsey, who had become Billy's closest advisor in the White House, called my sister to arrange a conference call for the four of us. Bruce and my sister had been friends for years. Bruce and my sister would have the direct conversations while Billy and I remained in the background for consultation, but off the telephone recordings.

There was a long, intriguing build-up to the consummation of "the deal." The purpose of the deal was to protect Billy from negative fall-out regarding the publication of my novel.

We agreed that in talking to publishers, in marketing my book, and in doing media interviews:

1. I would not tell publishers/media the full extent of my relationship with Billy;

2. I would paint only a broad-stroke picture indicating that Billy and I had a thirty-three year relationship that began when we were children;

3. I would be allowed to say only that the novel was semi-autobiographical and loosely based on my life history, as many first novels are;

4. I would be allowed to say that Billy and I had a sexual relationship from time to time, as long as I didn't give specifics about dates or locations, thereby giving the impression that perhaps we were both single on such occasions; and

5. I would specifically avoid using the A words *adultery* and *affair*.

After I agreed to everything that Billy wanted, I told him what I wanted:

1. In return for not telling the whole truth about Billy, I wanted him to promise that he "and his people" would not tell any lies about me; and

2. I wanted a way to confirm that our deal was in place and being honored.

Billy and Bruce conferred in the background for a few minutes and then proposed their agreement for an official White House position, as follows:

1. If any publisher or media person needs to verify the truth of what you have told them about your relationship with Billy, but within the agreed guidelines, you tell them to call the White House and ask for Bruce Lindsey.

2. The caller, of course, will assume that the official White House position regarding a relationship between Billy and Dolly will be a denial; instead, you tell them in advance that Bruce Lindsey will say, "Quote. The White House will have no comment. Unquote." That answer will be the sign that the deal is still in place.

I objected, via my sister, that Bruce's statement would be tantamount to a denial, but Bruce assured us:

"When you tell the publisher or the reporter what the exact words of the official White House position will be, and you include the words *quote* and *unquote*, then no one will think it's a denial. It is obviously something quite different. It is obviously a code of agreement. It's a deal."

Silly me. I believed Billy Clinton would honor the deal. When would I ever learn?

* * *

I was lulled into complacency because it seemed to me that the deal was working. I had no idea what was going on behind the scenes in the White House to destroy me over the next couple of years. Bill Burton, a fellow Arkansan and a former White House colleague of Lindsey, said, "There is no end to which Bruce wouldn't go for the president."

At the time, I did not realize that Hillary had her own "insanely loyal like Bruce Lindsey" sycophant in her half of the White House. Sidney Blumenthal was and still is one of Hillary's closest advisors.

When I filed my RICO (Racketeering Influenced and Corrupt Organizations Act) federal lawsuit against President William Jefferson Clinton and his lawyer Bob Bennett, his advisor Bruce Lindsey, the "journalist" Jane Mayer, and the *New Yorker* for tortuously interfering with the publication of my first novel, I did not know about the part that had been played by Sidney Blumenthal. If I had known then what I know now, I would have sued him too.

I wanted to sue Hillary in that same lawsuit, but my legal counsel thought it was unseemly to sue "the other woman" since she was the First Lady of the United States.

I don't know if any of the Clintons' plans to "destroy" me were aided by information from the FBI (Federal Bureau of Investigation). On the other hand, like other perceived enemies of Hillary, I received unwelcome correspondence from the IRS, the beloved Internal Revenue Service.

When co-president Hillary moved into the White House, she hired former bar bouncer Craig Livingstone as director of the White House Office of Personnel Security. Very soon, the former bar bouncer Livingstone requested and received from the FBI nine hundred files containing private information on Hillary's enemies, including members of both political parties.

When word of this wholesale invasion of privacy was discovered a couple of years later, there was a temporary media uproar. The big problem persists. Thousands of politicians in Washington still wonder what Hillary has on them. They don't know if they are in the nine hundred or not. If they have any secrets at all, they must live in constant dread of being publicly exposed.

Terrorism is the use of violence and intimidation for political aims. By this definition, Hillary Clinton is a terrorist. With her silent threats to the nine hundred, who is going make a peep?

Craig Livingstone resigned, taking full blame for whatever violations occurred. For a while, Hillary didn't know who he was; she certainly didn't hire him; she couldn't be responsible.

When the files were subpoenaed, Hillary fumed that she did not want reporters rummaging through her papers. That's when she famously declared, "We *are* the president."

The missing FBI files were subpoenaed, but they could not be located. It's important now to remember that right after deputy White House counsel Vince Foster died in the summer of 1993, boxes of papers were immediately removed from his office by Hillary's staffers.

The nine hundred files remained missing until Hillary "discovered" them on a table in the private quarters in the White House. The only fingerprints on them were those of Vince and Hillary, but she had no idea how the files came to be where they were.

A pile of a dozen manila folders on my desk is noticeable. I'm not sure how anyone could overlook a pile of nine hundred FBI files. I don't even know how nine hundred files of any size at all could be piled on a desk or tabletop without causing an avalanche that would crash to the floor and be noticeable to Hillary and to the cleaning crew. One can only presume that the cleaning people had not been upstairs in a couple of years.

There are so many curiosities about those FBI files.

Hillary was exonerated of any wrongdoing for having the files. Craig Livingstone took the fall for obtaining the files, but at least he could report that he had not been shot.

The media attached the word *gate* to the word *file* and then it all went away—except the lingering terror of exposure.

46

THE BIG PROBLEM

As I said earlier, the big problem in writing about Hillary Clinton is that the problem is so big. Who can comprehend it? The Clintons play by completely different rules.

Jay Leno did a funny bit about an aspect of Hillary's entitlement mentality on *The Tonight Show* on Thursday, June 19, 2008. Yes, it is "old news," as the Clintons would say, but Hillary's attitude has not changed since she ran for president the first time in 2008.

As Leno told it:

> Hillary Clinton is taking a month off from her job as senator to rest up from her [presidential] campaign. How does that work? You've been neglecting your job trying to get a better job. You don't get that job, so you to take a month off from the job you were trying to get out of and go on vacation. Imagine if you tried that with your boss. "Hey boss, listen—I've been looking for another job, and I'm exhausted. I want to take a month off. Here's where you can send my checks."

Jay Leno's monologues could be quite amusing, but we as voters need to take the underlying Clinton facts more seriously. Consider some of these facts about Hillary and her

Attacking and intimidating the sexual victims of her husband;

Bank fraud in Arkansas and in Washington;

Barry Seal;

Benghazi and the unnecessary deaths of four Americans, including a US ambassador;

Benghazi and the role of Sidney Blumenthal in planting lies;

Benghazi and the lies told to the families of the victims and the American people;

Benghazi and telling the truth to Chelsea Clinton at the time;

Bernard Nussbaum, White House counsel and Tripp's boss;

Betsey Wright and assaults on "bimbos," as she called them;

Bob Bennett, attorney who let his client Billy C. lie under oath;

Bill Clinton speech money and $165 billion okay'd by Hillary for arms sales;

Bill Duncan, IRS agent and Mena drug investigator;

Billy Dale and his travel office staff fired; lawsuit; settlement;

Black Panthers trial for torturing and killing a federal agent;

Blood Trail of infected blood from Arkansas prisoners;

Boeing's $10 million to the Clinton Foundation after which they got the green light to sell $29 billion in fighter jets to Saudis;

Boys on the tracks: Kevin Ives and Don Henry murders and nine witnesses dead;

Bruce Lindsey;

Health care, bungled attempts in Arkansas and for the USA;

California Communist Party internship with Bob Truehaft;

Camille Paglia, a true feminist, and her views of Hillary;

Cattle futures trading without the required minimum cash;

Cattle futures and making $100,000 off of a measly $1,000—and the futures broker losing his license and the firm paying fines (prelude to Clinton Foundation money);

Cell phone franchise deal worth $2,000 flipped for a $46,000 payoff;

Charles Matthews and Whitewater;

Cheryl Mills and Secretary of State emails;

Clinton Foundation money from ties to Algeria: Algeria was cleared to buy American-made weapons while the U.S. State Department had Algeria on its list of countries tagged for offenses ranging from corruption to violations of civil liberties;

Clinton Foundation money from ties to Kuwait: Kuwait was cleared to buy American-made weapons while the U.S. State Department had Kuwait on its list of countries tagged for offenses ranging from corruption to violations of civil liberties;

Clinton Foundation money from ties to Oman: Oman was cleared to buy American-made weapons while the U.S. State Department had Oman on its list of countries tagged for offenses ranging from corruption to violations of civil liberties;

Clinton Foundation money from ties to Qatar: Qatar was cleared to buy American-made weapons while the U.S. State Department had Qatar on its list of countries tagged for offenses ranging from corruption to violations of civil liberties;

Clinton Foundation money from ties to Saudi Arabia: Saudis were cleared to buy American-made weapons while the U.S. State Department had Saudi Arabia on its list of countries tagged for offenses ranging from corruption to violations of civil liberties;

Clinton Foundation money from ties to United Arab Emirates: UAE was cleared to buy American-made weapons while the U.S. State Department had UAE on its list of countries tagged for offenses ranging from corruption to violations of civil liberties;

Clinton Foundation and $165 billion in approved arms sales;

Clinton Foundation and the sellout of uranium to Russia;

Clinton Foundation is finally being investigated; pay attention;

Clinton Giustra Enterprise Partnership (CGEP) in Canada sent money from 1,100 undisclosed donors to Clinton Foundation;

Coattail clutching to

> a teaching job at UA Law School;
>
> a job at the Rose Law Firm;
>
> a partnership at the Rose Law Firm;
>
> a lucrative seat on Wal-Mart's board;
>
> the Legal Services Board of Directors;
>
> a seat in the United States Senate;
>
> a run at the presidency in 2008;
>
> a term as Secretary of State;
>
> a run at the presidency in 2016;

Connections to one hundred-plus witnesses who fled the country;

Craig Livingstone, bar bouncer and White House Security;

Dan Lasater;

David Hale and Whitewater;

David Kendall and Whitewater;

Dolly Kyle's federal lawsuit against Clinton and Cronies;

Eavesdropping on illegal wiretaps of political enemies;

Email server setup endangering the lives of Americans;

Email and

> question of where Hillary received top secret info;

> the definition of classified documents;

> lies about the classification of documents;

> wiping info before surrendering the server;

> felonious "de-classification" of forwarded emails;

> revelations about the Benghazi cover-up;

> Sidney Blumenthal's continuing role in cover-ups;

> Loretta Lynch's conflict of interest as a lawyer;

Eugene Fitzhugh and Whitewater;

Exports of sensitive technology to questionable purchasers;

FBI files subpoenaed, hidden, and later "discovered";

FBI files taken to be used for intimidating her "enemies";

Feminism and abuse of women;

Feminism and hatred of men;

Feminism and Camille Paglia;

First First Lady to be investigated for criminal activities;

Flip-flops on Israel;

Flip-flops on Black Lives Matter / Black Votes Matter;

Flip-flops on trade agreements;

Flip-flops on war;

Gary Johnson and videos of Clinton w/ Gennifer Flowers;

George Soros and Albania;

George Soros and Burma;

George Soros and donations to the Clinton Foundation;

George Soros and emails;

George Soros and his access to / influence on the Clintons;

Goldman Sachs and speech fees for undisclosed content;

Goldman Sachs and "conversations" worth over $200,000;

Guatemala Judge Iris Yassmin Barrios Aguilar and genocide;

Guatemala judge and emails with Ambassador Arnold Chacon;

Guatemala judge and emails "hidden" in Spanish;

Guatemala judge recommended for honors by Hillary;

Guatemala judge censured by Guatemala bar association;

Guatemala judge's illegal treatment of defendants and counsel;

Harold Ickes and communications about Linda Tripp;

Harry Thomason and political favors attempted;

Harry Thomason and the Lincoln Bedroom;

Hassan Abedin;

Herby Branscum Jr. and Whitewater;

Howard Shapiro, the FBI files and damage control;

Huma Abedin and FBI national security investigation;

Huma Abedin and questionable payments while on leave;

Huma Abedin and Secretary of State emails;

I don't remember – Hillary's testimony response 250 times;

Illegal campaign

    cash disguised as law firm double-billing;

    contributions "bundled" by various donors;

    contributions from James Riady;

    contributions from Henry Hamilton;

    contributions from Liem Sioe Liong

    contributions from Mochtar Riady;

    contributions from Yuen Hsu;

    contributions to get pardons for her brothers' friends;

    contributions to obtain a pardon for Marc Rich;

IRS audits of right-leaning nonprofit organizations;

IRS audits of women who spoke about Clinton abuses;

IRS official Paul Breslan admitted targeting Clinton foes;

James Carville, the Ragin' Cajun, trashed women for Clintons;

Jean Duffey, prosecutor;

Jim Blair, counsel for Tyson Foods,

Jim McDougal and Whitewater;

Judicial Watch and emails;

Judicial Watch and FOIA (Freedom of Information Act) suits;

Judicial Watch and its history of investigating the Clintons;

La Cosa Nostra;

La Cosa Nostra and Arthur Coia;

La Cosa Nostra and labor unions;

Lanny Breuer and communications about Linda Tripp;

Lanny Davis and communications about Linda Tripp;

Larry Flynt of *Hustler* and threats to Impeachment Committee;

Laughing after her legal attacks on a 12-year-old rape victim;

Laughing as a Black Lives Matter woman is escorted away;

Laughing behind the backs of African-American leaders;

Lawsuits by

> doctors to break secrecy of health care meetings;

> African-Americans over voting rights in Arkansas;

> Hispanics over racial profiling in Arkansas;

> Paula Corbin Jones against William J. Clinton;

> Linda Tripp against White House and Pentagon;

> Linda Tripp; personnel files; settlement;

Loretta Lynch, U.S. Attorney General, and conflicts of interest;

Loretta Lynch, U.S. Attorney General, in the decision seat;

Loss of congressional Democratic majority in 1994; the why;

Liza Featherstone and Hillary's "faux feminism";

Lying about her landing under sniper fire in Bosnia;

Lying about her political relationship with Sid Blumenthal;

Lying about her record in the Senate for introducing bills;

Lying about her use of a private email server while SOS;

Lying in statements to federal investigators;

Maggie Williams got $50,000 illegally from Johnnie Chung;

Maggie Williams hid Hillary's Rose Law Firm billing records; Maggie Williams removed files from Vince Foster's office;

Mail fraud in Washington;

Mary Mahoney, White House intern killed in a setup robbery;

Memoirs of "I don't remember" sold for $8 million;

Memoirs of "I didn't have sex…" sold for $12 million;

Mickey Kantor and communications about Linda Tripp;

Mitch Ettinger, attorney who knew Clinton lied under oath;

Nathan Landow and Kathleen Willey;

Nathan Landow and Vince Foster;

Norman Yung Yuen Hsu pardon from twenty-four-year prison sentence for illegal campaign contributions and political influencing that struck "at the very core of our democracy," said judge;

Operatives who covered Billy Clinton's sexual escapades:

Larry Nichols

LD Brown

Raymond "Buddy" Young

Operatives who threatened Bill Clinton's sexual victims, and/or covered his tracks, at the behest of Hillary:

Anthony Pellicano

Cody Shearer, who contracted for Terry Lenzer

Ivan Duda

Jack Palladino

Jerry Parks (murdered in 1993, knowing a lot!)

Mickey Kantor who pressured witness Julie Hiatt Steele

Ron Tucker

Terry Lenzer

Organized crime; Arthur Coia; speeches to his labor unions;

Paranoia and hiding what should have been public info;

Paranoia and shredding the governor's mansion visitor logs;

Paranoia and using a private email server in public office;

Paul Begala and communications about Linda Tripp;

Paula Jones sexual harassment lawsuit vs. William Clinton;

Paula Jones and attacks on her by James Carville, etc.;

Rahm Emanuel and communications about Linda Tripp;

REFCO, the trading firm fined for unethical futures trades;

Robert L. "Red" Bone, broker whose license was suspended;

Robert Palmer and Whitewater;

Rodham brother's $400,000 for seeking a presidential pardon;

Roger Clinton's seeking presidential pardon for Gambino;

Rosatom and the Russian uranium deal approved by Hillary;

Sam Houston, MD;

Sandy Berger took Top Secret documents relating to terrorism from the National Archives by "mistakenly" stuffing them into his pants before the 9/11 Commission Investigation;

Saul Alinsky and Hillary's thesis;

Secretary of State approves arms sales to foreign countries;

Selling overnight stays in the White House Lincoln Bedroom;

Selling seats on commerce department trade missions to China;

Senate 2000:

> Peter Paul's $700,000 illegal campaign donation;
>
> fined $35,000 by Federal Election Commission;
>
> Capricia Marshall involved in illegal fundraising;
>
> finance director David Rosen criminally indicted;
>
> Harold Ickes and ties to major crime families;
>
> Harold Ickes ran the campaign for Hillary;

Sharlene Wilson and cocaine connection;

Shredding of documents:

> governor's mansion visitor logs;

health care secret meetings in DC;

wiping server after subpoena;

electronic deletion of emails;

Sidney Blumenthal

as an early advisor to the Clintons;

feeding false stories to "journalists";

banned from State Department by Obama;

feeding anti-Semitic propaganda to Hillary;

giving Hillary a video "alibi" for Benghazi;

emailing Hillary about politics in DC;

and Jane Mayer;

and access to Pentagon files;

Speeches, called "conversations," earning over $20 million;

Stealing over $200,000 worth of White House furniture;

Stephens Inc. – Witt and Jack Stephens and $$ connections;

Strobe Talbott and connections with Russia;

Susan McDougal and Whitewater;

Taking influence money right before taking senate seat;

Tax evasion or "mistakes" admitted after being discovered;

Terry McAuliffe fundraising;

Tyson Foods and fines paid;

Tyson Foods and futures trading;

Tyson Foods and Jim Blair's investment advice;

Tyson Foods and political favors;

UAMS (emergency room) physicians threatened by Hillary;

Uranium sellout to Russia;

Vince Foster and what he died knowing;

Voting Rights Act of 1965 and Clinton violations in Arkansas;

Visitor Logs for governor's mansion ordered to be destroyed;

Visitor Logs for governor's mansion with women's names;

Wall Street firms, banks, and exorbitant speech fees;

Wal-Mart board service ignoring unfair labor practices;

Whitewater and the lies told to obfuscate the facts;

Worldwide Travel and campaign contributions;

Worthen Bank and $3.5 million line of credit for campaign;

and

Xi Jinping of China hosting a meeting on women's rights at the UN while persecuting feminists is something that Hillary Clinton called "shameless." What is truly shameless is Hillary's deliberate, ruthless, unceasing predictable attacks on her husband's female victims... and she started those attacks 30 years before Xi Jinping took office in China!

This incomplete list, ending with Xi Jinping's shameless treatment of women, brings us back to Hillary Clinton's attacks on the women who get in her way. Hillary's decades-long role of attacking women who dared to speak the truth is one of her most constant and overlooked themes.

Another common thread is that women who did reveal an incident about Billy and Hillary subsequently changed their stories. Almost all of the women who were subpoenaed to testify in the *Jones v. Clinton* lawsuit were pressured or threatened to keep them from testifying. A couple of them fled the country. Many then signed false affidavits that were prepared by Clinton's lawyers.

Never have so many women spontaneously exercised the female prerogative to change their minds.

Clinton's lawyers pressured me to file a motion to quash a subpoena so that I would not testify in the Paula Jones sexual harassment lawsuit. I refused to cooperate with them, and I did my duty as a citizen as well as an officer of the court, which is what lawyers are.

I testified truthfully in the *Jones* case about Billy Clinton's admission to me that he was a sex addict. A sexual addiction is a far cry from being a womanizer or a guy sowing his wild oats. It is a serious, uncontrollable force that led him into rape and sexual assault as well as to countless sexual encounters of various types over the decades that he was putatively married to the Other Woman.

There are many other women who had sexual affairs or were sexually attacked by Billy Clinton who are not known outside the small town of Little Rock. There are also plenty who do not even know that people know about them. I hope that others will be encouraged by the example of the brave women who finally made public what they had suffered at the hands of Bill Cosby.

Hillary shamelessly travels from town to town and looks into television cameras and tells the women of America that she has been "fighting" FOR them throughout her entire career.

I would like to know exactly which battle Hillary Clinton ever won on behalf of women.

47

MEDIA MAGIC

Readers may wonder why many of the hundred-plus items about Hillary that I listed in the previous chapter are unknown to them. I'm sorry to say that the mainstream media report the news that fits their political agenda, and do it with an unstated political slant. This is a very sad truth in our country today.

The Clintonistas would have us believe that the media were tough on President Clinton during the Monica Lewinsky scandal in the late 1990s. For a while there, the smell of blood in the water had even some of the liberal sharks circling. If Clinton was going to be dead meat anyway, they wanted a fresh bite. When it appeared that he would live to commit other atrocities, professional courtesy forced them to swim away.

After knowing for years that Billy Clinton was at best a woman-izer who had been accused in the *Jones* case of sexual harassment, the media chose to ignore the serious, credible, rape allegation against him by Juanita Broaddrick. Lisa Myers of NBC interviewed Juanita in a masterful piece of journalism, but the NBC higher-ups tried to bury the story. Internet users finally forced NBC to air it, but it was a one and done. (Currently, part of that interview can be seen on YouTube.)

When I filed a RICO lawsuit against President Clinton and his co-conspirators, the same Lisa Myers of NBC wanted to interview me in front of the federal courthouse in DC while I was there. The NBC higher-ups nixed it. Even after an issue in my case went to the U.S. Supreme Court (where I won), no one from the media wanted to report it. Or, I should say that most of the higher-ups in the media prevented their investigative reporters from publicizing negative truths about the Clintons.

The ultraliberal *New Yorker* magazine outdid itself when they joined the vast left-wing conspiracy operating from the Clinton's White House. I didn't realize when I sued the *New Yorker* that Sidney Blumenthal (Hillary's go-to gopher) was a big buddy of Jane Mayer who wrote the completely false story about me for the *New Yorker*.

Yes, it was completely false, based on *nothing* except Hillary's paranoid belief that I was trying to turn my first novel into some kind of political exposé of Billy. I wasn't. I didn't.

I sued Jane Mayer too, of course. Later, I found out that Jane Mayer was married to the editor of the *Washington Post*. It got cozier and cozier up there, while the truth got buried.

(Lorraine Adams, a reporter from the *Washington Post*, who worked closely at the *Post* with Bob Woodward of Nixon's Watergate fame, flew to Dallas to interview me for a front-page-worthy article. Subsequently, Lorraine called to tell me that the story would be relegated to being published as a fluff piece in the Sunday supplement section of the paper.)

The ironic thing is that the Clinton-Blumenthal-Mayer plot to trash me turned out to be the first domino to fall. They never saw it coming.

Evan Smith of *Texas Monthly* magazine in Austin saw the fabricated story by Jane Mayer in the *New Yorker* and he called me in Dallas for comment. After we talked (but still within "the deal" guidelines), Evan wrote a small piece in *Texas Monthly* and that article was seen by the first set of lawyers in the *Jones v. Clinton* sexual harassment case. Those lawyers did not call me, but they put the magazine clipping in her file.

Paula Jones then engaged other lawyers who did call me. After reading my novel, they asked me to testify about Billy's admission of sexual addiction, which was critical to their case.

When I told Billy (via my sister and Bruce Lindsey, as usual) that I was going to testify in the *Jones* case, Billy had his lawyers prepare documents saying that our sexual relationship was consensual and therefore had no bearing on a sexual harassment case.

Yes, I have the documents and the cover correspondence that was sent (via my sister's law office) on Billy's lawyers' letterhead. They wanted me to file a sworn statement about our *consensual* sex in federal court in a motion to quash the subpoena. They also sent a three-page brief in support of that motion to quash. I refused to file the motion because I had given my word to the *Jones* lawyers that I would testify.

Then, the *Dallas Morning News* printed an erroneous item about me in a page-five story about the fact that Gennifer Flowers was going to testify in the *Jones* case. I immediately called the reporter who had written the *DMN* story and asked him where he got his "fact" about me. He actually confessed, without any apparent shame, "I just assumed it." I was not at all surprised that the *DMN* refused to run a correction.

What should I say about the *Arkansas Democrat-Gazette*? My home state paper ignored me most of the time, which I did appreciate. The *AD-G*'s Clinton-loving Gene Lyons, however, expressed his opinion about me in an email to a friend of a friend. There's that Arkansas gossip thing again!

Gene Lyons said that I made the whole thing up and caused a scene at our high school reunion by confronting Billy, in front of witnesses, for *not* sleeping with me but having an affair with Gennifer.

Ann Gerhart, cowriter of *Washington Post*'s "Page Six" column, contacted me to do a feature piece after she heard about my novel, but she was skeptical about my long relationship with Billy (then President) Clinton. I referred her to Bruce Lindsey at the White House who told her "Quote. The White House will have no comment. Unquote."

Ann was blown away by the obvious arrangement that I had with the White House; she called me back immediately.

"This isn't a 'Page Six' story! It should be on page one!"

I suggested that she pass the news along to the editor. She did. It was much later when I discovered that he was married to Jane Mayer who wrote the fallacious *New Yorker* drivel. Ann wrote something for "Page Six," but that was the end of it.

Donald Van de Mark of CNN Business News called me on a Thursday afternoon and asked if we could have a ten-minute, live, telephone interview on Friday morning. I agreed, and he began to ask me some preliminary questions, at the end of which I gave him Bruce Lindsey's number at the White House.

Then I had another idea.

"If you will stand by your fax machine, I'll send you a copy of the prologue to my novel. Even though it's fiction, it will give you some ideas."

"Great," he responded, and he gave me his fax number.

The sixth of ten pages was still feeding into my fax machine when Donald Van de Mark called me back.

"Forget the telephone interview," he said.

"What?" I asked incredulously. "It can't be that bad."

"Bad? No!" He laughed. "It's terrific! I can't cover this story in a ten-minute conversation over the phone. I'd like to meet you in Dallas for an in-depth interview."

"Fine. When do you want to come?"

"Tomorrow."

I was taken aback by his sense of urgency, but we set an appointment to meet in Dallas the next day. In less than thirty minutes, he called again.

"The Washington bureau has heard about the story, and they want to be in on this, since it involves the president."

"Does that mean you're not coming?" I asked.

"I'll be there to do the interview, but they want to send someone from the DC bureau too, if that's okay with you."

"Sure," I said. How much more trouble could it be?

It wasn't too long before Donald called again.

"Same deal, but now with the Texas bureau. They want to send someone up from Austin to get the local angle."

After all that, the interview was moved from Friday to Saturday. I met Donald Van de Mark and his cameraman from New York at the Adolphus Hotel in downtown Dallas. The guys from Washington and Austin were there too.

We had a three-hour interview with the camera rolling. Donald and I had an instant rapport, which resulted in a well-documented piece that was at times amusing, and in other places quite moving.

At all times, it was candid and informative. Everyone involved was very pleased with our afternoon's work. We had a group hug when we parted.

Maybe you didn't catch it on CNN. That's too bad. I'm sure it would have been wonderful.

CNN didn't air a single minute of it. Poof! Media Magic! The entire story disappeared.

Perhaps we should ask for labels on all media news coverage, like on packages of cigarettes. WARNING: The news you are about to see is our liberal (or conservative) view of what should matter to you non-thinking Americans. Please sit quietly and suck your thumbs while we talk at you.

48

THE DEAL AND THE UNDERHANDED DEALERS

Ironically, it was Uncle Raymond Clinton who taught me to play poker and to watch out for underhanded dealing. In my interactions with Billy and Hillary Clinton, however, I never saw it coming.

We had a deal regarding the marketing of my first novel. Silly me. I did what I said I would do; they didn't.

At first, I had received encouraging responses about my novel from editors and publishers. Then, silence. At first, I had a close relationship with a literary agent. Then, silence.

When I saw and heard Linda Tripp on television talking about Jane Mayer of the *New Yorker* and the trash piece that she had written about Linda, it all became clear in that instant. Hillary and Billy had also trashed me by having Jane Mayer plant a completely fabricated story about me in the *New Yorker*. Knowing that most editors and publishers in New York would read the article, the Clintons did this in an effort to keep my novel from being published, even though it was a fictionalized story.

The bottom line of the deal was that I would not tell the whole truth about Billy if he and his cronies would not tell any lies about me. Ultimately, I filed a federal lawsuit against them, although I did not know about Sidney Blumenthal at the time; I would have sued him too.

If you never heard about my lawsuit, please be aware that the lack of publicity about it was due to media magic. However, thanks to the Internet, it is now possible to find archives that seemed to be lost at the time.

Everyone certainly heard about President Clinton's sexual abuse of Monica Lewinsky in the Oval Office. Investigative reporter Mike Isikoff of *Newsweek* was onto the Lewinsky story first, but the higher-ups at *Newsweek* sat on it. The news surfaced via the *Drudge Report.*

Billy lied about Monica Lewinsky while Hillary feigned shock. Hillary's outrage was real. Hillary began her typical trash campaign, calling Monica (who was about Chelsea's age) a "narcissistic loony toon."

Billy's semen on Monica's infamous navy-blue dress, which proved the allegations of their sexual encounters, did not stop coconspirator Hillary. She still persisted in her well-practiced, underhanded, media-supported smears of the young woman.

Hillary's point was not only to discredit Monica, but also to show other women what they could expect if they dared to talk about having sex with her co-president. Hillary assumed the role of the aggrieved but stalwart spouse. She took a poll to see if she would be better served politically with a divorce or with staying married to the sexual predator.

As Hillary discovered through the poll in Arkansas over a decade before, she did not have a snowball's chance in hell of being elected on her own.

It was never Billy's having sex with everyone else that bothered Hillary. It was his getting caught. Then she would have to deal with a potential threat to her own political career because of his out-of-control sex addiction. It was always about Hillary the Other Woman.

IMPEACHMENT OF A CO-PRESIDENT

You could rely on the mainstream media for their analysis of the Clinton impeachment, if you simply wanted to know what they had to say about it. You could rely on books written by Clinton apologists and sycophants, if you simply want to know what they had to say about it. You could even rely on some of the latest history textbooks that already contain the rewritten version of what happened in Washington during that very intense time at the end of the 1990s.

You could read the autobiographies written by Hillary and Billy Clinton, if you simply want to know what they had to say about the impeachment. You should now know they are liars.

If you want to know what really happened in 1998–99, you can't do better than reading David Schippers's book *Sellout: The Inside Story of President Clinton's Impeachment*.

While I charmed the retired gangster with the machine-gun nest in Hot Springs, Dave Schippers was fearlessly prosecuting mobsters in

Chicago. As he was in Chicago, Dave was in DC—fearless in his pursuit of truth as chief investigative counsel for the Clinton impeachment. Ultimately, he was disgusted with those who were afraid to look at the ugly Clinton truths.

Sellout gives an amazing, behind-the-scenes picture of the Clinton corruption and the cowardly complicity in it by politicians on both sides of the aisle. How many of them had secrets of their own? How many cowards in Congress were quietly terrorized by knowing that Hillary Clinton had seen over nine hundred FBI files that could contain information about them?

The Clinton impeachment was not about sex in the Oval Office. That trivialization of the crimes committed has been perpetrated on unthinking Americans for nearly two decades. I was there in Washington, waiting to be called as a witness by Dave Schippers, ready to tell the truth in the impeachment trial, just as I had done in my *Jones v. Clinton* deposition.

I had written proof, in Billy Clinton's own handwriting, of perjury, suborning perjury, witness tampering and obstruction of justice. Congress couldn't handle it. They were cowards. They were lily-livered, chicken-hearted, self-protective, weak, spineless cowards. Has Congress changed since then?

Is it any wonder that Americans of all political persuasions and of all ethnic, sexual, and socioeconomic groups are sick of the whole bunch in Washington? Somehow, there seems to be a collective awareness in 2016 that something is very wrong inside the Beltway, and we need to fix it.

Hillary Rodham Clinton is not trying to *fix* anything except her place in history. She has already managed to "fix" her finances. She went from being flat broke when she left the copresidency to amassing a $45 million personal net worth "on the side," while working for the government.

Hillary has already put in the "fix" for her email crimes against the country by counting on her old pal Loretta Lynch to look the other way when the FBI finishes its investigation.

Loretta Lynch is beholden to the Clintons for the federal judgeship that got her started on the road to being the Attorney General of the United States. As a lawyer, Lynch needs to recuse herself in the Clinton email criminal matter if, for no other reason, that there is the appearance of a conflict of interest. That is Ethics 101 for lawyers! Remind everyone of this fact via the Internet, which may be the best way for most of us to "fix" anything these days. Then, register and go vote.

THE UGLY CLINTON LIES AND TRUTH SUPPRESSION

An observant cowboy and his horse can tell when the lead cow in a herd is about to cut and run. Billy Clinton gets that same look in his eyes when he is lying or is about to lie.

Before writing this last chapter, I decided to review the previously mentioned video *The Man from Hope* again. Sure enough, there was that telltale look in Billy's eyes. I jotted down what he was saying: "I remember my grandmother and grandfather opposing the closing of Central High School to keep black students out."

This is typical of Clinton's pandering to black voters. He has always done this and gotten away with it (thanks, Media!). Despite his blatant racial discrimination against blacks, both as governor and as president, most African-Americans pay no attention to the detrimental laws he supported.

Billy's lie in *The Man from Hope* video is exposed by the facts that (1) Central High School was closed by the Democratic governor Orval E.

Faubus in September, 1958; and (2) Billy's grandfather James Eldridge Cassidy had died eighteen months earlier, on March 11, 1957.

Billy's blatant lie in the video is similar to Hillary's lies about being named after Sir Edmund Hillary (six years before he climbed Mt. Everest) or about dodging sniper fire in Bosnia. Hillary recently chided her Democratic opponent Bernie Sanders for being absent as she was "fighting" for health care for all Americans in 1993. One of Bernie's supporters immediately sent a photo that exposed her lie by showing Bernie standing right there with Hillary at the time.

Such lies as these are absolutely unnecessary, and they are a defining symptom of pathological lying.

In addition to being a pathological liar, Hillary may now be suffering from increasing cognitive impairment. The CDC (Centers for Disease Control) lists symptoms, including:

Memory loss. Hillary swore under oath 250 times: "I do not remember." Regarding Libya, she said "We didn't lose a single person." Where is Benghazi?

Repeating the same story over and over. Hillary told the (untrue) Bosnia sniper fire story countless times, and she repeatedly told made-up stories about events in Benghazi.

Vision problems. Although Hillary has always worn some type of corrective lenses, in the past couple of years, she has suffered from a peculiar type of double vision that requires Fresnel prism glasses. She has fallen several times (probably several more times than the public knows), and she has had at least one concussion from her unexplained falls.

Changes in mood or behavior. Hillary has always had at least two sides to her personality and has been known, and feared, for her sudden, screaming, foul-mouthed tirades over minor infractions by people around her. These behavior extremes are becoming more pronounced, as anyone can see, and she is not able to be around a lot of people for very long before she snaps.

Difficulty planning and carrying out tasks. This overlaps a bit with Hillary's inability to handle an emergency, as stated below. Hillary was not able to formulate a plan to evacuate or fortify the embassy or otherwise protect American lives and American interests in Benghazi. She failed to plan anything, despite having advanced warning and "intelligence" reports for at least a month before the massacres by terrorists.

Having trouble exercising judgment, such as knowing what to do in any emergency. This is of particular concern for a person who wants to have her finger on the nuclear trigger.

Hillary exercised the worst possible judgment by failing to aid our stranded American ambassador and our three other American citizens who died at the hands of terrorists in Benghazi.

Hillary was unable to formulate an appropriate emergency plan during the Benghazi attacks, despite having at her disposal every resource of the State Department. She didn't formulate any plan at all; instead, she turned over and went back to sleep. She is not able to handle emergencies.

There is another type of less dramatic emergency that Hillary has been unable to deal with lately. On a couple of occasions at recent campaign events, Hillary has been confronted by young women from the group Black Lives Matter. Rather than answer their legitimate questions, Hillary went into a panic, and desperately looked around for someone to remove the questioners.

Hillary's behavior after experiencing her little "emergency" encounters with these young black women has been completely inappropriate for an adult, much less for someone who wants to be the next president of the United States. In one of the incidents, Hillary imperiously said, "Let's get back to the issues" as the woman was escorted from the building; in another, Hillary derisively laughed at the woman behind her back. (That reminds me of Billy's and Hillary's laughing behind the backs of other minorities and calling Jesse Jackson "that G**damned nigger.") As far as Hillary is concerned, it's only black *votes* that matter. How the Clintons have managed to dupe so many for so long is truly astounding. Thanks, again, Media!

I'm sure that anyone who has been paying attention to the presidential campaign events can add other recent examples of Hillary's incompetent behavior that may be more signs of her increasing cognitive impairment. Despite Hillary's statement that she is not "a politician" like her husband, she has been on the trail in some way or other for over forty years. As a result, Hillary should be able to handle a few civil questions from women who are young enough to be her granddaughters.

The mere fact that Hillary cannot perform appropriately in the face of these very minor "emergencies" (where she is protected by the Secret Service!) is more than troubling.

* * *

Knowing that the Clintons are pathological liars is a step, but recognizing some of their "truth suppression techniques" is critical too. I paraphrased these with permission from Dave "DC Dave" Martin, who compiled the list many years ago.

As Dave said, the success of these techniques depends on a cooperative press and a mere token opposition party. It will be helpful if you, my readers, will be on the lookout for these ploys to start appearing against me as soon as this book is published.

I'm going to personalize this so you can see it easily:

1. *Dummy up.* If no one reports anything about Dolly, there is no news. This worked previously.

2. *Wax indignant.* How dare you, Dolly? What do you mean by calling Hillary "the other woman?"

3. *Characterize Dolly's words as rumors, or better, wild rumors.* This will be hard, since I have facts.

4. *Knock down straw men*, even if you have to make up the straw men. Deal only with the weakest aspect of the weakest charges. In my case, they will have to make up some weak charges, so watch for the lies to start. Standard operating procedure.

5. *Attach names* like nutcase, ranter, kook, crackpot, and their old favorite, bimbo. They might add "scorned woman" about me. They probably will avoid "old broad" since I'm six months younger than Hillary, but facts have never bothered them. They could use "narcissistic loony toon" that Hillary called Monica, but that's so last century.

6. *Impugn motives.* They will accuse me of being in this for the money! This is from Clintons who sold their lying-dog autobiographies for $8 million and $12 million, and who went from "dead broke" to a combined net worth of $90 million. I'd like to be able to give away the books, but they cost money.

7. *Invoke authority.* They have used the press for this in the past: If the *New Yorker* magazine says that I'm a lousy writer, am I a lousy writer? If the *Washington Post* says I'm a liar, am I a liar?

8. *Dismiss all the charges as "old news."* Absolutely! When you hear this truth suppression technique (which has always been a Clinton favorite), please remember that "past is prologue"; what they did in the past, they will do again. These people are not very creative; they will repeat themselves, over and over, exacerbated by cognitive impairment.

9. *Come half-clean.* This is the "confession and avoidance" technique used effectively by Hillary and Billy in their *60 Minutes* performance in 1992. They create the impression of candor and honesty while admitting only to generalized or harmless mistakes—like in their marriage and on tax returns.

10. *Characterize crimes as impossibly complex and the truth as ultimately unknowable.* I simplified the issues about Whitewater to overcome this one because it is another Clinton favorite.

11. *Reason backward.* We have a free press. If there were evidence of Vince Foster's "suicide" note being forged, the media would have reported it. If the media didn't report it, it didn't happen. (By the way, check out the twenty-one-page addendum that a judge allowed to be filed at the back of the official Starr Report on Vince Foster's "suicide." That wasn't reported either. Uh-oh, am I a conspiracy theorist? See how this works for them?)

12. *Require the other side to explain everything.* I don't think the Clintons will try this one with me because they know that I can—and I will, and I started it in this book. I invite a public debate on any of this, if Hillary and Billy are so inclined.

13. *Change the subject.* Billy bombed a small country to distract the public's attention from his emerging scandal over Monica. Neither Hillary nor Billy will want to talk about Dolly Kyle. They will do anything to change the subject. Watch for it.

14. *Lightly report incriminating facts and then make nothing of them;* referred to as "bump and run."

15. *Flood the Internet with agents.* Hillary used this one most recently in attacking the book *The Clintons' War on Women.* A dozen Amazon book reviews were traced back to one URL in Hillary's office. They may try that one again; watch for it.

16. *Send a bunch of their own stooges to start leaking news stories about scandals, and then discredit those scandals, making it appear that all new scandals are bogus.* It's a version of numbers 4 and 5 above, but it works quite well. You may suddenly see a lot of people on television and hear people on the radio saying that they knew Dolly Kyle and she's a _____ (pick from any list of epithets).

17. *Brazenly lie.* So far, this has been the Clintons' most reliable
tactic.

* * *

After all the time spent together in this book, we could be new friends—
even better than my new friends in Owney Madden's machine gun nest
back in Hot Springs when I was a kid. If so, I will appreciate hearing
from you, especially if you want to report the emergence of any of
the "truth suppression techniques." Feel free to report them to me by
number, like ordering burgers in a fast-food restaurant.

I still have enough material to write an encyclopedia about the
Clintons, but I'm getting very tired of them—and I hope you are too.
Whether we have become friends or not in this book, I'm sure I have
provided enough information to get a thinking person thinking.

INDEX

NOVELS BY DOLLY KYLE

PURPOSES OF THE HEART (1997)

PRISONERS OF THE HEART (2007)

PERJURIES OF THE HEART (2015)